"*A Psychoanalytic and Socio-Cultural Exploration of a Continent* provides a deep understanding of what is now happening in Europe, including growing national-fascist movements, the influence of modern globalization, current refugee problems and the impact of past historical events. This timely book clearly illustrates the intertwining of external and internal worlds of individuals and shows us how shared psychological elements give directions to societal and political movements."

— **Vamik D. Volkan**, MD, Emeritus Professor of Psychiatry,
University of Virginia, author, *Enemies on the Couch:
A Psychopolitical Journey Through War and Peace*

"Drawing on the work of several schools of thought, the authors of these deeply felt contributions have been inspired by their experiences both on the couch and in the circle. This imaginative and provocative use of hypotheses from psychoanalysis and group analysis helps us to understand more deeply and confront more fully the central political project of the Western world today: the continuing civilisation of Europe in response to the regressive attacks upon it. Our leaders would benefit from the insights into the unconscious dynamics of persons and their groupings that are so well elaborated in this European book."

— **Earl Hopper**, PhD, psychoanalyst, group analyst and
organisational consultant in private practice in London,
editor, *New International Library of Group Analysis*

"This rich and thoughtful book will reward its readers well, be they clinicians, historians, commentators or, can we hope, our political leaders. *A Psychoanalytic and Socio-Cultural Exploration of a Continent* provides incisive understanding of the conscious and unconscious group psychological forces that inflame much of the psychological, sociocultural and political upheaval the world is experiencing today."

— **Molyn Leszcz**, MD, FRCPC, CGP, DFAGPA,
Professor of Psychiatry, University of Toronto,
President-Elect, the American Group
Psychotherapy Association

A PSYCHOANALYTIC AND SOCIO-CULTURAL EXPLORATION OF A CONTINENT

This important book gathers a set of influential international contributors with psychoanalytic and group analytic knowledge to provide a wide-ranging critical analysis of the present state of Europe.

Europe is facing huge challenges: waves of immigrants are reshaping its identity and testing its tolerance; Brexit is a destabilizing factor and its outcomes are not yet clear; economic crises continue to threaten; the resurgence of nationalism is threatening an open-borders one-continent ideology. This book tackles some of these challenges. Divided into two parts, the first analyses the current social, political, cultural and economic trends in Europe using psychoanalytic and group analytic concepts, while the second concentrates on existing applications of psychoanalytic and group analytic concepts to help manage national and international change in individual countries as well as on the continent as a whole, including groups for German, Ukrainian and Russian participants; groups organised in Serbia in order to overcome the recent, traumatic past; and the "Sandwich model", developed to enhance communication in situations of conflict, trauma and blocked communication. When we feel threatened, we cling to our in-group and its members. We want to think the same and be the same as our neighbors, but this group illusion of homogeneity conceals the fact that we are different. While homogeneity offers stability, it is diversity that offers freedom.

This book will be of great interest to researchers on the present state of Europe from across a range of different disciplines, from psychoanalysis to politics, sociology, economics and international relations.

Anna Zajenkowska, PhD, is Adjunct Professor and head of the Department of Social Psychology and Doctoral School of the Maria Grzegorzewska University in Warsaw. She is a trained group analyst and board member of the IGAR (Institute of Group Analysis RASZTÓW). She also has several years of international experience in business (Poland, Austria and Korea), which she uses while conducting intercultural trainings.

Uri Levin is a clinical psychologist, group analyst and organizational consultant. He is a board member of the EFPP (European Federation of Psychoanalytic Psychotherapy), and a member of IIGA, GASi and IAGP. He teaches and supervises both in individual and group settings. He works mainly at his private practice in Tel Aviv with adults, couples and adolescents.

The EFPP Monograph Series
Anne-Marie Schlösser (Series Editor)

A series of Monographs produced in conjunction with the European Federation for Psychoanalytic Psychotherapy (EFPP). Each volume brings together writings on a particular topic by authors from several European countries. The EFPP promotes communication and discussion between psychotherapists across national boundaries in the child and adolescent, adult, family and group sections of the organisation, through its conferences and seminars on topics of interest in contemporary psychoanalytic psychotherapy. The organisation represents some 13,000 psychoanalytic psychotherapists in twenty-two countries in Western, Central and Eastern Europe and is concerned with many matters which are relevant to the profession, such as training and registration.

Recent titles in the series include:

A Psychoanalytic Exploration on Sameness and Otherness
Beyond Babel
Edited by Anne-Marie Schlösser

A Psychoanalytic and Socio-Cultural Exploration of a Continent
Europe on the Couch
Edited by Anna Zajenkowska and Uri Levin

A Bridge Over Troubled Water
Conflicts and Reconciliation in Groups and Society
Edited by Gila Ofer

For further information about this series please visit www.routledge.com/The-EFPP-Monograph-Series/book-series/KARNACEFPPPM

A PSYCHOANALYTIC AND SOCIO-CULTURAL EXPLORATION OF A CONTINENT

Europe on the Couch

Edited by Anna Zajenkowska and Uri Levin

LONDON AND NEW YORK

First published 2020
by Routledge
2 Park Square, Milton Park, Abingdon, Oxon OX14 4RN

and by Routledge
52 Vanderbilt Avenue, New York, NY 10017

Routledge is an imprint of the Taylor & Francis Group, an informa business

© 2020 selection and editorial matter, Anna Zajenkowska and Uri Levin; individual chapters, the contributors

The right of Anna Zajenkowska and Uri Levin to be identified as the authors of the editorial material, and of the authors for their individual chapters, has been asserted in accordance with sections 77 and 78 of the Copyright, Designs and Patents Act 1988.

All rights reserved. No part of this book may be reprinted or reproduced or utilised in any form or by any electronic, mechanical, or other means, now known or hereafter invented, including photocopying and recording, or in any information storage or retrieval system, without permission in writing from the publishers.

Trademark notice: Product or corporate names may be trademarks or registered trademarks, and are used only for identification and explanation without intent to infringe.

British Library Cataloguing-in-Publication Data
A catalogue record for this book is available from the British Library

Library of Congress Cataloging-in-Publication Data
A catalog record has been requested for this book

ISBN: 978-0-367-18274-8 (hbk)
ISBN: 978-0-367-18277-9 (pbk)
ISBN: 978-0-429-06044-1 (ebk)

Typeset in Bembo
by Apex CoVantage, LLC

CONTENTS

Foreword by Morris Nitsun	*x*
Acknowledgments	*xiii*
About the contributors	*xiv*

Europe on the couch: the breaking of a homogeneous
group illusion   1
Anna Zajenkowska and Uri Levin

PART ONE
General reflections   **5**

1 Learning from history? The crisis and future of the
European project   7
Aleida Assmann

2 A way of seeing some effects of globalization and new
technologies in Europe   20
Maria Eugenia Cid Rodríguez

3 Relationality in the age of neoliberal dispossession:
Protecting the "other"   32
Marianna Fotaki

viii Contents

4 My Europe: a continent between rejection and
re-inclusion: a discussion with Dr. Robi Friedman 44
Anna Zajenkowska and Uri Levin

PART TWO
Particular understanding **55**

5 The image of Europe in the social unconscious of Israeli Jews 57
Haim Weinberg

6 Poland and the other – the other and Poland: a dialogue
between a newcomer and a native 67
Ziad Abou Saleh and Bogdan de Barbaro

7 The German "Welcoming Culture" – some thoughts about
its psychodynamics 85
Regine Scholz

8 Norway: between grandiosity and inferiority 99
Thor Kristian Island

9 Far from the madding crowd: pre to post Brexit Britain 112
Halina Brunning and Olya Khaleelee

10 Will Brexit brake the EU? 124
Shmuel Bernstein

PART THREE
Practical interventions **133**

11 National nightmare: thoughts on the genesis and legacy of
perpetrator trauma 135
M. Gerard Fromm

12 Social memory of the Holocaust in Poland 147
Katarzyna Prot-Klinger and Krzysztof Szwajca

13 Negotiation between three ambivalently connected
nations: finding common ground through metaphors in
multinational large group sessions 163
Marie-Luise Alder and Stephan Alder

Contents **ix**

14 The Balkans on the Reflective-Citizens couch unraveling
social–psychic–retreats 175
Marina Mojović

15 Europe on the couch in Social Dreaming Matrices 188
Gila Ofer

Index *199*

FOREWORD

Europe on the couch

I write in London, UK, in early March 2019, in the midst of the ever-deepening Brexit crisis. We are now only weeks away from the deadline of departure, 29th March 2019, and still there is no clear way ahead. I cannot remember a time of greater confusion and fragmentation in the United Kingdom and, more generally, on the European stage. It is not only the complexity of the issues but the extreme division between parties, people and points of view that is so bewildering. A common response amongst friends and colleagues, indeed the public at large, is one of exasperation and futility. "Wake me up when it's all over", a friend uttered recently, expressing a wish to forget, to withdraw. "Let them get on with it", he said, "just don't expect me to stick around". That intelligent people, responsible, thoughtful citizens who normally are engaged with current affairs should have reached a point of such weariness and resignation is significant – and worrying.

While there is now an enormous amount of literature on the political and historical background to the European crisis, it is striking how little has been written on the psychological aspects, in particular the group processes at work in the mess that is currently Europe. Not only is there a lack of integration and coherence in actual day-to-day affairs, but also a lack of cogent analysis of the group processes that both generate the conflict and are triggered by them in a circular process. Amongst the shouts of political dogma and dissension, of pro-European and anti-European rhetoric, of left- and right-wing ideology, there appears to be no voice reflecting an in-depth psychological perspective that might help to make sense of the mess. For this reason, the initiative of putting "Europe on the couch", as this book sets out to do, is timely and appropriate. Europe can indeed be seen as a patient, a tired, worn-out, confused patient, prone to splitting and dissociation, unconsciously suicidal or destructive and in need of help. However, we also have

Foreword **xi**

to be careful not to pathologize, since many of the issues we face in Europe are the consequences of major anxiety about survival and continuity in a very uncertain, constantly changing world, of the escalating pressures of population growth and immigration, of rampant technological progress and the globalization and "virtualization" of our very existence.

It is encouraging that group analysis, psychoanalysis and related disciplines have in this book risen to the challenge, have come together as a body of thinkers and writers to try and understand and unravel the predicament we are in. Group analysis and psychoanalysis have increasingly ventured outside the consulting room, addressing social and political developments, past and present, and trying to throw light on the kinds of issues that tend to escape rational structural analysis. We need insights drawing on both conscious and unconscious processes, on notions of group inclusion and exclusion, on the dynamics of conformity and compliance, on the genesis of prejudice and hatred. In terms of my own concept of the anti-group (Nitsun, 1996, 2015), I see a gross enactment of pro-group and anti-group forces, of groups breaking up or clinging together, of a yearning for belonging and a revulsion at belonging, with fears of smaller groups being swallowed up by the larger group, with projection onto the "other" group of all that is undesirable, and on the implosion and disintegration of groups that have once known unity and now face breakdown. Much of this evokes fears of extinction, influenced by the shadows of two destructive world wars that loom large in a dangerous age of political power play and technological transformation.

Once the Brexit dust has settled, assuming it does, what chances are there of stability and coherence in the hothouse of Europe? There are reasons to be pessimistic: the swing to right-wing authoritarianism and control; the looming threat of left-wing insurgency. But, as with all crises, there may also be opportunities. If we can see the crisis as an inevitable part of history, of the ongoing dynamics of group and anti-group in a changing world ecology, there may also be forms of understanding and facilitation that make the ride a little bit less frightening. Further, and in spite of crises, there are of course enormous resources in Europe, at all levels of country and culture. To this end, I welcome the sections of this book that offer the hope of positive, practical intervention, that apply theory in the interests of adding coherence and containment and that draw on our shared humanity and ultimately common purpose of survival and growth. Europe, the patient on the couch, may never be the same again, but from the chaos and confusion may emerge new potentials and possibilities.

There is wisdom in Winnicott's notion of creative destruction (Winnicott, 1974), the idea that growth processes paradoxically entail destructive processes and require the testing out of destructive forces. Although Winnicott focused on infant development and the dynamics of the mother-child pair, much of what he said relates to wider social processes. I have several times drawn on this idea in my own work and writing on groups (Nitsun, 1996, 2015) and I suggest that it is very applicable to Europe on the couch. In some ways, what we are now experiencing may be an inevitable part of the undoing process of history, of the destruction of the old in

xii Foreword

order to create the new. This book, I propose, is a valuable part of the dialogue that supports such a creative, if painful transition. The editors of this searching and original book, Anna Zajenkowska and Uri Levin, have drawn together a group of eminent writers in the field and are to be congratulated on a considerable achievement.

Morris Nitsun

References

Nitsun, M. (1996). *The anti-group: Destructive forces in the group and their creative potential*. London: Routledge.

Nitsun, M. (2015). *Beyond the anti-group: Survival and transformation*. London: Routledge.

Winnicott, D. W. (1974). *Playing and reality*. London: Pelican.

ACKNOWLEDGMENTS

We are grateful to the European Federation of Psychoanalytic Psychotherapy (EFPP) and to all its board members, for supporting the process of writing this book.

We are especially thankful to Ms. Anne-Marie Schlosser, past-president of the EFPP and the editor-in-chief of the EFPP books series, for her continuous encouragement.

From the outset, the publisher gave us most valuable and appreciated support. Elliott Morsia and Russell George from Routledge were extremely helpful in the last stages of production. Without them, it would have been impossible to conclude the work.

Ms. Monika Stolarska was responsible for the long and creative process of designing the book's front cover. She was always sensitive to our needs and professional in her replies.

We were assisted by Dr. Gila Ofer's trustworthy advice and optimistic spirit, by Dr. Robi Friedman's hospitality and spurring attitude, and by Dr. Morris Nitsun's engagement and commitment.

The authors of the chapters collectively produced an experienced ensemble of knowledge and wisdom. We heartily thank them for the effective and productive communication along the Sisyphean editing process. Their patience and tolerance to our requests were key factors to keep the work joyful and playful.

Last but not least we wish to thank our families and good friends for giving us the space and time we needed for our work, as well as for believing in our project and in us.

ABOUT THE CONTRIBUTORS

Marie-Luise Alder holds a Master's Degree at International Psychoanalytic University Berlin (IPU) with a Master's thesis about Psychoanalysis in Istanbul. Alder is a scientific research assistance in the CEMPP Project (Conversation Analysis of Empathy in Psychotherapy Process Research) at IPU (2014–2017). Since 2017, Alder has been in psychotherapeutic/psychoanalytic training. She is an active member of the research group under Prof. Michael B. Buchholz at IPU.

Stephan Alder is Medical Doctor, Psychiatrist, Neurologist, Psychotherapist, Psychoanalyst (German Society of Psychoanalysis, Psychosomatic and Depth Psychology, DGPT), Jungian Psychoanalyst (German and International Society of Analytical Psychology, DGAP-IAAP) and Group Analyst (German Society for Group Analysis and Group Therapy, D3G, Group Analytic Society International, GASi).

Aleida Assmann is Professor Emeritus of English Literature and Literary Theory at the University of Konstanz, Germany. She held guest professorships at Rice, Princeton, Yale, Chicago, Vienna, Mainz and Lucerne. Main areas of research: historical anthropology, media history and cultural memory. Recent publications: *Memory in a Global Age: Discourses, Practices and Trajectories* (ed. with Sebastian Conrad, 2010), *Cultural Memory and Western Civilization: Functions, Media, Archives* (2012), *Memory and Political Change* (ed. with Linda Shortt, 2012), *Introduction to Cultural Studies: Topics, Concepts, Issues* (2012), *Shadows of Trauma: Memory and the Politics of Postwar Identity* (2016).

Bogdan de Barbaro is a clinical psychiatrist, psychotherapist and a supervisor of psychotherapy and family therapy. de Barbaro is also currently Professor of psychiatry and Director of Department of Psychiatry in Collegium Medicum of the Jagiellonian University, Krakow, Poland.

About the contributors **xv**

Shmuel Bernstein is Supervising Clinical Psychologist, Jungian Analyst, President ISAP, Past Director of the Adolescents Unit, Summit Institute Jerusalem, and Past Director of Psychotherapy in the Adolescents Program under the auspices of the Sigmund Freud Centre in the Hebrew University of Jerusalem and Summit Institute.

Halina Brunning is Chartered Clinical Psychologist, Freelance Organizational Consultant and Accredited Executive Coach. Brunning published extensively on clinical and organizational issues and edited several books for Karnac including *Executive Coaching: Systems-Psychodynamic Perspective* (2006), translated into Italian in 2009. Between 2010 and 2014 Brunning conceived of and edited a trilogy of books which analyses the contemporary world through a psychoanalytic lens: *Psychoanalytic Perspectives on a Turbulent World*.

Marianna Fotaki is Professor of Business Ethics at the University of Warwick Business School and holds a PhD from the London School of Economics and Political Science. She has published over 70 articles, book chapters and books on gender, inequalities and the marketization of public services. Marianna currently works on whistleblowing (funded by the ESRC and British Academy/Leverhulme Trust), solidarity responses to crisis and refugee arrivals in Greece.

Robi Friedman is Clinical Psychologist, Group Analyst, and Co-founder and Past Chair of the Israel Institute for Group Analysis. Friedman is also Past President of the Group Analytic Society (International). He is Teaching Group Analyst at SGAZ (Zurich Institute for GA) and writes on relational aspects of dreamtelling, disorders, soldiers' matrix and the large group.

M. Gerard Fromm, PhD, is Distinguished Faculty and Former Director, Erikson Institute of the Austen Riggs Center. Trained in psychoanalysis, Jerry is the current President of the International Dialogue Initiative, an interdisciplinary group that studies the psychodynamics of societal conflict, and a Past President of ISPSO.

Thor Kristian Island, MD, is a psychiatrist, psychotherapist, supervisor and training group analyst in private practice in Oslo, Norway. He is Co-founder and Previous Director of Institute of Group Analysis (Norway). He was also Co-founder and Previous President of the Norwegian Group Psychotherapy Association.

Olya Khaleelee is a corporate psychologist and organizational consultant with a particular interest in organizational and societal transformation. She was for many years Director of OPUS: an Organisation for Promoting Understanding of Society, which seeks to enhance awareness of our roles as citizens.

Uri Levin is a clinical psychologist, group analyst and organizational consultant. He is a board member of the EFPP (European Federation of Psychoanalytic

xvi About the contributors

Psychotherapy), and a member of IIGA, GASi and IAGP. He teaches and supervises both in individual and group settings. He works mainly at his private practice in Tel Aviv with adults, couples and adolescents.

Marina Mojović is a psychiatrist, psychoanalytic psychotherapist, training group-analyst and organizational consultant; Member of GASi, IAGP, ISPSO, OPUS, EFPP. In GAS-Belgrade: Founder of Psychosocial/Systems-Psychodynamic Training, Social Dreaming Training, and Serbian Reflective-Citizens Koinonia. Special interests: large groups, social unconscious, social trauma, "black holes" and "gangs" in foundation matrix. Author of the concepts "social-psychic-retreats" and "conception-trauma".

Gila Ofer, PhD, is a clinical psychologist, training psychoanalyst and group analyst. She is Co-founder and Past President of Tel-Aviv Institute of Contemporary Psychoanalysis (TAICP) and a founding member of the Israeli Institute of Group Analysis (IIGA). Ofer is also Lecturer and Supervisor in the Program of Psychoanalytic Psychotherapy at Tel-Aviv University and is on the faculty of TAICP and IIGA. She is convening training in group analysis in Istanbul and in Bucharest and is Coordinator of Eastern European countries EFPP and the Editor of the *EFPP Psychoanalytic Psychotherapy Review.*

Katarzyna Prot-Klinger is a psychiatrist, psychotherapist and Professor at Maria Gregorzewska University. She conducts individual and group psychotherapy of Holocaust survivors and is the author of many publications.

Maria Eugenia Cid Rodríguez is a clinical psychologist, trained in Madrid and London at the Tavistock Clinic. She is a psychoanalytic psychotherapist, founding member of the AMPP of which she is currently teacher, supervisor and president. Additionally, Rodríguez is Member of the Board of the AEPP and EFPP delegate, and she's Associate Member of the APM (IPA). Private practice.

Ziad Abou Saleh is Doctor of Sociology, researcher and lecturer at the SWPS University of Social Sciences and Humanities and Higher School of Banking in Wrocław. Saleh is an expert on Polish-Arabic dialogue and negotiations and a Polish citizen of Syrian origin.

Regine Scholz, PhD, is a group analyst and licenced psychotherapist in private practice, specialized in trauma treatment. Scholz is a former member (2010-2017) of the MC of the Group Analytic Society International (GASI), member of the editorial board of the journal *Group Analysis*, founding member of the German Society for Group Analysis and Group Psychotherapy (D3G) and IDI fellow. Her publications are mainly about the psychic impact of culture and collective trauma.

Krzysztof Szwajca, MD, is a psychiatrist, psychotherapist and psychotherapy supervisor. He is Employee of the Department of Child and Adolescent Psychiatry, Jagiellonian University Medical College, and a head of the Home Treatment Team in the Clinic. Szwajca is a student of Professor Maria Orwid and a member of the team founded and headed by her, which works with chronic war trauma. He is a co-author and author of about 50 scientific publications.

Dr. Haim Weinberg is a psychologist, group analyst and Certified Group Psychotherapist in private practice in California. Weinberg is Past President of the Israeli Association of Group Psychotherapy and of the Northern California Group Psychotherapy Society. He co-edits a series of books about the social unconscious, wrote a book on Internet groups and co-authored a book on fairy tales and the social unconscious.

Anna Zajenkowska, PhD, is Adjunct Professor and head of the Department of Social Psychology and Doctoral School of the Maria Grzegorzewska University in Warsaw. She is a trained group analyst and board member of the IGAR (Institute of Group Analysis RASZTÓW). She also has several years of international experience in business (Poland, Austria and Korea), which she uses while conducting intercultural trainings.

EUROPE ON THE COUCH

The breaking of a homogeneous group illusion

Anna Zajenkowska and Uri Levin

Is Europe a 'sibling orientated' or an 'authority orientated' group? That is a question that emerged during a discussion described in the book by Robi Friedman and us, the editors. This question mirrors the current situation in Europe, which resembles a constant fight between the separation-individuation desire and symbiotic needs (Mahler, 1968).

Symbiotic needs were clearly visible in the 60s, 70s and 80s of the last century when two major processes pushing in the direction of homogeneity pervaded Europe. Eastern Europe was still under the 'artificial' unity forced on it by the Soviets, the western part the European Union consolidated in response to adding new member countries. The fall of the iron curtain on the one hand, and now Brexit on the other hand, tell us we might be reaching the end of the illusion of homogeneity in Europe, and represent strong separation-individuation desires.

The book gathers authors with psychoanalytic and group analytic knowledge that is used to obtain better understanding and insight into what has been happening in Europe recently and what the future might bring to this disquieted land. We believe that theories created to give us better tools for treating the symptoms of the psyche can also be beneficial in analyzing political, social, cultural and economic structures. And how can individual and group psychological practitioners contribute to citizens of the continent? No doubt, Europe is facing huge challenges, just to name a few: waves of immigrants are reshaping its identity and testing its tolerance; Brexit is a destabilizing factor and its outcomes are not yet clear; economic crises are still breathing down numerous countries' necks. The resurgence of nationalism is promising for many and threatening the open-borders-one continent ideology.

The nationalistic remake on the European scene seems to contradict everything else that opposes its values and norms. It is being activated and strengthen by awaken fear and traumas from the past (Volkan, 2001). When people feel threatened, there is a tendency to cling to in-group members and 'melt' with others. That creates a feeling of oneness and "members seek to join in a powerful union with an omnipotent force, unobtainable high, to surrender self for passive participation, and thereby feel existence, well-being, and wholeness" (Turquet, 1974, p. 357). Hopper (2003) writes that under certain circumstances a group is not really a group, but is either a mass or an aggregate, which reflects a bi-polar form of dysfunctional incohesion. The oscillation between these bi-polar intra-psychic constellations of Aggregation/Massification, which is derived from a fear of annihilation, is a characteristic of traumatized people, groups, organizations and even societies. The feeling of oneness is however an illusion, because we are different. Baumeister (2005) claimed that people balance on a tightrope between stability and freedom. Homogeneity offers relative stability but it is diversity that is related to freedom. That is why we can either reflect after we fall from the tightrope on how not to fall again (freedom direction) or practice how not to lose balance and fall (stability and safety).

This book, with its group of contributors, theories, conceptualizations and reveries, will try to cope with the challenge of better understanding the psychological processes underpinning Europe's contemporary tectonic movements.

Europe – a group

Europe is a group of countries. Group members create bonds and relations with each other. People who value groups tend to share a communal orientation that stresses a focus on others, which is a common factor with collectivism (Wojciszke, 2010). Psychological studies have shown that when activating the idea of collectivism, more emphasis is placed on social or relational identities and also on closeness and obligation to other group members, and that sensitivity to their needs and goals will increase (Oyserman & Lee, 2008). That would be the idealistic orientation for the European countries.

Nonetheless, the human self comprises many subsystems or parts, like for example an individual-self, which lets people feel that they are unique and different from others, with just their own experiences and characteristics (Sedikides, Gaertner, & O'Mara, 2011). We could use this idea and think about individual countries in Europe trying to preserve their national culture and identity.

The problem is that the individual-self is rather resistant to unfavourable feedback but is open to positive opinions. That is why people would be motivated to protect and preserve the positive idea about the individual-self, which would influence the attribution process. For instance, people would claim more personal responsibility for dyadic or group successes, at the same time they would apportion the responsibility for failures in both dyadic or group members (Alicke & Govorun, 2005; Sedikides & Gregg, 2003). Doesn't that match how European countries perceive their own actions?

Thankfully, the human self is composed of 'multiple selves', which are interconnected and individuals are able to switch between them depending on the context (Messer & Warren, 2000). We have both the individualist part, which when we think about countries could be called the national identity, but we also have the communitarian one, stressing the great importance of relationships, for example, within the EU but also between EU and non-EU countries. That is the reason for the book, to create relationships, at the micro level, between all the people engaged in its creation, but at the macro level, between different social group members – the readers of the book.

The Poland on the Couch project

The idea of the book is closely related to the Poland on the Couch project, which is an initiative of group analysts aimed at building a safe space for conversation – the basis of social life.

Its roots date back to 2014, when an international conference, 'Poland on the Couch – about the strength and fragility of the individual in the contemporary global world seen from the perspective of social and psychodynamic psychology', was held. During the conference, analysts together with representatives of the world of science and the media discussed what is happening in Polish society.

The conference has become an inspiration for the organization of the Reflective Citizens workshops held in different cities in Poland, in which representatives of different environments can have an opportunity to reflect on social processes. One part of the workshops is a Large Group, which creates a space to ask questions and look for answers. During one of the last workshops in 2018, a question regarding the role of psychoanalysts and psychotherapists was raised: what can psychotherapists do in the public space? That is why the current book consists of three parts: General Reflections; Particular Understanding; and Practical Interventions. The first and second concentrate on analyzing processes and dynamics, utilizing psychoanalytic and group analytic concepts, from the macro, that is more a European level, and from the micro, that is a specific country-level perspective. The third part presents some of the current applications of psychoanalytic and group analytic concepts as tools for enhancing national and international change in countries as well as on the 'continent as a whole'.

Content of the book

We cordially invite you to reflect and think together with the authors of the book about the issues described in each of the chapters. In the 'General Reflections' part, Aleida Assmann writes about the importance of history and collective memory, Maria Eugenia Cid Rodríguez concentrates on challenges related to the globalization and technological development that European citizens are facing. Marianna Fotaki presents a very simple yet important solution to address most of the challenges, that is the importance of relations and interdependence. Finally, a discussion with Robi Friedman aims to integrate different theoretical concepts and perspectives on the current processes in Europe, utilizing insider and outsider perspectives on Europe.

The second part deals more specifically with relations between different nations and peoples. Among chapters presenting a country-focused view, Haim Weinberg

4 Anna Zajenkowska and Uri Levin

writes about the trauma of the war and genocide reflected in the Social Unconscious of Israeli Jews. In a fascinating dialogue, Bogdan de Barbaro and Ziad Abou Saleh discuss the attitude of Poles towards the Other, as a Pole and Syrian respectively. Regine Scholz focuses on the perspective of the German 'Welcoming Culture', whereas Thor Kristian Island reflects on the attitude towards the Other with regard to feelings of inferiority and superiority. Finally, this part is concluded with two chapters dealing with the current issues of Brexit. Halina Brunning and Olya Khaleelee closely analyze the social processes leading to it, and Shmuel Bernstein asks if one country leaving the EU can break it.

The last part introduces psychological interventions aimed to facilitate dynamic social processes. M. Gerard Fromm presents an idea of a conference working on perpetrator trauma. Katarzyna Prot-Klinger and Krzysztof Szwajca show how to work with descendants of both perpetrators and victims. Stephan Alder and Marie-Luise Alder describe their experience with Trialog Conferences, where Germans, Russians and Ukrainians meet and talk about their relations, history and future. Marina Mojović describes the use of Reflective Citizens' workshops to support the harsh process of recovery of a country which experienced a civil war. This part, and also our book, is concluded with Gila Ofer's chapter on dreams (Social Dreaming Matrix) revealing at least part of Europeans' unconscious.

References

Alicke, M. D., & Govorun, O. (2005). The better-than-average effect. In M. D. Alicke, D. A. Dunning, & J. I. Krueger (Eds.), *The self in social judgment* (pp. 85–106). New York: Psychology Press.

Baumeister, R. F. (2005). *The cultural animal: Human nature, meaning, and social life*. Oxford: Oxford University Press.

Hopper, E. (2003). *Traumatic experience in the unconscious life of groups: The fourth basic assumption: Incohesion: Aggregation/massification or (ba) I: A/M* (Vol. 23). London and Philadelphia: Jessica Kingsley Publishers.

Mahler, M. S. (1968). On human symbiosis and the vicissitudes of individuation. *Infantile Psychosis*, 1.

Messer, S. B., & Warren, C. S. (2000). Understanding and treating the postmodern self. In J. C. Muran (Ed.), *Self-relations in the psychotherapy process*. New York: Guilford Press, 2001.

Oyserman, D., & Lee, S. W. (2008). Does culture influence what and how we think? Effects of priming individualism and collectivism. *Psychological Bulletin, 134*(2), 311.

Sedikides, C., Gaertner, L., & O'Mara, E. M. (2011). Individual self, relational self, collective self: Hierarchical ordering of the tripartite self. *Psychological Studies, 56*(1), 98–107.

Sedikides, C., & Gregg, A. P. (2003). Portraits of the self. In M. A. Hogg & J. Cooper (Eds.), *Sage handbook of social psychology* (pp. 110–138). London: Sage Publications.

Turquet, P. M. (1974). Leadership: The individual and the group. In G. S. Gibbard et al. (Eds.), *The large group: Therapy and dynamics*. San Francisco and London: Jossey Bass.

Volkan, V. D. (2001). Transgenerational transmissions and chosen traumas: An aspect of large-group identity. *Group Analysis, 34*(1), 79–97.

Wojciszke, B. (2010). *Sprawczość i wspólnotowość. Podstawowe wymiary spostrzegania społecznego (Agency and communion: Basic dimension in social perception)*. Gdańsk: GWP.

PART ONE

General reflections

1

LEARNING FROM HISTORY? THE CRISIS AND FUTURE OF THE EUROPEAN PROJECT

Aleida Assmann

Can we learn from history? I am sure you are all familiar with the standard answer to this question: All we learn from history is that we learn nothing from history. Thinkers as different as Hegel and George Bernhard Shaw agreed on this point. Reinhart Koselleck later added a specific reason for this negative answer: We cannot learn from history because modernity is a dynamic process propelled by constant innovations and radical change. The effect is that old lessons can no longer be applied to new problems (Koselleck, 1989). Paul Valéry also belonged to those who could not imagine that history was a teacher of life. In 1931, after the First and before the Second World War, he observed how the European nations geared up their past, transforming it into an explosive weapon of propaganda.

> History is the most dangerous concoction that was ever created by the chemistry of the intellect. Its effects are well known. It makes the nations dream, transports them into ecstasy, creates fabulations, heightens their reflexes, keeps their wounds open, stirs them from their rest, leads them to megalomania, and is the cause that nations become embittered, boasting, obnoxious and vain.

And he continues: "History justifies whatever you like. It does not teach anything, because it contains all and provides examples for everything."[1]

Learning from history after 1945

Valéry did not live to see the end of the Second World War. I want to argue that Europeans did indeed learn from history after the war, but the lessons that were absorbed differed with shifting contexts. When we think about learning lessons from history, we have to be aware of the fact that these lessons change over time. For this reason we need to pay attention to the historical contexts and frames in

8 Aleida Assmann

which they develop. The emergence of a new value system is a complex, continuous and contingent process that is facilitated by internal developments and pushed by sudden shifts and external pressure. To better understand the long-term project of the EU, I shall retrace some of the steps to observe more closely which lessons from history the EU has heeded at what time.

After 1945, all energies were focused on the forging of a new beginning. Elementary principles of justice were re-established in the Nuremberg trials. With these trials, the allies cleared the ground and granted West Germany the license for a new start. To achieve this goal of a new beginning, one had to look forward. Looking backward was not an option, as Churchill clearly explained when he spoke to young students in Zurich in 1946:

> We must all turn our backs upon the horrors of the past and look to the future. We cannot afford to drag forward across the years to come hatreds and revenges which have sprung from the injuries of the past. If Europe is to be saved from infinite misery, and indeed from final doom, there must be an act of faith in the European family and an act of oblivion against all the crimes and follies of the past.[2]

It is important to understand these words in their historical context that jar today with our historical sensibility. After 1945, the politicians did not argue for a memory culture. On the contrary: The first lesson from history that Churchill learned after the war was *to forget*. He was aware that the Germans had turned what they called 'the shame of Versailles' into a propaganda memory that mobilized hate and resentment which helped Hitler to fanaticize the Germans and lead them directly into the Second World War. Historical memories therefore were deemed highly dangerous. Like Valéry, Churchill considered them as a toxic element in the chemistry of the spirit and as explosive fuel unleashing further violence.

The first lesson to be learned from history after 1945 was to create peace among Western European neighbors and the way to consolidate this peace was through a pact of silence and a culture of forgetting. The framework of this peace was not very peaceful however; it was the Cold War that called for a strong Western military alliance against the Eastern alliance of the Soviet Union. The Western alliance started in 1950 as a European community of coal and steel. There was a clear aim in this economic and political collaboration, which was the taming of Germany. What had to be avoided at all costs was a Germany that would once more build up a heavy industry and start another war. The economic community of the six member states, Belgium, Germany, France, Italy, Luxemburg and the Netherlands, was installed to secure peace. Germany, which had started the Second World War and unleashed so much excessive violence across Europe, had to be contained and controlled in this process of integration.

The Western European community saw rapid economic growth thanks to the American investment of the Marshall Plan, its integration into NATO and a strong Western Alliance. The nations were quickly modernized in this period of economic boom when the past was forgotten and all energies invested in the future. 'Development' was the magic word of the time; growth seemed endless and the words 'future' and 'progress' were synonymous.[3] The rapid modernization process, aimed at economic prosperity and the enlargement of the EU market, continued in the 1970s. Through the accession of Denmark, Ireland and England, the number of member states grew to nine. By the 1980s, the last West-European dictatorships, Portugal, Spain and Greece, had turned into democracies. With their membership, the political zone of the European market was further homogenized and enlarged.

Learning from history after 1989

This continuous development was crossed by an historical event that nobody had anticipated. After the collapse of the Berlin Wall and the Iron Curtain in Europe, the politics of the Cold War came to an end. This led eventually to the unexpected growth of the EU beyond its Eastern borders. In 1995 three more Western European states joined the EU, Finland, Austria and Sweden, and a decade later in 2004 and 2007, twelve Central and Eastern European states followed. What Putin registered in 2005 as the greatest geopolitical catastrophe of the 20th century could equally be called the greatest success story in the second half of the 20th century, spanning the Cold War and the new millennium. This perspective, however, has not really been rooted in the minds and hearts of Europeans. The EU has been reluctant when it comes to expressing a clear-cut self-image, let alone a notion of its identity. We have to come back to this historical moment to discover the foundational values of the EU that can serve as the yardstick for its development and orientation. The EU was not only enlarged after the fall of the wall, it was also genuinely reshaped and reconstituted in a rapid and deep process of transformation. This was a moment when old lessons from history were confirmed and new ones were added. Let us focus on these lessons, which to my mind create the frame and foundation of the European project.

The European dream

Nation states, as Ernest Renan already knew, are held together by a 'national myth' (Renan, 1882). Myth in this sense is not the opposite of factual history but a foundational narrative. Such a narrative may be grounded on the past or on a vision of the future. American literary critic Leslie Fiedler has emphasized that in contrast to the British or French nation the American nation is not unified by a common memory but by a shared dream. "As Americans," he wrote, "we are inhabitants of a shared vision and not of a common history" (Fiedler, 1988, p. 73). This vision is the 'American Dream', which is promised to Americans as individuals and not as a collective. He or she who works hard can get ahead and rise to the top of the social hierarchy.

Thinking along the lines proposed by Fiedler we may say that the Europeans are inhabitants both of a common history and a shared vision of the future. Past

10 Aleida Assmann

and future are directly linked in what I call 'the European Dream'. It is no less remarkable than the American dream because it is addressed to both individuals and nations. It refers to two impressive transformations:

> – *From war to peace, showing how deadly enemies can be transformed into friendly neighbors and collaborating partners.*
> – *From dictatorships to democracies, showing how totalitarian coercion cedes liberty and individual rights.*

Indeed most of the 28 EU member states have had experience with dictatorships, of the fascist and the Stalinist version. These two transformations have entered the DNA of the EU, but they could be much deeper anchored in the consciousness of its citizens who tend to take these gifts and achievements thoughtlessly for granted. The European dream should be clearly defined and recognized by everyone for what it is: a high good and prized asset those generations of young Europeans have enjoyed and profited from, growing up into a region without menacing borders, offering not only individual mobility but also intellectual and cultural liberty and transnational exchange. Recent regime changes in Hungary or Poland have shown, however, that democratic structures are not written in granite but a precarious good that needs to be defended and protected. The uniformity of state-sponsored media, the return to an autocratic legal system, the monologic message of public monuments and museums and the growing infringement of citizen participation – these are alarming signals that the gifts of democracy can easily be taken back step by step.

Two more lessons

Form war to peace and from dictatorships to democracies – these lessons from history were learned already after 1945 and re-confirmed after 1990. What is less known, however, is that after 1990 the EU learned two more lessons that are as central for its constitution and have also become part of its DNA. These lessons have become manifest in two new phenomena that reinforce each other: the adoption of a new 'memory culture' (Erinnerungskultur) and the implementation of a human rights regime.

(1) A new memory culture

When the wall came down and communism ended, voices were heard that proclaimed 'the end of history'. It was not history, however, that came to end, but the time regime of modernity, which received a severe blow. Together with the expectation of a bright future, the vision of progress, steady growth and reliable resources faded.[4] As the future lost its glamor, the past returned with a vengeance. Not only in West Germany, the informal consensus to turn one's back to the dark past came to an end. The time obviously had come for the EU to learn a new lesson from history. While after 1945 the lesson had been *to forget*, the lesson was now *to remember*.

The new German 'memory culture' (Erinnerungskultur) was a historical novelty in that it was based on the 'negative memory' of excessive violence that Germans had perpetrated on innocent victims and civilians during the Second World War. It focused on the atrocities of the war that were now perceived as an unfathomable crime that had to be remembered. Forgetting suddenly appeared as a second murder that happens when the nameless dead that had been murdered are forgotten. The genocide should not be followed by a 'mnemocide'. Framed by the new concepts of responsibility, accountability and empathy, a transnational memory of the Holocaust was inscribed into the constitution of the EU.

In the late 1980s and 90s, a phrase was often repeated that expressed a temporal paradox, and perhaps even a temporal pathology: 'The further the Holocaust is retreating in time, the more closely is it approaching us'. Traumatic violence is impossible to process; it silences both the victims and the perpetrators. While the victims, however, regained their voices and developed forms of a memory culture, the perpetrators profited from the social consensus of forgetting and 'communicative silence'. In Germany, this pact of silence was broken when the 'generation war' stepped back and their sons and daughters, the 1968 generation, took over responsibility and offices in the 1980s and 90s. Trauma has been defined as "a past that does not pass".[5] If trauma is silenced, time itself does not dissolve it. It warps time and chronology, leaving a black hole that disrupts the linear flow of time. Instead of disappearing with time, trauma produces periods of latency after which the past suddenly returns and invades the present with undiminished impact.

The memory of the Holocaust returned in the 1980s and 90s as the unacknowledged aftermath of the Second World War. It had been given a name in the 1960s, but it had not yet found a place in Germany's political system and in the general consciousness of the society. The shared transnational memory of the Holocaust was inscribed into the DNA of the EU with the Stockholm declaration in 2000 and a further UN-declaration in 2005. What had been forgotten, dropped, repressed and silenced eventually returned with a strong affective impact.[6] While there are no direct links between the history of the Holocaust and other events such as slavery or colonialism, the discursive framework of the latter was taken over as a template to articulate also other historical wounds and traumas. In the wake of the recovery of the memory of the Holocaust, the task of taking responsibility for crimes against humanity in the course of their national history has spread also to nations all over the globe who are currently in the process of transitioning from autocratic regimes to democracy. This cumulative effect caused a shift in the construction of national memory and identity from heroic to post-heroic narratives.

Some historians saw their professional authority endangered by the new memory boom. This new memory culture, however, did not challenge, let alone repeal the standards of historical scholarship. On the contrary, historical research took an active part in the effort to recover a previously ignored or denied historical truth. The moment for facing the historical truth had come for Germany immediately after the War together with the opening of the concentration camps and the global publicizing of the shameful atrocities. For other European countries, it came after

12 Aleida Assmann

1990 with the opening of hitherto sealed Eastern European archives.[7] Archival documents, historical research, historical commissions and the collection of oral testimonies enlarged historical knowledge and increased the scope and complexity of Holocaust memory, challenging some firmly established national self-images and causing the revision of national narratives. Here are a few examples: New documents about Vichy and the history of anti-Semitism in East Germany put an end to the self-image of France or the GDR as pure resistors; after the scandals about the Nazi past of Austrian president Kurt Waldheim and information about a Polish pogrom in Jedwabne, Austria and Poland were no longer able to claim exclusively the status of victim, and even the seemingly neutral Swiss was confronted with its own 'sites of memory' in the form of their banks and borders. In contact with the crime of the Holocaust, national memories became more dialogic, integrating also negative instances of the past into the national narrative.

(2) The re-implantation of human rights

This shift in memory politics was framed by the human rights regime, which is the other new lesson to be learned by the EU from history after 1990. Human rights had of course been declared various times at the end of the 18th century and also after the Second World War, but it is important to note that they were implemented and claimed by new historical actors only in the 1980s. After a long rhetorical and declarative incubation period, the active history of human rights stated with NGOs such as Amnesty International and Human Rights Watch who systematically observed human rights violations and used new communication technology to mobilize a larger public in the digital global arena. One of its first manifestations were the demonstrations of the 'mothers and grandmothers on the Plaza de Mayo' in Argentina who claimed their disappeared husbands, children and grandchildren. These political actors were women with white scarfs, looking very different from the usual icon of the revolutionary hero, but their persistent collective moral force brought the dictatorship to an end and initiated a process of political transition and commemoration – along the lines of human rights claims.

In the West, the end of the Cold War brought to an end the unquestioned dominant time regime of modernity, and in the East the equally future-oriented political ideology of communism/Stalinism. This produced a crisis of orientation as it left a cognitive and emotional vacuum. I want to contend that this vacuum was soon filled with the human rights paradigm that offered itself as a political substitute in this period of transition. Samuel Moyn has referred to the human rights paradigm as a 'last utopia' (Moyn, 2010). After the collapse of communism the time was ripe for the new 'era of human rights'. Adopting human rights as a yardstick of political practice was not just another lesson learned by the EU after 1990. It rather became the core value that confirmed, supported and framed all the other lessons learned from Europe's violent history.

While communism had been built on a narrative of progress that mobilized the masses and advocated a violent struggle for a better future, the regime of human rights intervenes on behalf of the victims of history, including those of communism, and emphasizes the protection of the vulnerable individual. As communism is a political ideology that is emphatically future-oriented, it has blind spots when it comes to the past, rendering it virtually incapable of critically assessing its past and of acknowledging its own victims of violence. As the new human rights regime started to replace the older frameworks within which power struggles used to be debated in terms of class struggles, national revolutions or political antagonisms, historical violence could be newly addressed and criticized. By resorting to the universal value of bodily integrity and human rights, the new terminology introduced a new universal moral standard that criminalized the violations and led to the elaboration of new memory policies (Jelin, 2003). It was indeed the re-implantation of the human rights paradigm that for the first time provided a framework within which historical crimes could be addressed and 'normative violence' could be exposed and criticized (Butler, 1999, p. xx; Lloyd, 2007, p. 136).

More generally speaking, coming to terms with historical crimes, atrocities and massive human rights violations in the past became a new issue and project in various post-colonial countries that responded to their own injustice and engaged in healing historical wounds. The new consensus backing up the new memory culture and the human rights regime was that from now on "the road to the future runs through the disasters of the past."[8] Extending national accountability from the present to the past led to a rewriting of the national past to include also the victims' experience.

Different lessons from history

The EU member states have absorbed lessons of history, but they have not all learned the same lessons. Germany with its massive historic guilt of having started the Second World War and having initiated and fervently pursued the Holocaust had obviously most to learn from history and has therefore turned into the most dedicated member and supporter of the EU. The lesson of the Holocaust learned by Germans is 'never again become perpetrators!', which blocks their desire for heroic valor, impressive weapons which they rather produce and export than put into practice in armed conflicts. The lesson learned by Israelis, on the other hand, is 'never again become victims!', which explains their striking display of power and strong desire for safety and security. Within the EU, the lessons learned from history also differ considerably. Germany, which had suffered from an overdose of nationalistic and imperialist obsessions, was eager to overcome this past and to embrace a reduced from of nationhood that privileges the transnational over the national. Central and Eastern European nations like Poland and the Baltic states, on the contrary, had had a shortage of nationhood which had been withheld from them through periods of violent occupations, which explains that they were moving in the opposite direction. Instead of grading down their desire for nationhood in the EU, they considered the EU as a frame of protection for strengthening their national ambitions. They chose the memory of collective victimhood as the defining element in the process of their new nation building. It is entrenched in their national museums that have telling names such as 'The House of Terror' in Budapest, the 'Occupation Museums' in Riga and Tallinn and the 'Museum of Genocide' in Vilnius.

While the Jewish victims have entered into a dialogic memory with the nation of their former perpetrators, this has not happened in the case of the victims of Stalinism. On the contrary: Stalin as the hero and the cult of war has moved into the center of Russian commemoration, which prevents any signs of a 'politics of regret' (Olick, 2007) and a more self-critical and inclusive approach to its own past. The possibility of the EU as a frame for encouraging more dialogic memories is further blocked by deeply rooted psychological constraints that have not yet received much attention. They ought, however, to be clearly identified, analyzed and discussed in order to be processed and worked through. Vamik Volkan introduced the term 'chosen trauma' to describe nations like the Serbs who cultivated the experience of a mythic defeat, which 600 years later was politically instrumentalized by Slobodan Milosevic to mobilize hatred and violence against the Muslim Bosnian population in former Yugoslavia (Volkan, 2006). Other psychological blockages may develop in nations that have become the target of excessive violence and genocide. These nations remain extremely vulnerable to re-traumatization and are therefore not readily capable for empathy with other victims, a syndrome that might explain the relation of Poles vis-à-vis Jews or in the approach of Israelis towards Palestinians.

After 2015: the humanitarian crisis and future of the EU

Ingeborg Bachmann has remarked: "history teaches all the time, but it finds no students". The EU has learned enough lessons, and it is now time to heed them and to apply them. 'The European dream' of democracy and peace was shaped after 1945 and reshaped 1990, and is now in a further process of reshaping. The EU is presently undergoing a crisis due to strong centrifugal tendencies of nations that are either breaking away to assert national sovereignty and independence (like the UK) or pushed by a strong religious fervor or fierce nationalism (like Poland and Hungary) that leads to the replacing of democratic structures by autocratic rule. Another even more excruciating challenge is currently hitting the core of the EU value system. This is the arrival at the borders and coasts of Europe of more than a million refugees who have made Europe the goal of their destination as they are fleeing from war, terror and violence. The arrival of masses of refugees at European borders has been perceived in an alarmist framework as a triple threat: the threat of losing one's national identity, the threat of material loss and the security threat. The refugee crisis has split the very core of the EU's value agreement by pitting humanitarian transnational commitment against a commitment to national identity and security. Altruistic and egocentric values clash at the borders of Europe where refugees are detained in camps because no agreement can be reached about their distribution and integration process across the European nations. The situation is

Crisis and future of the European project **15**

continuously exacerbated through terrorist attacks that harden mental borders and dramatize the conflict between us and them, friend and foe, pitting human rights claims and security claims as contradictory and irreconcilable goals. In diplomatic encounters with autocratic states like China and Turkey, however, the EU still refers to itself as a community of values that is united by its firm commitment to human rights. But this also means that the attitude towards refugees has become the ultimate test case for the self-image of the EU and what it stands for.

After 1990 and the abrupt end of the Cold War, the EU has shared its dream and lessons learnt from history after the Second World War with Eastern states from the Soviet Bloc. Today the member states do not need further lessons; instead, they should remember, embrace and apply the old and new lessons. The refugee crisis is indeed the test case whether the lessons that have been absorbed and built into the foundations of the EU are actually put into praxis and working as orientation for the future. To react to this situation by resurrecting proud and self-contained nations and shutting the borders is to quit the European project at this critical stage of transformation. If Europe is to be saved and continued, it is not by withholding the European dream from others and by forgetting its commitment to human rights but by sharing it with others who are eager to embrace the same lessons and values.

The consequence of this impasse is a humanitarian tragedy. What is deeply forgotten at this moment of crisis is the common European history of forced migration. Religious and national wars have led in Europe to forced migrations, frequent regime changes have triggered violent expulsions and genocides like that of the Armenians and of the European Jews have produced deportations and death marches. Today, however, there is as yet no shared European memory of this experience in which millions of Europeans have been actively and passively involved. If the nations of the EU are hesitant right now to respect human rights and share their dream with migrants who are fleeing from war and terror, this is the consequence of a deep historical amnesia. A shared European memory of this experience is not in sight; yet it could raise more awareness and empathy, strengthening solidarity and a common orientation for the future.

In such a situation of impasse, it becomes the project of the arts to bring to the attention of the society from what it averts its eyes and to remind it of what it prefers to forget. In February 2006, during the Berlinale Film Festival, Ai Weiwei brought to Berlin thousands of swimming vests and mounted these last relics of drowned refugees in conspicuous places in the city: the concert hall at the Gendarmenmarkt in the center of Berlin, and, shaped as lotus flowers in the park of the Belvedere in the center of Vienna. The humanitarian tragedy of the refugees is also visibly acted out by a group of artists who call themselves 'Center for Political Beauty'. According to their own self-description, this organization functions as "a think tank which links interventional art, politics, and human rights and attempts to gain the attention of digital media in order to protect human lives."[9] They actually brought back some of the dead bodies of refugees from the periphery of Europe

16 Aleida Assmann

into the capital city of Berlin where they buried them observing ritual ceremonies in a space in front of the Bundestag and the Chancellor's office. By staging symbolically what the society prefers to forget they intervened into the actual political situation, showing what is disappearing from sight within a framework of 'normative violence' (Butler, 1999, p. xx; Lloyd, 2007). With their scandalous and deeply irritating interventions this group is performing a symbolic act on two levels: in burying the actual dead drowned in the Mediterranean they are giving them back their names and, at the same time, remind the society of an age-old cultural duty and a humanitarian right, which is to receive a proper burial.

Europe's others – extending the bounds of EU memory

When speaking of 'Europe's others', many think today of the migrants that are now heading towards this region, desperately trying to salvage lives and existences that were wrecked by war and violence. The EU may forge a link to these others not only by creating and empathic memory of flight and expulsion, but also by addressing another historical amnesia that concerns Europe's colonial history. It is amazing how strong the barriers still are that prevent European nations from critically reflecting on this defining history and forming it into a memory of the EU. Europe is connected to the world through a long history of colonization and colonialism. Reaching into so-called 'new worlds' and extending its realm of power and influence beyond its borders was one of Europe's defining features. This history started in early modernity at the time of the reformation and peaked in the 19th century when European empires fought in fierce competition over far-away territories. The devastating wars of the 20th centuries were global wars, implicating regions and nations that were far removed from the continent of Europe. While in the meantime the murder of European Jews has become a shared memory of the EU, the post-imperial nations are still far from forming a shared dialogic memory of this history together with the former colonized.

Here is just one example. When Pierre Nora's volumes on *Lieux de mémoire* met with great resonance in the 1980s and 90s, few readers noticed that only one of his 100 listed sites of memory of the French nation dealt with French colonial history. In 2005 a 'memory law' was passed in France stipulating that French colonialism was to be presented only in a positive light. The law met with heavy resisted by historians and was repealed two years later.

What is hardly known and discussed today, for instance, is that colonial history did not end abruptly after the Second World War. After the scramble for territories came the scramble for resources. In a recent study entitled *Eurafrica: the Untold History of Integration and Colonialism*, Peo Hansen and Stefan Jonsson have shed light on the continuity of colonial projects in the post-war era (Hansen & Jonsson, 2014a, b). They have shown that the peace project of integration in the European Economic Community (EEC) went hand in hand with a geopolitical and economic effort to retain colonial influence in Africa. The integration of Europe happened together with the decolonization of Africa in the 1950s and 60s. Both processes, however, were connected by a neo-colonial Eurafrican vision, as the strategy papers of the early post-war years reveal:

> Europe as an entity will be viable only if the links which unite it with countries and dependent territories [. . .] are taken into account. The era of national ownership of colonial territories is past. [. . .] From now onwards a common European policy of development for certain regions of Africa should be taken in hand.
>
> *(Hansen & Jonsson, 2014a, pp. 8–9)*

Another quote by Heinrich von Brentano, German minister of the exterior in the Adenauer era, made the point even more explicit:

> The resources of raw material, variegated and abundant, which the overseas territories dispose of, are likely to ensure for the entirety of the European community of the common market the indispensable foundation for an expanding economy.
>
> *(Brentano, 1957, p. 10)*

As I already emphasized, 'development' was a key concept of the 1950s and 60s, enforcing modernization and progress. This was aimed at by the member states by extracting from the African continent the necessary resources for the expanding economy of the European market. In other words, modernization and globalization were pushed in the Cold War by neo-colonial strategies. Recovering Europe's long colonial history and forging a self-critical European memory of the way in which it continued into the founding years of the European Economic Community could lead to a more dialogic relationship with Europe's Others in general and a future agenda of stronger commitment to reconciliation, restitution and collaboration with African states.

Conclusion

The EU differs from nation states in that its existence can never be taken for granted. It has existed for more than 70 years now, and it has seen ruptures and shifts over time. This transnational community has undergone remarkable changes at historical turning points. Its future, however, is open, because it was created as an experiment and founded on a shared project. It was invented after 1945 and re-invented after 1990, so it is only logical that it will have to be re-invented once more after 2015. In order to secure a future for the European project it will have to heed the lessons learned from history, to preserve the European dream of peace and liberty, to reinforce and expand its self-critical memory and to strengthen the commitment to human rights. We can also put it this way: the EU is a story with an open end, and it is us Europeans who bear the responsibility for whether and how this story is being continued.

Notes

1 P.Valéry (1931). Extrait. De l'Historire. In *Regards sur le monde actuel*. Paris: Librairie Stock, Delamain et Boutelleau (translation AA).
2 R. S. Churchill (Hg.). (1948). *The sinews of peace: Post-war speeches by Winston S. Churchill* (p. 200). London: The Riverside Press.
3 G. Wood (2017). Beyond colonialism: Continuity, change and the modern development project. *Journal Canadian Journal of Development Studies, 38*(1).
4 A. Assmann (2019). *Is time out of joint? The rise and fall of the time regime of modernity*. New York: Cornell University Press.
5 The quote refers to Ernst Nolte, whose article appeared under this headline in the Frankfurter Allgemeine Zeitung on 6 June 1986 and started what was later called 'the historians' debate' in West-Germany.
6 German national memory is built on the experience of two dictatorships. The first ended with a trauma of violence and guilt and a passive nation that had to be liberated from itself by the allies. The end of the second dictatorship was different: ended with the fall of the wall with the triumph of self-liberation.
7 A detailed account of this shift can be found in T. Judt (2005). *Postwar: A history of Europe Since 1945*. New York: Penguin.
8 J. Torpey (2006). *Making whole what has been smashed: On reparations politics*. Cambridge: Cambridge University Press, S. 19, 6.
9 Homepage Center for Political Beauty.

Bibliography

Assmann, A. (2019). *Is time out of joint? The rise and fall of the time regime of modernity*. New York: Cornell University Press.

Brentano, H. (1957). *Letter to Konrad Adenauer*. Retrieved from www.divaportal.org/smash/get/diva2:621898/FULLTEXT01.pdf

Butler, J. (1999). *Gender trouble. Feminism and the subversion of identity*. Tenth anniversary edition. London: Routledge.

Churchill, R. S. (Ed.). (1948). *The sinews of peace: Post-war speeches by Winston S. Churchill*. London: The Riverside Press.

Fiedler, L. (1988). Überquert die Grenze, schließt den Graben. Über die Postmoderne. In Wolfgang Welsch (Hg.), *Wege aus der Moderne. Schlüsseltexte der Postmoderne-Diskussion* (pp. 57–74). Weinheim: VHC (transl. A.A.).

Hansen, P., & Jonsson, S. (2014a). *Eurafrica: The untold history of European integration and colonialism*. London: Bloomsbury Publisher.

Hansen, P., & Jonsson, S. (2014b). Another colonialism: Africa in the history of European integration. *Journal of Historical Sociology, 27*(3), 442–461. Retrieved from www.divaportal.org/smash/get/diva2:621898/FULLTEXT01.pdf

Jelin, E. (2003). *State repression and the labors of memory*. Minneapolis: University of Minnesota Press.

Judt, T. (2005). *Postwar: A history of Europe since 1945*. New York: Penguin.

Koselleck, R. (1989). Historia Magistra Vitae. Über die Auflösung des Topos im Horizont neuzeitlich bewegter Geschichte. In R. Koselleck (Ed.), *Vergangene Zukunft. Zur Semantik geschichtlicher Zeiten* (pp. 38–66). Frankfurt am Main: Suhrkamp.

Lloyd, M. (2007). *Judith Butler: From norms to politics*. Cambridge and Malden, MA: Polity Press.

Moyn, S. (2010). *The last Utopia: Human rights in history*. Cambridge: Harvard University Press.

Olick, J. (2007). *The politics of regret: On collective memory and historical responsibility*. New York: Routledge.

Renan, E. (1882). *What is a nation?* Lecture delivered at the Sorbonne. Retrieved from https://web.archive.org/web/20110827065548/www.cooper.edu/humanities/core/hss3/e_renan.html

Valéry, P. (1931). Extrait. De l'Historire. In *Regards sur le monde actuel*. Paris: Librairie Stock, Delamain et Boutelleau.

Volkan, V. D. (2006). Slobodan Milošević and the Serbian chosen trauma. *Clio's Psyche, 13*(1), 19–22.

Wood, G. (2017). Beyond colonialism: Continuity, change and the modern development project. *Canadian Journal of Development Studies, 38*(1), 3–21.

2

A WAY OF SEEING SOME EFFECTS OF GLOBALIZATION AND NEW TECHNOLOGIES IN EUROPE

Maria Eugenia Cid Rodríguez

—To my mother Elva
—and my father Antonio

We are living in a historical period probably only comparable to the Industrial Revolution (Stapley, 2006), a time which brought about a new economic and social paradigm in which social classes, wealth, the bourgeoisie, the proletariat, the unions, inequalities and redistribution took on the leading roles. Similarly, the magnitude of the changes that have taken place in recent decades leads us to believe that we are going through a new major paradigm shift. This time, however, the protagonists are the technological and information revolution; the expansion of the global market; the separation of labour relations from social relations of production; the transformation and in some cases the destruction of social categories, both of social classes and movements as well as of institutions and other socialising agents such as the traditional school and family (Touraine, 2005). And in the midst of it all is the subject, caught in the crossfire of a network of global connection-disconnection, fighting for its survival, seeking new references that sustain and help its vital and emotional development.

The changes that are taking place are of such magnitude, both in their content and in the speed at which they are implemented and developed, that the subjects are faced with the feeling of living in a continuous crisis, not always one involving growth, and with a high cost of suffering that is not always acknowledged. Of course, societies have always developed in processes of continuous change and transformation. They would not exist if not. But what makes the current changes so different?

The conjunction of globalization and the technological revolution constitutes a phenomenon that has provoked a violent disruption in the previous social system.

All change, whether it be in the mind, in groups or in society, supposes an agitation of this calibre if growth is to take place. But the *catastrophic change* (Bion, 1965; Grinberg, 1972) that we now face does not always seem to find in Europe, both as a continent and as a container, the support needed for what is new to transform into true growth. Rather, the new often seems to run up against broken, fragmented containers, such that their contents spill out onto the lives of societies and people, causing a suffering that cannot be felt or thought about. In the worst cases, the contents of the unconscious fantasies of all times take hold of the reins, thereby becoming the container and causing harm. This violent turbulence also seems to affect *invariance* (Bion, 1965; Grinberg, 1972; López Corvo, 2002; Sandler, 2005), that is, those elements that must remain unchanged for societies to be able to continue to recognise themselves amidst these changes. The new style of life seems to wave between the death of the previous one (Stapley, 2006) and the lack of pre-conceptions, unconscious expectations of a humanised future. It is always difficult, individually and socially, to abandon the known and face the terror of the unknown, such that the invariance, the expectations of encountering something good internally and externally, the negative capability and tolerance of frustration, all help to face the unknown without a true catastrophe taking place. But these emotional security systems sometimes seem to be bankrupt, making insecurity, uncertainty, confusion, chaos, the sensation of fragility, fragmentation and vulnerability predominate in those states of expectation and confrontation with the unknown. Those are very primitive human emotions, but I think they are deeply present in these times without being sufficiently acknowledged.

I propose using this emotional perspective to observe some social phenomena such as financial bubbles, corruption, terrorism and refugees in the European landscape. Beyond the beneficial and developmental effects globalization and new technologies have brought, I believe the phenomena I will be exploring here are some of the ways how the catastrophic effects produced by globalization and new technologies become manifest in their ability to stimulate mankind's most primitive anxieties, emotions and behaviours. Psychoanalysis also has a responsibility for thinking about this facet of human experience. I hope to convey my way of seeing it.

A brief historical note

After the Second World War, with the atomic bomb and mankind having shown their ability for annihilation, the world decided to contain its destructiveness with the Cold War, of which the Berlin Wall was its visible representation, maintaining a balance, although fragile because, as Segal says, "the Cold War was not really so cold, and the nuclear threat had not really disappeared" (Segal, 2007a, p. 40). Simultaneously and in parallel, Europe and the Western world seemed to be recovering from the devastation. There followed a boom of construction, of economic development, of reparation of the damage with profound social reforms, of the development of democracy in a great many countries. Europe, and the Western world headed by the

United States, looked out on a better future: the so-called Welfare State was being built, albeit in some countries more than in others.

However, in the 1970s there was a depletion of the economic system that led to a serious financial crisis with its epicentre in the United States. This was joined by the oil crisis, causing the crisis to spread worldwide. The debacle was compounded by the stock market crash in 1987. Political leaders found themselves powerless and overwhelmed. It was from within this failure, initially imperceptible but nonetheless unstoppable and implacable, that the seeds of globalization slowly began to sprout. It was thought necessary to invent a large-scale response that would allow the economy to produce the benefits needed to maintain the welfare state of modern society . . . at any price.

A number of American and European mercantile minds had the brilliant idea of globalization to get out of the crisis, turning the market into the motor of the world and a solution to all its ills, underlying the belief that globalization would bring growth, wealth would spread and inequalities would decrease. International relations would be expanded; it would take democracy where it did not heretofore exist; it would bring about the integration of markets and of nations to a point never seen before; it was an opportunity to reform the economic, political and social landscape by eliminating the barriers of time and space that separated peoples (Stapley, 2006; Stiglitz, 2002). It was panacea.

Parallel and synchronously, the technological revolution brought e-mail and the World Wide Web, which rapidly began to develop in the 1980s and provided the indispensable conditions for globalization to develop. A world without borders was contemplated in which people, capital and goods moved freely through the web; companies and people would no longer be tied down to a single place and its restrictive traditions. The Internet would turn unconscious fantasies into reality as needed to achieve the global objective.

It is true that globalization and the World Wide Web brought outstanding improvements to the world and to Europe: greater life expectancy; the sciences developed to an unimaginable level; the chance to develop the most sophisticated forms of talents and creativity; for most citizens to have access to knowledge, something unthinkable years ago; economic development in some poorer places. Indeed, globalization and the World Wide Web have contributed to reducing the feeling of isolation of the most disadvantaged countries; European and international institutions were created that have benefited the interrelations among peoples and the development of human rights and democracy (Stiglitz, 2002). In all this, Europe has been both a great promoter and a beneficiary at the same time. Nevertheless, not all that glitters is gold.

When I try to gain a psychoanalytic understanding of the emergence of globalization with the help of new technologies as a solution to a deep crisis, Melanie Klein and her conceptualization of the two types of reparation, depressive and manic, come to mind (Klein, 1935, 1940). The depressive mental states are essential for human beings to be able to develop, especially in times of crisis and change. It

Effects of globalization and new technologies **23**

means being able to feel and sustain the depressive anxiety that has to do with the damage done to the others, whether in the unconscious or conscious fantasies or in reality. This type of anxiety leads to feelings of responsibility for that damage and for trying to repair it, to sublimation or to any form of creativity.

One might think that after the Second World War the Western world gave ample and profound evidence of this capacity for mourning and reparation in the reconstruction of its European and North American societies. Successful depressive behaviour fostered creative growth. However, it seems that the exhaustion of the economic system in the 1970s also brought about depletion in this depressive capacity to sustain the pain, necessary to grow, and manic reparation began taking control. Not being able to rely more on their constructive and reparative feelings, with crises emerging everywhere, manic and obsessive omnipotence seems to have settled in as a predominant mental-social functioning in the minds of political and economic leaders, and in the peoples, to deny the persecutory fears and the guilt derived from the devastation caused by the destruction of the moment and the past.

Continuing with Klein (1935, 1940), we may say that a certain degree of manic reparation was normal and necessary at times when other resources were lacking. However, it would seem that globalization, boosted by new technologies in the omnipotent satisfaction of group unconscious fantasies and their leaders broke with the benignity of some manic reparation and this was installed as a form of control and denial of pain. This type of reparation is dominated by the desire to triumph over the other, who is viewed with contempt, and therefore fails to alleviate guilt and restore the damage. On the contrary, there is a resurgence of hatred, of complaining and avoiding the responsibility of facing internal and external reality. I would say that this type of manic reparation is one of the emotional elements that lie beneath the binomial globalization-www and its consequences.

Financial bubbles

Globalization and the Internet have worked hand in hand in the construction of the global solution but also in the construction of bubbles: the real estate bubble at the end of the 1980s, the dotcom bubble in the 1990s, the subprime bubble in the first years of the 21st century, with devastating effects on the countries of southern Europe and beyond. Indeed, globalization itself and the Internet seem like bubbles themselves.

It may be best to try to get inside a globalised bubble to understand it from emotional and unconscious assumptions. One of the fundamental tasks of groups is to contain and manage anxieties, mainly the deepest and most disturbing ones that are too difficult to sustain individually (Bion, 1961). Under normal circumstances, when the containment system works properly, the most primitive aspects are contained in the group, who can transform them and give them more benign expressions. For example, we all crave revenge when someone hurts a loved one, but it is up to the group to restrain our crazed desire for revenge and turn it into justice. But now we are experiencing social moments of broken, fragmented, damaged containers that fail in their transformative function; and where there is no containment, the contents of the most primitive unconscious fantasies roam freely in group operations. This is the case of bubbles. If someone is told that a person is working individually with a mental dynamic as little in touch with reality as the one in the subprime mortgages, also aptly known as trash mortgages, one would say that person is functioning psychotically. And yet, within the global mentality, it seemed perfectly normal: the financiers, the banks, the governments, the peoples, all hooked on the same unconscious fantasies of manic reparation, of omnipotent magical thinking, that growth is infinite, living in the belief of the existence of an inexhaustible breast, the saviour of the crisis and depression, resisting to think that bubbles are whatever takes us away from true, sustained economic and social development and emotional well-being (Tuckett & Taffer, 2008; Cid Rodríguez, 2010).

Here we may take John Steiner's notion of psychic retreats (Steiner, 1993) to continue thinking psychoanalytically about the bubbles of globalization. Steiner understands that these are mental states to which we withdraw to avoid anxiety and mental pain. They are defensive, pathological mental organizations that play a very particular role in the universal problem of dealing with primitive destructiveness; they are a defence against destructiveness, providing areas of relief and sense of protection, but at the same time they are also an expression of destructiveness, because they attack the ability to think and keep the individual away from contact with reality and with others. The retreat serves as an area in the mind where reality does not have to be faced, where unconscious fantasy and omnipotence can exist without being contrasted and where everything is allowed. This is what makes the retreat so attractive.

It seems that these financial bubble-retreats have been populated with what Tuckett and Taffer (2008) have called 'phantastic objects', an expression of the primitive infantile phantasies of possession of the primary object the mother and her attributes, her body and parts of it. In the invention of new financial products, new emotional products were likewise invented at the same time that were unconsciously grasped by the groups as having qualities of these primary object relationships, so that these financial products turned into phantastic objects, generating great excitement and enthusiasm, but with the consequent action of anti-thought, anti-pain, anti-growth.

Europe lives in a world ravaged by violence in its most diverse expressions: crisis, terror, ecological disaster, child abuse, corruption, inequalities, negligence, all of which make fertile ground for the search for these refuges, bubbles in which individual fears are denied, but also in a broader way, group fears of destructiveness, mass annihilation and depression are also denied. But the relief achieved in these financial retreats, or retreats of any other kind, comes at the cost of isolation, stagnation and non-development, because these states have no ability to metabolise the primitive anxieties of those who try to flee; far from transforming anything, the bubbles become vehicles for the action of destructive elements.

Effects of globalization and new technologies **25**

It is difficult to know why these bubbles, past and future, explode. But perhaps we can think that the bursting occurs when this pathological defensive system breaks. It cannot be split or denied any longer, and the split content returns violently and vengefully. Everything that was always there in the bubble, but did not want to be seen because it broke the idealised and euphoric love affair (Tuckett & Taffer, 2008), came back in force in the crisis. The euphoria gave way in Europe to persecutory depression, thereby releasing the most devastating phantasies and realities: unemployment, inequalities, poverty together with intense anger; feelings of harm; revenge and blame. These are realities and emotional contents that, in the most paranoid-schizoid European landscape, are felt most acutely by the countries of the East and the South.

New solutions that were as pathological as they were ineffective arose from part of the mentality of globalization, this time in the form of a primitive, cruel, omnipotent and sadistic superego, so alien to human suffering, with the face of *austericide*. This is a term used in some Southern European countries to express a homicidal austerity of killing by excessive austerity, such is the experience and suffering these peoples have had because of the Europe's economic solutions to the recession. These solutions, which advocate recovery and growth, have not only fostered an economic rift between peoples, North and South, rich and poor, East and West, but I believe have also contributed to exacerbating the most primitive social mental operations such as projective identifications, mutually acted out among peoples. In other words, in this projective movement, the split differences seem to have been trapped by the group mentality to perversely act out all sorts of aggressive, envious unconscious fantasies of mutual rejection.

The cruel superego, arising from the confusing consequences of this excessive use of pathological projective identifications, imposes its destructive superiority and is governed by moral norms that do not even include notions of good and bad (Grinberg, 1972, p. 42). It is this kind of superego that in phantasy and in reality, punished some European societies more than others.

Thus it seems that globalization and new technologies are not providing any truly reparative, depressive, integrative solutions to the woes all this causes in people. I can only wonder what new bubbles are brewing.

Corruption

Corruption is perhaps another manifestation of the negative and catastrophic effects of globalization and the Internet that populate the current European landscape.

Contact with reality and truth is always painful. As a result, the human mind is always in a position to create lies to avoid that pain; but the excess of lying destroys mental growth. The so-called *post-truth* culture, in which systematic repetition of a lie makes it true, is part of current European society and an expression of this anti-growth activity. Evasion, distortion and falsification of reality and truth are all variations of perversion. In the perverse mental state, reality is recognised but, at the same time, it is denied because it is about obtaining individual or group pleasure at the expense of a more general good, to the point, sometimes, of not recognising the existence of the other or of the others, or of recognising them but as objects to be used. The abuse of others is the essence of this type of relationship (Long, 2008). Obviously, this type of relationship has always existed among humans, but the perverse use of new technologies and the global mentality favours not recognising the other as a person so as to make it easier to use and manipulate him.

In a social functioning, at one extreme would be fraud and corruption, where all the facts of reality are not only consciously known but are knowingly evaded. We find European examples in the use of public money for private profit purposes; in labour reforms touted by the mercantile mind of globalization, which use and abuse people for the satisfaction of the few. The very idea that globalization is progress and prosperity, denying poverty and inequalities it has generated not only in underdeveloped countries but on European soil as well, is yet another example of this perverse culture, as are the policies of cutbacks in attending to the basic needs of European citizens, knowingly yielding to private, commercial and financial interests (Stiglitz, 2002, p. 31).

Islamic terrorism

On September 11, 2001, the planet watched terrified, overwhelmed and confused, as a few insignificant airplanes made mockery of technological omnipotence, penetrated into the bowels of the great financial empire and disintegrated them. A few miles away, the Pentagon was also wounded, though not mortally. The omnipotent unconscious fantasies of invulnerability of the superpowers were severely attacked on their own soil. The blast waves of the explosion reached Europe. The world saw its most primitive terror broadcast live and direct: personal disintegration imbued with hostility (Segal, 2007a). The world looked on in dread how yet another unforeseen effects of globalization and new technology exploded: Islamic terrorism.

This was not the first jihadist attack, but the first that was broadcasted live by all the global media. It represents a milestone, a before and after of terrorism in the era of globalization and new technologies. In 2004, it struck European soil through Madrid and spread out dramatically thereafter: Spain (206 victims), France (251), United Kingdom (90), Belgium (32), Germany (15), Sweden (6), Denmark (3), Italy (2), Bulgaria (9) and thousands of injured (Infolibre, 2018).

The effects the attacks had on the invariance, continuity, cohesion and coherence in the identities of the peoples, under the auspices of globalization and the World Wide Web, have also become globalised; they have crossed the boundaries of the Western world and have reached non-Western societies (Stapley, 2006), who have felt themselves deeply attacked to the very foundations of their identity. The secular paranoid-schizoid gap between the Western and Muslim worlds has not only widened, but it seems that the Muslim world, in this new global colonization, feels attacked and dominated by a persecutory, intrusive global object that undermines their particular faith and lifestyle. The amalgam of the basic assumptions of fight-or-flight and messianic dependence (Bion, 1961) seems to underlie the reaction of the Islamic world, which rigidly defends itself against catastrophic change, sometimes psychotically clinging to the past depository of values threatened in the present. In this intersection of pathological projective manoeuvres of our times, we find similarities on the European side in the resurgence of a worrisome xenophobic, anti-Islamic sentiment. Admittedly the gap is not only between the West, Europe and Islam, but also between modernity and traditionalism (Varvin, 2017) in both worlds; and here again we find similarities on the European side, where an ultra-nationalist malign ideology, political parties and extreme right groups with all their outpouring of collective violence against the new and the different are gaining in strength and power.

This is a very complex issue, perhaps too broad to develop here, but as far as this chapter is concerned, I would now like to see how it happens that Islamic terrorism in Europe is perpetrated mostly by young European Muslims.

We can think that these are young second- or third-generation immigrants, generally members of disadvantaged groups, who feel rejected and stigmatised by a society in which they do not feel integrated, young people that do not feel the benefits of globalization. These are vulnerable young people, their adolescence as a broken mental state; in the midst of a crisis of individual and collective identity, in search of an identity, which leads them to taking refuge in their ancestry, which gives them a sense of belonging. We can assume that in the fanatical mind of the terrorist a *constellation of death* is enclosed (Williams, 1998, p. 30). This is a pathological mental organization characterised by the domination of envy, hatred, violent unconscious fantasies and cruelty, with emptiness in the capacity of containment and failures in their ability to think in an abstract level. They have habitually suffered from early experiences of cruelty and death. They show obedience to a leader outside the self or to an intrapsychic sadistic leader. It is a mind dominated by persecutory anxiety, confusion and chaos, unable to pass through the depressive mental work. This prevents such a person from digesting this constellation of death. If he does not find anyone or anything, inside and outside himself, that will help him transform, the psychic indigestion will put him in a position to act violently. This indigestion can be suspended, encapsulated in time and in any type of personality and pathology, until an emotionally disturbing moment arrives, from the internal or external world, which can trigger the violent act.

What has been said so far would be common, with variations, to every criminal mind. But the terrorist mind also aims to kill not just an individual but a group or a society and what it represents. And this is where I think European society could do well to think about how and to what extent it is contributing to this disaster rather than only rigidifying the paranoid systems of control and security. Perhaps Islamic terrorism in Europe is to a certain extent one of the cruel expressions of the inability of the European mentality to detoxify those social mental states dominated by this constellation of death, encapsulated in pathological organizations which are not depressively digested, and which is acted upon by vulnerable, criminal, fanatic mentalities. In what way does the European mentality nourish the death instinct in these pathological organizations? To what extent does globalization, with its

28 Maria Eugenia Cid Rodríguez

devastating arrogance toward differences, contribute to this terrorism? ISIS proclaims "its worldwide triumph of the Islamic law, expression of absolute and divine truth" (Varvin, 2017, p. 17). I find the parallels with the pathological and malign areas of the mentality of globalization to be quite shocking.

Much clearer and more explicit is the participation of the Internet in the dissemination of terrorist propaganda, the recruitment, financing and radicalization of these terrorist groups. The parallelism between the structure of the terrorist group ISIS and the structure of the Internet is very curious: a transnational network that does not understand borders, with a sense of community, which is not directed by any one centralised power but by horizontal cross-links (Cid Álvarez, 2018). The perverse use of the Internet has made it a means without borders for the death instinct that nourishes terrorism emotionally.

Refugees

Migration and its reception is a very complex issue. Let's just focus on the Mediterranean Sea. The Europe of globalization and the Internet without limits, forgetting its own history of migration, an integral part of its identity, does not want to see that the Mediterranean has become a graveyard.

In the ambiguity of the perversion of how conscious or unconscious our knowledge of reality is, we find the phenomenon of *turning a blind eye*. Steiner defines it as mental situations "in which we seem to have access to reality, but we choose to ignore it because it is convenient to do so" (Steiner, 1993, p. 161). We are aware that we choose not to look at the facts of reality without being fully aware of what we are evading. Europe turns a blind eye to the Mediterranean Sea.

Some brief statistics: According to the United Nations High Commissioner for Refugees (UNHCR), in 2018 alone there were one million refugees who tried to cross the Mediterranean (ACNUR, 2018). According to the International Organisation for Migration (IOM), an UN-related organisation, the number of people who drowned in the Mediterranean exceeded 15,000, which was more than 50% of all refugee deaths worldwide in the last four years (Público.es). According to reports from Amnesty International that come from the IOM, EU policies, such as the increase in hostility of some countries toward migrant rescue boats; the support of the Libyan Coast Guard that intercepts the exodus and return the people to refugee camps that violate human rights; the agreements made with Turkey and so on, are responsible for the deaths of 1,111 people from January to June 2018 and another 721 deaths in the months of June and July 2018 (The Guardian, 2018; Amnesty International, 2018).

In his Bionian analysis of the emotional experiences of immigrants, Grinberg (1989) illustrates the vicissitudes that can occur in the encounter between the immigrant (i.e., the new, the different, the contained) and the host community (i.e., the container). In the failure of its mental function, Europe the container cannot contain the catastrophic change, the arrival of refugees experienced as a tsunami, and instead is turning it into a real humanitarian catastrophe. Of the multiple

Effects of globalization and new technologies **29**

possibilities of interrelation, the one now occurring is the most serious. "The contained element may, by sheer disruptive force, pose a threat of destruction to the container. An excess of rigidity or fear may drown the contained and thus stymie his development" (Grinberg, 1989, p. 82). When seen from the Mediterranean, the literalness of Grinberg's words is startling.

We might say that it is very interesting, if it were not so painful, to observe how the European economic and political giant, the result of globalization and the Internet, feels so threatened by refugees, most of whom are children. It seems that the potency of the most primitive emotional phenomena of pathological projective identification is on a par with economic power, so that the 'contained', the refugees, has become the recipient of the most destructive, voracious and envious unconscious fantasies (Klein, 1957), turning them into intruders who come to deprive Europeans of their assets, into terrorists who come to attack the purity of European identity, culture and tranquillity. "The villagers' persecutory life experiences are so strong that they need to dehumanise the immigrant and reduce him to an inanimate object, denying his status as a person (they turn him from someone into 'something') after having tried to ignore his existence entirely" (Grinberg, 1989, p. 84). Europe has projectively turned refugees into a kind of "biodegradable category" (Garzón, 2018, p. 215), into real living zombie objects waiting to be extinguished.

At a time more than any other in its history, in which it can have access to the reality of what is happening, Europe instead turns a blind eye to the Mediterranean. Perhaps in doing so, it wants to avoid having to face its darkest side, its most "*uncanny*" (Freud, 1919) that underlies its emotional network, choosing to encapsulate it and keep it at a distance, under the sea or in refugee camps, with walls and barbed wire so that the projected will not come back. Europe wants to drown the *nameless dread* (Bion, 1962) in the Mediterranean Sea, the emotional experience not contained, not thought of or transformed in the vertiginous changes that it experiences . . . and without witnesses to observe it, grieve over it and tell about it. The humanitarian organizations deployed at sea, the ones that represent the part that is depressive, supportive and empathetic with the refugees' pain and their desire and right to live, are disappearing on account of pressure from the states. In an excess of perverse institutional distortion, these organizations are now being criminalised and some are being tried for human trafficking. Is this how Europe demonstrates its strength and its power?

In this way of seeing the effects of globalization and the Internet in the European landscape, the coloured figures of life instinct, which oscillate dialectically with destructive emotions, seem to have been eclipsed. But when at times this group life force seems to fade, it reappears with new pushes toward transformation. Women, the elderly, young people and citizens are taking to the streets of Europe denouncing the excess of globalization, demanding reparation for so much damage, demanding that lies be revealed, promoting solidarity and empathy with human suffering. In this dialectical tension between paranoid-schizoid and depressive forces (Klein, 1946; Bion, 1963), we all have the responsibility to construct thought, to seek truths with a small 't' (Segal, 2007b); to contribute to the care of containers under transformation, to search for solutions, also with a small 's'; to learn from experience and to try not to continue with the construction of Truths and omnipotent, fanatical and dogmatic magic Solutions that have brought us here. In this era in which we are transforming ourselves into *homo digitalis* (Lassalle, 2018) with robotisation riding at a steady pace, we must take care of the invariance of humanity by containing emotions and transforming them into thought, in order to grow during catastrophic changes.

Translation: John F. Nelson Yonan

References

ACNUR. Retrieved from www.acnur.org/noticias/press/2018/8/5b6625294/muertes-en-el-mediterraneo-sobrepasan-las-1500-acnur-lanza-alarma.html

Amnesty International. (2018). Retrieved from www.amnesty.org/es/latest/news/2017/17/control-mediterranean-death-toll-soars-as-eu-turns-its-back-on-refugees-and-migrants

Bion, W. R. (1961). *Experiences in groups and other papers*. London: Tavistock Publications.

Bion, W. R. (1962). A theory of thinking. In *Second thoughts*. London: Maresfield.

Bion, W. R. (1963). *Elements of psycho-analysis*. London: Maresfield.

Bion, W. R. (1965). *Transformations*. London: Maresfield.

Cid Álvarez, S. (2018). *Terrorist Propaganda. Terrorism and organised crime*. Universidad Europea de Madrid. Unpublished.

Cid Rodríguez, M. E. (2010). Crisis económica y destructividad. *Revista de Psicoterapia Psico-analítica AMPP, 8*, 45–61.

Freud, S. (1919). The *"Uncanny"*. S.E., 17 (pp. 217–252). London: Hogarth Press.

Garzón, B. (2018). *La indignación activa*. Barcelona: Planeta.

Grinberg, L., & Grinberg, R. (1989). *Psychoanalytic perspectives on migration and exile* (N. Festinger, trans.). New Haven, CT: Yale University Press.

Grinberg, L., Sor, D., & Bianchedi, E. T. (1972). *Introducción a las ideas de Bion*. Buenos Aires: Nueva Visión.

The Guardian. Retrieved from https://theguardian.com/world/2018/org/08/eu-policies-to-blame-deaths-at-sea-mediteaanean-amnesty-international-report

Infolibrewww. (2018). Retrieved from infolibre.es/noticias/politica/2017/08/17/los_prin cipales_atentadoseuropa_desde_2004_68693_1012.html

Klein, M. (1935). A contribution to the psychogenesis of manic-depressive states. In *Love, guilt and reparation and other works 1921–1945: The writings of Melanie Klein* (pp. 262–289). London: The Hogarth Press.

Klein, M. (1940). Mourning and its relation to manic-depressive states. In *Love, guilt and reparation and other works 1921–1945: The writings of Melanie Klein* (pp. 344–369). London: The Hogarth Press.

Klein, M. (1946). Notes on some schizoid mechanisms. In *Envy and gratitude and other works, 1946–1963: The writings of Melanie Klein. 3* (pp. 1–24). London: The Hogarth Press.

Klein, M. (1957). Envy and gratitude. In *Envy and gratitude and other works, 1946–1963: The writings of Melanie Klein. 3* (pp. 176–235). London: The Hogarth Press.

Lassalle, J. M. (2018, Abril 10). "Big deal" y "fake humans". *El País, Opinión*, p. 11.

Long, S. (2008). *The perverse organization and its deadly sins*. London: Karnac.

López Corvo, R. E. (2002). *Diccionario de la obra de Wilfred Bion* (pp. 190–191). Madrid: Biblioteca Nueva-APM.

Público. Retrieved from www.publico.es/sociedad/migrantes-y-refugiados-muertes-medi
terraneo-superan-3000-cuarto-año-consecutivo.htmc

Sandler, P. C. (2005). *The language of Bion: A dictionary of concepts* (pp. 360–362). London: Karnac.

Segal, H. (2007a). September 11. In *Yesterday, today and tomorrow*. London: Routledge. First written 2001.

Segal, H. (2007b). Reflections on truth, tradition and the psychoanalytic tradition of truth. In *Yesterday, today and tomorrow* (pp. 69–78). London: Routledge. First published 2006, *American Imago*, *63*(3), 283–292.

Stapley, L. F. (2006). *Globalization and terrorism: Death of a way of life*. London: Karnac.

Steiner, J. (1985). Turning a blind eye: The cover-up for Oedipus. *The International Journal of Psychoanalysis*, *12*, 161–172.

Steiner, J. (1993). *Psychic retreats*. London: Routledge.

Stiglitz, J. E. (2002). *El malestar en la globalización (Globalization and its descontents)*. Buenos Aires: Taurus.

Touraine, A. (2005). *Un nuevo paradigma para comprender el mundo de hoy*. Barcelona: Paidós.

Tuckett, D., & Taffer, R. (2008). Phantastic objects and the financial market´s sense of reality: A psychoanalytic contribution to the understanding of stock market instability. *International Journal of Psychoanalysis*, *89*(2), 398–412.

Varvin, S. (2017). Our relationship with refugees: Between compassion and dehumanisation. In *Psychoanalysis in Europe* (Vol. 71, pp. 10–24). Bulletin European Psychoanalytic Federation. Luxembourg: Weprint.

Williams, A. H. (1998). *Cruelty, violence and murder*. Understanding the Criminal Mind. London: Karnac.

3

RELATIONALITY IN THE AGE OF NEOLIBERAL DISPOSSESSION

Protecting the "other"

Marianna Fotaki

Introduction

We are now witnessing the highest levels of displacement on record in world history. An unprecedented 68.5 million forced migrants are seeking new lives, including nearly 25.4 million refugees, half of whom are under the age of 18 (UNHCR, 2018). The arrival of over a million refugees into the European Union, mainly from Syria, Iraq, and Afghanistan, during a short period of a few months in 2015 highlighted the urgency and magnitude of this phenomenon. Rather than being a short-term emergency, international organisations warn that this is likely to be a new structural condition, and that large flows of dispossessed people fleeing war, poverty, and climate change will continue in the coming years. This situation calls for a coordinated and collaborative global response, since such mass movements often fuel a sense of anxiety about migration (OECD, 2015). In addition to the perception of refugees and migrants as threats to the economy and security, such anxiety is often attributed to concerns surrounding globalisation and multiculturalism (Dempster & Hargrave, 2017).

Much less attention has been given to how anti-migration sentiments may be a form of anxiety displacement arising from the dislocation experienced by citizens in economies with decreasing opportunities for meaningful employment and an increasingly privatised welfare state. Yet this seems to be the situation in many developed European countries. In addition to the consequences of the financial crisis, the most recent such dislocations include the retrenchment of the welfare states, as a consequence of the neoliberal shift in public policy over the past few decades. At the most simple level, neoliberalism is a policy model aiming to curtail the role of the state to that of a modest regulator only securing "private property rights, free markets, and free trade" (Harvey, 2005, p. 2). It propagates fiscal austerity and greatly reduced government spending with the police and the military, representing core

Relationality in the age of dispossession **33**

and limited functions of the neoliberal state. The shift to normative neoliberal doctrine in public policy meant introducing deregulation and privatisation of public services under the guise of New Public Management (Jingjit & Fotaki, 2011), financialisation of the economy (Haiven, 2014), shifting risk to individuals (Martin, 2002), along with the global flow of capital, and extraction of resources and wealth from the many to accumulate them in the hands of the few. The consequences are inequality spiralling out of control (see Fotaki & Prasad, 2015 for a review), expulsions from land, and ubiquitous forms of dispossession around the world (Sassen, 2013). This not only creates an ever-growing class of the global poor who are forced to migrate for survival to the global North, but also brings a threat of deprivation to the middle classes of industrialised countries by inculcating a politics of fear as the dispossessed on the move "embody all our fears" of losing everything (Bauman, 2016).

At the same time, numerous local and individual initiatives are rejecting the state's claim to a monopoly over concern and care, or are simply stepping in to address problems emerging from the state's inaction. This response may also occur in the face of perceived incapacity or negligence by official authorities. Such actions are exemplified by the volunteer organisations set up in local communities to address the most urgent needs of over a million refugees and forced migrants reaching the shores of Greece and Italy in 2015 (Fotaki, 2017a), and many others offering help on their journeys toward Northern European countries; in some instances, villages in Italy and Greece have also integrated refugees as contributors to local communities (BBC, 2017; Canal, 2017). Taken together, such opposite reactions pose the question of how solidarity with or rejection of dispossessed people arises. For instance, what impact have the financial crisis and anti-migration discourses by politicians and the media had on people's attitudes and behaviours? Psychoanalytically speaking, how do individuals internalise the dominant ideological narratives, and what intra- and inter-psychic mechanisms do they deploy to sustain them?

The chapter addresses these questions by offering a psychosocial approach to understanding how various emotions, including care for the unknown other, co-exist with a feeling of threat from the other in the context of the neoliberal onslaught on entire populations globally, culminating in the global financial crisis of 2008. The aim of the chapter is twofold. First, it argues for consideration of the psychosocial dynamics of the deeply emotional reactions underpinning anti-migration attitudes and hostility toward refugees as being rooted in a fear of dispossession and dis-identification with "othered", dehumanised human beings under conditions of growing precarity. Specifically, I show that, by rejecting precarity and vulnerability as defining features of the human condition and the indispensability of care this necessitates, neoliberalism encourages and gives us moral licence to reject and stigmatise the weak (i.e., refugees, the unemployed, and the mentally ill; see Tyler, 2013). I argue that the neoliberal doctrine evades the issue of responsibility for the other by imposing an image of a subject whose needs for social bonding are replaced by consumerist wants, and by dehumanising the dispossessed whom it helps to create. This, I propose, is meant to distract citizens from their own unmet needs for care amid the ever-increasing precariousness that they themselves are

34 Marianna Fotaki

experiencing, and to encourage them to project their related fears and anxieties onto the growing populations of dispossessed.

The second and related objective is to debunk this fantasy of the disembedded and disembodied consumer enacting our desire for invincibility. I do so by elucidating the political objective underlying denial of vulnerability and precariousness as a rejection of the reliance on others that makes us human. I contrast this with the feminist ethics of relationality, which acknowledges and brings back the idea of responsibility for the unknown "other", thus counteracting the neoliberal attack on solidarity with others.

The next sections outline the established explanations of anti-migration and anti-refugee politics to foreground the proposed psychosocial approach, and discuss how neoliberalism affects these attitudes. In the second part of the chapter, I draw on feminist psychoanalytic approaches to shared precarity as foundational to the human condition and propose an ethics of relationality as a way of counteracting the rejection of the dispossessed and needy.

Accepting or rejecting refugees and forced migrants: why and how this happens

Researchers have identified a range of social and individual factors that may facilitate or impede willingness to receive refugees and migrants into our societies, falling into the broad categories of economic, security, cultural, and integration threats (Dempster & Hargrave, 2017; Esses, Hamilton, & Gaucher, 2017). Underlying these are complex psychosocial processes of categorising belonging and who is deemed to be an outsider. Such processes neither necessarily nor exclusively involve rational evaluations and calculative thinking, but are often driven by unconscious affective dynamics that are central to defining both who counts as deserving, and the level of help that individuals are willing to provide to them.

Contrary to popular belief, the availability or scarcity of resources is only one, and not even the most important, factor influencing such decisions. Consistent evidence shows little correlation between immigration attitudes and personal economic circumstances, but rather with national-level impacts, whether cultural or economic (Hainmueller & Hopkins, 2014). Various factors that coexist with economic fears and threats may also positively affect people's attitudes toward refugees and migrants. In a recent study from Germany, for instance, most respondents agreed that accepting refugees was a national obligation – a result of a complex combination of feelings, including obligation, scepticism, fear, empathy, and guilt (Purpose, 2017). Moreover, individuals with a prosocial orientation are more likely to provide help to refugees, even if it is costly (Böhm, Theelen, Rusch, & Van Lange, 2018), while for others, such actions may be about embodying the universal values of humanitarianism and international citizenship (Foucault, 1979). Overall, people tend to be more favourably disposed toward those recognised as refugees than they are toward asylum seekers and other migrants who are not seen to be beneficial to one's own country (Bansak, Hainmueller, & Hangartner, 2016).

Public attitudes are also shaped by a number of other key influencers, notably politicians, government policy, media reporting, other members of the public, and refugees and migrants themselves (Dempster & Hargrave, 2017). Among these influences, framing of the debate by political leaders and the media is key. Arguably at least in part following their governments' policies and pronouncements, the public in receiving countries such as Germany and Sweden have enthusiastically welcomed hundreds of thousands of people in 2015; but the reverse is also true. For instance, whilst accepting virtually no Syrians, Afghans, or Iraqis, leaders in Britain and Poland have reacted with considerable hostility (Karakayali, 2018) and virulent oratory against them. Such political speechifying may give voice to pre-existing concerns in their constituencies, but it also allows politicians to speak their own minds about real or imaginary fears that refugees and migrants could pose for their societies. Hence, politicians and the media may contribute to radicalising these debates.

McHugh-Dillon (2015) describes this relationship as bi-directional: while political narratives are heavily influenced by what politicians think the public feels about these issues, they also establish a backdrop against which public attitudes are formed. Information environments and elite rhetoric play central theoretical roles in explaining attitudes toward immigration, and especially their dynamics (Hainmueller & Hopkins, 2014). For instance, how migration is covered and how refugees and migrants are portrayed in the media broadly determine the overall shape and content of public debate (OECD, 2011; Duffy, Frere-Smith, & Friess, 2014). The economic threat (e.g., concerning job competition or fears of disintegration of the welfare state) is often collapsed together with the security threat (Long, 2012), prompting an ever more aggressive reaffirmation of national borders. Such narratives mobilise affect by evoking fears of annihilation by mass arrivals of aggressive and culturally alien newcomers bent on destroying Christian civilisation and/or liberal Western ways (Huntington, 1993).

I suggest that political leaders often mobilise these discourses to detract their constituents' attention from their own policies which fail to provide services that are important for their survival, such as good-quality free and universal health and social care for the elderly, education, affordable housing, and opportunities for meaningful employment for the younger generation. The causes of precarity to which populations are increasingly exposed in developed economies, including affluent European countries, are thus evaded or projected onto less fortunate others to maintain an illusion of security. For instance, fear of refugees and migrants, stoked up by the Sweden Democrats, a party with Neo-Nazi roots, seems to have grown in the context of the decaying Swedish welfare state (Nilsson, 2018). It is also partly because people tend to understand their shared political identity very much in nationalist, and thus more exclusionary, terms, even in the universal welfare state of Sweden (Sandelind, 2018). At the same time the system built to support its citizens appears to have turned against them, and is now failing to provide dignified care for its elderly (Widmalm, 2018). In the aftermath of the neoliberal drive for efficiency and the marketisation of public services the public spending has decreased.

In Germany, the rise of the anti-migration party has also been associated with a general feeling of decline: "One has to remember that the German party Alternative für Deutschland [AfD] was founded initially as a reaction to the euro crisis" (Karakayali, 2018, p. 609). Party activists are refusing to "pay" for the failure of the Eurozone periphery, and specifically that of Greece. This ultra right-wing populist party has thus emerged in response to the alleged loss of the country's sovereignty, although it is now widely accepted that the bail-out funds did not save the Greek economy, but rather safeguarded the German banks and their depositors from bankruptcy (Stiglitz, 2011). Meanwhile, the countries of the southern frontier of the European Union, and particularly Greece, which has undergone the longest and deepest recorded economic depression during peacetime (Coppola, 2018), are experiencing refugee and migration arrivals as a lived crisis within a larger economic, social and political crisis (Lafazani, 2018). Various extreme-right and neo-Nazi political formations, which were hitherto heavily marginalised, have risen to prominence in Greece and Italy on their xenophobic rhetoric, when the financial crisis coincided with the arrival of hundreds of thousands of refugees and forced migrants.

As Max Haiven (2014, p. 69) aptly puts it, "To the extent that we are more and more precarious, we brew an existential anger, a self-loathing that can easily be displaced onto others." This also helps explain the growing virulent disdain for the poor, refugees, and those "at risk" (ibid.). In other words, the refugees and migrants escaping abject poverty are spectral figures haunting those who are not yet dispossessed. The ruling elite, including politicians and the media, are regarding and casting them as a threat to the social order that they themselves have disrupted by abdicating their responsibilities to their own citizens, such as protection of the vulnerable and ensuring meaningful employment and opportunities for future generations. These threatening figures are embellished through various ideological discourses (e.g., by deploying racialised tropes) as utterly and irreconcilably different from ourselves. The fear and disgust that this mobilises allows the not-yet-dispossessed of the developed countries to be distanced from the all-too-human suffering. This leads to a decrease in solidarity with uprooted people and greater exploitability of migrants (Cholewinski & Taran, 2009), while detracting the citizens of affluent European countries from holding politicians to account for their policy choices.

Next, I outline key shifts in public policy following the ascendance of the neoliberal ideology that have contributed to the growing insecurity and sense of precarity in the populations of the industrialised countries. These include privatisation of public services, and the consequences of turning these into consumerist market commodities, such as denial of the need for care, the financialisation of all forms of social life, and shifting risk onto individuals.

Major shifts in public policy under the neoliberal ideology

New Public Management, which introduced business methods to deliver public services in the UK and other developed countries, signalled a sharp shift in favour of the market rather than relying on public policy for social transformation. This

Relationality in the age of dispossession **37**

shift, initiated almost four decades ago, challenged the notion of the state's responsibility for ensuring comprehensive welfare provision for all who need it, and it has now been adopted by all mainstream parties across the political spectrum (Fotaki, 2011). In addition to privatising services and tightening eligibility criteria, coupled with various measures of intrusive surveillance (see e.g., Rizq, 2013), freedom of choice and user autonomy increasingly occupy more prominent positions than equity of access or equality of opportunity on policy makers' agendas in many countries.

Yet, as I have argued elsewhere (Fotaki, 2014), rather than facilitating the conditions necessary for a transformation toward empowered citizens who shape their services, these shifts tend to create responsibilised users who are increasingly expected to deal on their own with issues of ill health, and who have little or no control over the services from which they are supposed to "choose". Making users and patients responsible for their illness or disability, and making health status an issue of lifestyle and choice, signifies a refusal to accept the crucial effect social inequalities have on health outcomes. The drive to privatise public services, predicated on a policy of individualistic consumerist choice, is also insidious, as it may also tap into an unattainable existential fantasy that fulfils other, less obvious, functions of an escapist desire to avert the human predicament of disease and dying (Fotaki, 2006), or to assuage the fear of uncertainty following rapid change. Susan Long (1999) draws on psychoanalysis to explain how practices emerging from consumerism and economic rationalism often act as unconscious organisational and social defences against such anxieties. The social cost of shifting to individualised consumerism produces a corrupt way of thinking in which any sense of greater good is sacrificed to fulfilling individual wants. This perverse state of mind often characterises individuals and groups in corporate life (Long, 2008).

Yet the same discourse has colonised the areas of public policy that were until recently defined by the notion of care, solidarity, and responsibility for the other, such as health and social care (Fotaki, 2010). Neoliberal ideology, and its successful metastasisation from finance and economic governance into all walks of life, is underpinned and held together by a set of fantasmatic constructs, among which the fantasy of consumerism occupies a central position. Max Haiven (2014) explains that this is a result of a wider trend whereby popular culture and everyday life are being transformed by the logic of financial capital, which depends on such transformations in the realms of social action, representation, and subjectivity. In the brave neoliberal world there is no need for care, other than as a service or commodity to be bought and sold in the marketplace according to individual preferences. The so-created financialised imaginary is beholden to the system of reproducing financialised capitalism with everyone performing the entrepreneurial self.

In short, neoliberalism propagates and creates new types of subjectivity. On the one hand, it models people's behaviours on abstract assumptions of self-interested individuals who are rational decision makers motivated solely by the need to enact their preferences and maximise utility through acts of consumption in every circumstance and at all times. However, such an ideological proposition bears little resemblance to most empirical findings in the fields of biology, neurology, and even

38 Marianna Fotaki

descriptive psychology (Fotaki, 2010). Yet ideologies have a performative effect because they are stitched and held together through various affective attachments to desirable states of being, such as for instance the idea of the customer as sovereign and free or the illusory notion of freedom of choice meeting the allegedly unlimited individual wants.

This has dark and pernicious consequences for both how we feel about ourselves and how see ourselves in relation to others. If everything is a matter of personal choice and striving to fulfil our own preferences, then all successes and failures are our responsibility alone. Neoliberalism ignores not only pre-existing inequalities of birth and geography, but also fundamental facts of the human condition that we are all experience at some point in life, such as disease, frailty, and death (Money-Kyrle, 1971). In other words, it refuses to accept the precarity of life and the human body, our infinite capacity for injury, and how we all depend on each other for survival.

The worldwide dominance of such paradigm has also drastically altered the terms of the debate on collective responsibility, the need to care for the dispossessed, and how we should share our resources with others. On the one hand, the global supply chains of transient and cheap migratory labour are essential for late capitalism to continue to produce goods to fuel consumption ad infinitum and fulfil the allegedly insatiable desires of the customers. Various forms of expulsion described by Sassen (2013) are then seen as unavoidable for feeding this insatiable consumerism, despite creating a growing number of dispossessed in the developing world who are joining the ranks of underpaid and disposable labour in developed countries. On the other hand, the rapid pauperisation and impoverishment of the middle classes in the developed world, who can no longer afford to act as consuming subjects since the financial crisis, creates conditions in which the newly poor may compare themselves with migrants. This could give rise to both hostility and solidarity. To prevent the latter outcome, the dispossessed, the new poor, the refugees, and the forced migrants must be constituted as abject (Tyler, 2013). Yet when precarity becomes so widespread and random, people may choose to collaborate and care for each other. Humans are wired to cooperate on a larger scale than most other mammals, but in contrast to them, people regularly cooperate with many unrelated individuals from the time of foraging societies (Boyd & Richerson, 2009). Therefore, I suggest that the real and ultimate aim of introducing consumerism as an overriding governing principle of neoliberal shift in public policy is to replace the notion of a basic inclination for care of others. This is achieved through attacks on our connections with one another, and on the welfare state, which is a societal arrangement embodying this collective responsibility. To counteract this, I propose a feminist poststructuralist frame of relationality, as discussed in the next section.

Relationality counteracting neoliberal dispossession and attacks on life

Relationality is the foundational concept in feminist thinking. It gives meaning to our individual experiences and transforms us into social beings (Butler, 2004). The

Relationality in the age of dispossession **39**

psychoanalytic understanding of relationality elucidates how it is primarily concerned with intersubjectivity (Benjamin, 2004), while encompassing both intrapsychic and interpsychic reality. According to Freud, social life depends on individuals' ability to sublimate their sexual instincts and use them to bond within successively larger communal groupings (Freud, 1920). Jacques Lacan extended his theory by elucidating why we cannot exist socially except in relation to an important other. People who care about us early in life, and with whom we form libidinal ties, are the literal others, while social institutions and symbolic values onto which we transfer our affect are the big Other standing for a given symbolic order (Lacan, 2006). It is in relation to literal (loved ones) and symbolic 'others' (community, nation, etc.) that we strive to remake the world that surrounds us when we engage in political activities (Fotaki, 2010).

Judith Butler, a feminist poststructuralist philosopher, draws on the key Lacanian idea of the individual's desire for recognition in the symbolic order to explain how our own precarity binds us to others (Butler, 2004). She elucidates how we all depend on the other under conditions that are inevitably precarious, and how fears about our own survivability link us to others whom we do not know (Butler, 2004). In other words, the existence of the other is a pre-condition for our own literal and symbolic survivability: "who 'I' am is nothing without your life, and life itself has to be rethought as this complex, passionate, antagonistic, and necessary set of relations to others" (Butler, 2009, p. 44). This is not about an identification based on empathy according to Butler, whose idea of relationality is about an ethical obligation toward the irreducible other. She takes inspiration from Emmanuel Lévinas, regarding the face of the other belonging to the sphere of ethics, when she posits that our infinite capacity for being injured obliges us to protect the other.

Yet the face of the other, in its defencelessness and precarity, is at once a call to kill and a call for peace (Benjamin, 2004). In her own conception of relationality as a psychoanalyst feminist, Benjamin offers a clinical category that she terms "thirdness", as a space where the subject and the other are intertwined, without one prevailing over the other, because such space is governed by patterns of recognition and co-creation involving rapture and disruption that repairs. New insights from psychoanalytic feminist thinking develop these ideas further by proposing an ethics of "difference", which is based on connectedness, co-existence, and compassion toward the other, grounded in our corporeal and embodied connections.

One of the most innovative theories on relationality to emerge recently is that of the matrixial borderspace and "trans-subjectivity" developed by Bracha Ettinger (2006), a French-Israeli psychoanalyst, philosopher, and artist who works with various media, including painting, video, graphical works, diaries, and notebooks. These ideas of trans-subjectivity and the matrixial borderspace, which denote both a symbolic and material entity, imply an absence of separateness of the subject from the other. Matrixial trans-subjectivity denotes that "I" is always inextricably linked to the unknown "non-I" or the Other/(m)other that co-emerges through the process of cohabitation in the womb. The subject is therefore always a partial subject, comprising the symbolic and the material remnant of the mother, and of the baby that

40 Marianna Fotaki

cohabited with her (see Kenny and Fotaki (2015) for more details). Ettinger's idea of the subject co-emerging through an encounter with an unknown other presents us with a compelling ethical proposition that connects Lévinasian responsibility for the other with the feminist thought of the other defined as "becoming together" (Fotaki & Harding, 2017, Chapter 6). In invoking the idea of co-habitation and the joint relational space, it raises the concept of compassionate borderspaces (Kenny & Fotaki, 2015) as a new ethical proposition that acknowledges our shared predicament as humans.

The relational reconsideration of subjectivity vis-à-vis the other outlined above, which brings together insights from diverse feminist psychoanalytic thinking, also has implications for care. This is because caring and relating share conceptual resonance: care is everything we do, and is also a way of knowing that is based on ontological rather than moral groundings (Puig de la Bellacasa, 2012). Neoliberalism has no capacity for care because it operates at the level of normative abstractions when referring to live human beings. Put differently, it cannot see persons from inside and cannot understand them, care about them, or assess their moral character that the father of economics, Adam Smith, advocated for (Collier, 2018). Under neoliberalism, therefore, we are witnessing a rapid increase in various categories of undeserving "others", such as the new poor in affluent Western societies, who are pitted against the dispossessed refugees and forced migrants from the developing world to compete relentlessly under conditions of an induced scarcity and ever-increasing precarity. Excluded others are seen as absolute "monstrous others" and as people with no human rights worth protecting.

However, drawing on our shared notion of vulnerability may be useful in reframing the "migration issue" from an abstract global debate to something that resonates in people's lives, thus challenging the perception of the refugee as an unrelatable "other". This, I suggest, can be counteracted by relational care, defined as "*everything that we do* to maintain, continue and repair 'our world' so that we can live in it as well as possible" (Puig de la Bellacasa, 2012, p. 198). But care is political as it implies distribution and asking broader social and political questions to contextualize caring within them (Tronto, 1993). It is therefore important not to rely simply on people's ethical values, but to promote policies and politics that account for our shared precariousness and the uncertainty we all face under the neoliberal regime. Such a re-positioning of responsibility for the other has important implications for understanding and rethinking developments in public policy (Fotaki, 2017b). It urges us to make the role of governments explicit in how people understand, treat, and relate to one another, and to explain why public policies must emerge from recognition that all our lives are precarious, and that we all depend on society for survival.

Conclusion

This chapter has argued for the utilisation of psychoanalytic ideas of human development along with feminist conceptions of embodied affect and care to reframe subjectivity in relational terms and to better understand how our sociality is always defined vis-à-vis the others. As Ahmed (2004, p. 1) puts it, "emotions work to shape the 'surfaces' of individual and collective bodies. Bodies take the shape of the very contact they have with objects and others." Such theorisation enables us to consider how we live politics through the body and everyday practices, and how neoliberalism taps into our fears and desires by aligning subjects with collectives when we attribute "others" as the "source" of our feelings (Ahmed, 2004). In reality, affective politics are about how we live our lives in relation to others, and how we share the world with others. We therefore owe protection to the dispossessed within and outside our borders, because their fate concerns us all. By offering it, we value their lives as equal and accept their vulnerability as our own. Public policies are key in helping us to recognise this, and that we all depend on each other for survival.

References

Ahmed, S. (2004). *The cultural politics of emotion*. Edinburgh: University of Edinburgh.

Bansak, K., Hainmueller, J., & Hangartner, D. (2016). How economic, humanitarian, and religious concerns shape European attitudes towards asylum seekers. *Science, 354*, 217–222.

Bauman, Z. (2016). *Strangers at our door*. Cambridge: Polity Press.

BBC. (2017, July 12). The Greek island where Syrian refugees are welcome. *BBC News*. Retrieved from www.bbc.co.uk/news/av/world-europe-40586229/the-greek-island-where-syrian-refugees-are-welcome

Benjamin, J. (2004). Beyond doer and done to: An intersubjective view of thirdness. *Psychoanalytic Quarterly, 73*, 5–45.

Böhm, R., Theelen, M. M. P., Rusch, H., & Van Lange, P. A. M. (2018). Costs, needs, and integration efforts shape helping behavior toward refugees. *Proceedings of the National Academy of Science of the USA, 115*, 7284–7289.

Boyd, R., & Richerson, P. J. (2009). Culture and the evolution of human cooperation. *Philosophical Transactions of the Royal Society B: Biological Sciences, 364*, 3281–3288.

Butler, J. (2004). *Precarious life: The powers of mourning and violence*. London: Verso.

Butler, J. (2009). *The frames of war: When is life grievable?* London: Verso.

Canal, G. (2017, April 19). Refugees brought this small, dying Italian village back to life. *Global Citizen*. Retrieved from www.globalcitizen.org/en/content/refugees-brought-this-small-dying-italian-village/

Cholewinski, R., & Taran, P. (2009). Migration, governance and human rights. *Refugee Review Quarterly, 28*(4), 1–33.

Collier, P. (2018). *The future of capitalism: Facing new anxieties*. London: Allen Lane.

Coppola, F. (2018, July 31). The greatest depression. *Forbes*.

Dempster, H., & Hargrave, K. (2017). *Understanding public attitudes towards refugees and migrants*. ODI Working Paper 512. London: Overseas Development Institute.

Duffy, B., Frere-Smith, T., & Friess, H-J. (2014). *Perceptions and reality: Public attitudes to immigration in Germany and Britain*. London: Ipsos MORI.

Esses, V., Hamilton, L. K., & Gaucher, D. (2017). The global refugee crisis: Empirical evidence and policy implications for improving public attitudes and facilitating refugee resettlement. *Social Issues and Policy Review, 11*, 78–123.

Ettinger, B. L. (2006). *The matrixial borderspace (Essays from 1994–1999)*. Minneapolis: University of Minnesota Press.

Fotaki, M. (2006). Choice is yours: A psychodynamic exploration of health policy making and its consequences for the English National Health Service. *Human Relations, 59,* 1711–1744.

Fotaki, M. (2010).Why do public policies fail so often? Exploring health policy making as an imaginary/symbolic construction. *Organization, 17,* 703–720.

Fotaki, M. (2011).Towards developing new partnerships in public services: Users as consumers, citizens and/or co-producers driving improvements in health and social care in the UK and Sweden. *Public Administration, 89,* 933–955.

Fotaki, M. (2014). Can consumer choice replace trust in the National Health Service in England? Towards developing an affective psychosocial conception of trust in health care. *Sociology of Health & Illness, 36,* 1276–1294.

Fotaki, M. (2017a). *TEDx talk: Turning fear to purpose.* TEDxVlerickBusinessSchool [video]. Retrieved from www.youtube.com/watch?v=-aP_Ug11La4

Fotaki, M. (2017b). Relational ties of love: A psychosocial proposal for ethics of compassionate care in health and public services. *Psychodynamic Practice, 23,* 181–189.

Fotaki, M., & Harding, N. (2017). *Gender and the organization: Women at work in the 21st-century.* London: Routledge.

Fotaki, M., & Prasad, A. (2015). Questioning neoliberal capitalism and economic inequality in business schools. *Academy of Management Learning & Education, 14,* 556–575.

Foucault, M. (1979). Michel Foucault on refugees – a previously untranslated interview from 1979. *Progressive Geographies.* Retrieved September 29, 2015, from http://pro gressivegeographies.com/2015/09/29/michel-foucault-on-refugees-a-previously-untranslated-interview-from-1979/

Freud, S. (1920). *Beyond the pleasure principle. S. E.,* 18. London: Hogarth.

Hainmueller, J., & Hopkins, D. J. (2014). Public attitudes toward immigration. *Annual Review of Political Science, 17,* 225–249.

Haiven, M. (2014). *Cultures of financialization: Fictitious capital in popular culture and everyday life.* Basingstoke: Palgrave Macmillan.

Harvey, D. (2005). *The brief history of neoliberalism.* Oxford: Oxford University Press.

Huntington, S. P. (1993).The clash of civilizations? *Foreign Affairs, 72*(3), 22–49.

Jingjit, R., & Fotaki, M. (2011). Confucian ethics and the limited impact of the new public management reform in Thailand. *Journal of Business Ethics, 97,* 61–73.

Karakayali, S. (2018).The *Flüchtlingskrise* in Germany: Crisis of the refugees, by the refugees, for the refugees. *Sociology, 52,* 606–611.

Kenny, K., & Fotaki, M. (2015). From gendered organizations to compassionate borderspaces: Reading corporeal ethics with Bracha Ettinger. *Organization, 22,* 183–199.

Lacan, J. (2006). *Ecrits: The first complete translation in English* (B. Fink, trans.). New York: W.W. Norton & Company.

Lafazani, O. (2018). *Κρίση* and *Μετανάστευση* in Greece: From illegal migrants to refugees. *Sociology, 52,* 619–625.

Long, K. (2012). In search of sanctuary: Border closures, "safe" zones, and refugee protection. *Journal of Refugee Studies, 26,* 458–476.

Long, S. (1999). The tyranny of the customer and the cost of consumerism: An analysis using systems and psychoanalytic approaches to groups and society. *Human Relations, 52,* 723–743.

Long, S. (2008). *The perverse organisation and its deadly sins.* London: Karnac.

Martin, R. (2002). *Financialization of daily life.* Philadelphia, PA: Temple University.

McHugh-Dillon, H. (2015, April). If they are genuine refugees, why? Public attitudes to unauthorised arrivals in Australia. *Foundation House.*

Money-Kyrle, R. (1971). The aim of psychoanalysis. In D. Meltzer (Ed.), *The collected papers of Roger Money-Kyrle* (Chapter 33). Strath Tey: Clunie Press, 1978.

Nilsson, P. (2018, October 9). Opening the door to the far right. *Jacobin Magazine*. Retrieved from www.jacobinmag.com/2018/09/sweden-election-sap-sweden-democrats-immigration-far-right

OECD. (2011). Public opinions and immigration: Individual attitudes, interest groups and the media. In OECD, *International migration outlook* (pp. 116–156). Paris: OECD.

OECD. (2015). *Is this humanitarian migration crisis different?* Migration Policy Debates No. 7. Washington, DC: OECD.

Puig de la Bellacasa, M. (2012). "Nothing comes without its world": Thinking with care. *Sociological Review, 60*, 196–216.

Purpose. (2017). *Attitudes towards national identity, immigration, and refugees in Germany*. London: Purpose Europe.

Rizq, R. (2013). States of abjection. *Organization Studies, 34*, 1277–1297.

Sandelind, C. (2018). Constructions of identity, belonging and exclusion in the democratic welfare state. *National Identities, 20*, 197–218.

Sassen, S. (2013). *Expulsions: Brutality and complexity in the global economy*. Cambridge, MA: Belknap.

Stiglitz, J. E. (2011). Rethinking macroeconomics: What went wrong and how to fix it. *Global Policy, 2*, 165–175.

Tronto, J. (1993). *Moral boundaries: A political argument for an ethic of care*. London: Routledge.

Tyler, I. (2013). *Revolting subjects: Social abjection and resistance in neoliberal Britain*. London: Zed Books.

UNHCR. (2018). *Figures at a glance: Statistical yearbooks*. London: UNHCR UK. Retrieved from www.unhcr.org/uk/figures-at-a-glance.html

Widmalm, S. (2018). The ideology of economism can explain the rise of right-wing populism in the upcoming Swedish elections. *Respons*, 3. Retrieved from http://tidskriftenrespons.se/artikel/ideology-economism-can-explain-rise-right-wing-populism-upcoming-swedish-election/

4

MY EUROPE: A CONTINENT BETWEEN REJECTION AND RE-INCLUSION

A discussion with Dr. Robi Friedman

Anna Zajenkowska and Uri Levin

AZ and UL: Let us open by thanking you Robi, for your hospitality, letting us have the interview in your cozy clinic in Haifa, Israel, and for your readiness to share with us some of your ideas and conceptualisations, as well as your personal insights and feelings. For our readers who do not know you, we would like to briefly introduce you. You are a clinical psychologist, a group analyst, and a co-founder of the Israeli Institute of Group Analysis, as well as one of its past Chairs. You are also a former President of the Israeli Association for Group Psychotherapy, and a Past President of the International Group Analytic Society (GASi). You have written extensively on group analysis. You were also a gifted volleyball player and coach. Groups play a major role in your personal as well as in your professional life.

You have a fascinating history, and although you were born in South America, you are deeply rooted in Europe. Your mother escaped from Prussia during World War II (WW2), and your father, South Hungary. If the war had not started, your life would have probably gone on a completely different route.

Would you like to add more for our readers about your sense of belonging to Europe; about 'Your Europe'?

RF: It strikes me how much I feel 'at home' in European groups, where I work. It seems to enter the Danish or Swiss way of thinking and feeling for boundaries, responsibility or humility, just to give some examples, which match part of my upbringing. Especially the German culture, in which I was raised by my mother's family, feels very accessible. Sometimes, I even wonder if it is possible that I am part of the German Matrix, including my ambivalence towards it. Europe has a strong intergenerational heritage, a cultural and social history which influences persons in every corner of the world.

AZ: During our background conversation, you differentiated between the Group Analytic culture, which is 'sibling oriented', and other group settings, which are more 'authority oriented'. Looking at Europe, we can identify some nations with more hierarchical and collectivistic characteristics, like Greece or Poland, in comparison to those nations showing more egalitarian culture – Norway for instance. At the same time, egalitarian values seem to be shared to a greater extend by EU.

RF: I also thought about it, but I have some different ideas regarding this issue. I am not sure if what we see from the outside as egalitarian (in regard to EU) is such in reality. Some countries like Germany or France hold a more superior position. The easiest way to bridge between two different conflicting cultures is actioning lawful agreements. Even if they are negotiated between the highest level by ruling parties, resolving disagreements by signing papers alone does not have, by itself, an influence on the population. It takes many generations of interaction for a society to really agree to lawful agreements, if ever.

When I participated in a team with some members of the IDI (International Dialogue Initiative) in Northern Ireland in 2012, we convened a meeting with the five largest parliamentary groups. The Irish were great in achieving the Good Friday Agreement. However, there still is a big wall in Belfast's middle, separating the 'agreeing' parties. Protestant and Catholic citizens would not do sports together, would not go to school together, would not marry if they came from the other group. In order to really agree, people in conflict, in their thousands, have to meet in real life and communicate. It is a big challenge to organise such interactions. That is the reason we promote large groups of hundreds of participants, which are very important and provide an opportunity for every group analyst to intervene. We also have media to provide meetings to a large number, but that only helps when people love each other. Otherwise, media's distance only intensifies conflicts.

AZ: What you said resonates with my idea, that it seems that we – Europeans (if I may use a generalisation) are not yet a sibling-oriented group. We are trying more to establish and create a relation with an external authority. That is a first phase of a group process development, which eventually, if properly facilitated, can lead to a differentiation phase, where we would be more capable of dealing with each other despite many differences in norms and values.

RF: Imagine that you are more an authority-oriented country, e.g. Poland, and you meet a sibling-oriented one, like Norway. People from Poland would get scared, they would perceive the other culture as an anarchy, they could feel that their culture is endangered. This danger, for example, results in the fear from refugees and by closing the borders. Such reactions are related to the feeling of security. Basically, the less secure a society feels, the more authority-oriented it becomes. These attitudes toward authority are unconsciously part and parcel of our foundation, dynamic and individual matrix. The problem is the lack of a real dialog between different countries, for example, Germany and Poland, and if there is not enough dialog, there is distance, which usually increases further distance and splitting.

46 Anna Zajenkowska and Uri Levin

UL: What you say is interesting. I think of Germany and of Angela Merkel. Is it possible that she made a mistake opening the borders the way she did – not dialoging with the German society and other societies, which were more fearful than her?

RF: Well, it was a more political than social decision, and therefore the massive immigration was not digested by large parts of the local society. My opinion is that her doings also mirror emotions based on the transgenerational transfer of guilt and the need for reparation of the past. She comes from the East part of Germany, with the narrative that they were the 'good-doers', very social, with the Nazi matrix largely repressed. In my opinion, one more problem is that her good intentions clash with conflicting West and East German perspectives, which partly are challenged in what seems to be very different opinions about themselves.

AZ: It seems that citizens lack a space to express their fears, including being afraid of other people. Perhaps, it would be vital if authorities could find out what the citizens are afraid of and why, and then address it?

RF: Yes, very much so. In addition, what you say in-between lines is also related to the fact that leaders being in power experience more glory than trauma. People in power do not experience depression; that is often the experience of the civil society.

UL: Groups, as well as the relations between 'leaders' and 'citizens', seem to play a major role in your life.

RF: Indeed, groups are very important to me, probably because of my rather complicated and challenging family. That is why I wanted to be in a group, and always tried to be in a good group. I was sent by my mother to a German school in South America, in which most of my classmates were children of escaped Nazis. It was very difficult there, as every day I had to fight, because I did not want to run away all the time. The children's and their families' rejection became an incentive for me to try to enter groups. I tried to overcome this rejection; of course, other people react differently.

AZ: Why did you feel rejected?

RF: Because they were, both children and sometimes teachers, openly anti-Semitic. I knew that after my first five minutes at school. I will now tell you a personal story, which I have never told in public, but I decided that I am old enough to share it with you. My mother brought me to my first day in school, which had started a week earlier; I was five years old back then, my father had just died, and everyone had returned from summer vacation before me. I entered the class and sat down, and when my mother left, the teacher asked me in a disgusted and surprised tone: 'Isn't your mother a Jew?' I got up and threw my chair at her. The teacher sent me to the director's office.

AZ: Why did you throw the chair?

RF: Because she actually humiliated me; it was in her tone, and because in this German Nazi culture, in which I was put in, to say: 'you are a Jew' was like saying 'you are an animal'. I could not stand it; actually, my mother was also rejected from her school in Nazi Germany, where she lived until 1942.

Continent between rejection and re-inclusion **47**

AZ: Is it possible to look at this situation from a different perspective or just as a sign of anti-Semitism?

RF: I wish it was possible. That it was me who misinterpreted the situation; maybe it was my own envy that *they* were the real Germans and I was not, which brought up my rage. But maybe it is difficult for today's generations to understand how it was before, and just after the war; it happened in 1952 – anti-Semitism was so deep, it could not stop from one day to another. When I was in Germany in 1962, in public toilets you could still see many painted swastikas. . . . But I also wish to mention that when we grew up and became teenagers, the confrontation between my friends and their parents began, as they started asking about what the parents actually did during the war. That helps me to talk about social changes. I think Germans did an amazing job in changing from a Nazi, a hating and rejecting matrix, to a democratic inclusive matrix, different than any other nation in the world, not only in Europe.

UL: You refer to the fact that Germans are constantly working through their history?

FR: Yes, it seems that even if the fighting generations identified with Nazis and did not want to feel guilty, their children felt guilty 'for' their parents.

I have been supervising in a psychiatric department in Germany, which helps refugees who are suffering from many emotional distresses. In my opinion, all the people working with refugees there or elsewhere in Germany, do at the same time engage in important political work. Only two generations ago, such refugees, who are now met and cared for, would be, in the best case, kicked out of Germany. They repair the sickness of a whole nation who suffered from what I call the second Relation Disorder – the Rejection Disorder. Many of our societies are currently suffering from this disorder.

UL: In some of your papers, you differentiate rejection from exclusion. You argue that rejection is social expulsion from a group or community, while exclusion is more 'normal' marginalisation in the group. In your Foulkes Lecture in May 2018 you stated: 'Rejection and chronic exclusion make you sick. Inclusion cures. Rejection is trauma, inclusion is glory – extremes in a possible dialogue'. When you look at Europe today – Brexit, refugees, the rise of right-wing politics – do you identify a 'possible dialogue' or rather split or broken communication between people, societies and nations?

RF: This is a good question. Let us say you come to Germany as a refugee from Afghanistan. You might not be greatly welcomed and possibly not immediately included, but you get a chance to stay, get a place to live, and get some work, although very often below your qualifications. Still, it is quite different from other countries, which would not let such a person in, which would reject her/him. People want to be seen and acknowledged. In my therapeutic group, I have a patient from Ethiopia. He tried to buy a house, in a shitty place, but they do not let him. That is rejection, they do not mind him working here for them, in an under-paid job, but they do not want to include him in their vicinity. Exclusion is active – 'I do not give you the power, even if you are intelligent, I do not want to hear you'. Excluded people feel depressed when their exclusion becomes chronic, until somebody comes and mobilises them. To keep such an 'exclusion-order', societies need secret police and an army, which makes them a Soldier's Matrix. This is the concept I use to describe the human dynamics in a society under threat or a wish for glory. These fighting communities over-identify with the fighting leadership, and progressively experience less ability to feel guilt, shame and empathy. This loss disinhibits aggression and hate towards different 'Others'. Everyone then, women, children and men, are enlisted in excluding parts of their society. Rejection on the other hand means: 'I do not want to see you ever again'.

AZ: That reminds me of large groups, which we conduct in Poland as part of the 'Poland on the couch' project. Very often people are afraid of discussing contradictory ideas with each other. It seems that when somebody's point of view is being 'rejected', immediately the fear appears they there will be a horrible fight, and 'we will kill each other'. It seems like anger and aggression are mixed.

RF: Yes, this happens, when a culture has a tradition of fearing their own aggression. It reminds me why I like discussions with Italians. They have a culture which can get heated when in conflict, they may even shout when angry, but are usually not physically violent. Among other possibilities, it can be connected to elements which disinhibit aggression, as the consumption of alcohol, and the culture of obedience to authority. In Italy, in the many years I worked there, I got the feeling that usually people drink alcohol more lightly and seem to respect less authority. This results in relatively higher levels of empathy, guilt and shame than in more aggressive cultures.

UL: In 2015 you offered a new concept – the Soldier's Matrix – 'to promote thinking about societies and their individuals under the influence of war threats, existential anxieties and hopes for glory'. In a different terminology, you argue that the 'dynamic matrix' takes over both the 'foundation' and the 'individual' matrices. Can you tell us how you came up with the idea of Soldier's Matrix?

RF: I started working in Germany about fifteen years ago. I remember one particular moment when I walked into Berlin with a German colleague. I saw something looking like an army garrison (you know I can smell the army from anywhere). The strange thing was that the entrance was not protected by a soldier, but by a private guard. When I asked about it, my colleague replied that 'We (Germans) do not like to see soldiers'.

I found it fascinating and specific about the German culture with its hundreds of years of war history: in this matrix, soldiers and what they represent must stay unseen. Another example could be a German psychoanalytic society, dominated during the war by Nazi German ideology. Only about twenty years after the war, during which the psychoanalytic community had not spoken about this subject, members of another community, representing a different matrix, came and attacked them: 'Are you crazy? How can you not talk about your past?'.

Continent between rejection and re-inclusion **49**

UL: What is your opinion about using Group Analysis as an intervention tool in a time of a social crisis?

RF: I wrote about it in my paper about indications and counter-indications in small group therapy (Friedman, 2013). Usually, you need to wait at least two to three months to the end of the acute part of the crisis before you can accept someone in the group. This often is also true in large groups, which are 'hard to sell'. I am working constantly on 'marketing' them and prepare the societies for the large group as an intervention tool. We had a large group with Israeli teenagers which was done in a high school about two years ago, and it went very well. The youngsters know how to 'tweet' and not give long speeches. Large monologues, which convey 'me' and 'not listening to you' influence the group's dynamic by disturbing the development of a dialog culture. I think we are progressing towards having group-analytic large groups in the elaboration of social crisis.

AZ: It's interesting. In Poland during the 'Poland on the Couch' workshops, people often gave speeches, especially at the beginning of a large group. 'Tweet and Listen' is a good idea . . . although long speeches are probably in a way a defense mechanism, that protects from open and deep contact with the newly acquainted others. . . . Getting back to listening: in your paper about Relational Disorders you ask three questions: What is the disorder that needs to be treated; what is the optimal therapeutic space; and when should a specific optimal space be recommended? If you were to refer these questions to the current situation in Europe, what would be your answers?

RF: I wrote about four Relational Disorders. The first Relational Disorder I wrote about has to do with an interaction between deficiency, i.e. being weak, with a potent group. One part is 'lacking' while the other part is 'full of'. So, you have a victim, or you are a victim, which is often the norm. I remember an intervention I made when I was conducting a large group in a conference in Athens. They seemed to feel that they were the victims of Europe and their own government, but they themselves told the large group that they do not want to pay taxes. The Greek are always deficient thus, this Greek large group, maybe representing the Greek Matrix, held the strongly to the position of the deficiency Disorder. They were in constant complaint towards Europe for killing their ancient tradition. Of course, the Greek never were only victims. So, for me, the Greek psychological culture is an example of what I have termed 'deficient disorder', which can change into more pro-active involvement, in a way, what they actually were trying to do in the last years, from a psychological point of view, may be seen as curing the 'Deficiency Relation Disorder'.

'Rejection Disorder' is what happens in some European countries, where they do not want any refugees, no matter how much and from where. Behind rejection, there is hatred and scapegoating. But tolerating and even using and learning from the different, the 'others', usually has a developmental aspect. Closing the society is often not really emotionally or socially helpful.

Then there is the Relation Disorder of the 'Selfless/Selfish', which you usually find in societies and systems organised in hierarchies. You see it in Japan,

50 Anna Zajenkowska and Uri Levin

where the culture is one of extreme obedience in all organisations, including university. The more autocratic and paternalistic societies are, the more selflessness is required from the civil society, without real gains. In the end, patriotism ends in war and/or in a poor personal or family life.

The forth Relation Disorder is 'Marginalisation'. It has to do with 'who has the power', 'who is the authority in the society'. In some societies, you find chronic marginalisation, which of course has its counterpart: chronic centralisation. In most European countries, you can guess beforehand when you go to a restaurant who will serve you and who will clean the dishes in the kitchen, or what will be the skin colour of those who do serving jobs on the streets and buildings. If this situation changes, and the cleaning personnel becomes (again) doctors, bus drivers and managers of restaurants, I would think that such a society is healthier than one where the margins are kept away from better jobs and power.

AZ: So according to what you say, the more chronic the situation, the more disordered the society. Would you agree that the disorder shows itself not only through the characteristics of a society, but also through not being willing to reflect upon the situation, to get into a dialogue about the possibility to change?

RF: Today, when I teach about the Relational Disorders, I relate not just to pathology but also to health. 'What does it mean to be a healthy society?' For me, the possibility of social mobilisation is a character of health. A healthy society is a society in which Relation Disorders are not chronic. We can be more optimistic about a society, where one can be more integrated, be more central and be able to lead. I consider it part of life to sometimes be weak, sometimes to feel afraid of rejection, to identify 'too much' with your community or sometimes to feel marginalised. Always being in these situations causes mental and physical sickness.

UL: The idea of a European Union was in a way a group analytic endeavor, a post–two world wars attempt to create a more open continent, less national, more egalitarian and based on exchange. But maybe the 'therapy' did not work; maybe the 'rejected', 'excluded' countries won't continue taking part in these dynamics?

RF: My generation was convinced that the EU was established because wars should 'never again' happen. My grandfather, who was a German soldier, said: 'there will *never* be peace between France and Germany'. Fortunately, the idea of 'NOT HAVING WAR' prevailed and became an important ideal for the post-war generation, who were willing to pay a high price for this peace. Indeed, the last seventy years were relatively peaceful. So maybe for the young generations today, born and living in peaceful times it seems obvious and natural, and they are less afraid than the older generations of power conflicts that could shake the EU. This is certainly true, in my opinion, of the Brexit UK.

AZ: Relationships in the EU were once based on fear and not on a genuine belief in cooperation. A few generations ago, the fear of war in Europe was very vivid. Today, for most of the young generation, war is probably unimaginable and not an option.

RF: You are not afraid of war?

AZ: Personally I am. My grandparents survived the war, my grandfather even two wars – WW1 and WW2. They told me a lot of terrifying stories, which definitely made me afraid of war and what people can do to each other. At the same time, it seems to me that when I talk to my students, and ask them if they are afraid of war, the majority answers: 'no'. Of course, that is not a representative sample, more my subjective opinion based on some conversation with people in their twenties.

UL: This optimistic stance of your students, Anna, connects me, Robi, to your own personal optimistic attitude towards large groups.

RF: If you look at the EU as a large group, there is a lot of exchange between the countries. There is also an enormous amount of money invested in projects aimed at enhancing democracy, liberalism, freedom and equality. I do have an optimistic view, that if you take many people, let them sit together and organise the setting in a good way, people will come out feeling that they are more tolerant. By meeting in the large group, something interpersonally good will happen to the members. But we have to remember that for many people, the setting of the large group is too difficult, at least in the beginning. This is one of the main reasons I developed the 'Sandwich Model', in which a large group session is sandwiched in between two small group sessions. If you gather a hundred members of the civil society and you start immediately with a large group, you may lose a lot of people. You first have to explain the large group setting to people, help them and even educate them to stay, to hold on and start with a small group. Otherwise, they might prematurely abandon the process. If you use this 'Sandwich Model' in a conflicted society, you will also have to work with the 'organisation' to help people to commit themselves to stay, because when the conflict is opened in the large group, the leadership's holding attitude is a key success factor to this process.

AZ: Robi, I agree, but one of the obstacles I see is that we need to learn, what is the benefit of being an active citizen?

RF: Once people get over the idea that they do it to get over fear, they feel that they are courageous, and they like it, especially the participation in large groups. They suddenly wake up and reflect: 'why for example did I watch a scapegoating event, and did nothing?'. Now they feel they can do something, and they feel they are growing. Once you help them grow, you will grow together. In many countries young people do not vote, but for instance in Switzerland there are at least six referendums a year, people learn how to be active, they decide. You know, in Switzerland they do not have a president. There is a cabinet with seven members, and each year one of them takes the lead, with the rule: primus inter pares. They are all equal (well, except the banks, which are a bit above 1☺). They try not to make majority decisions, but always get to a consensus. The culture is: 'let's do it together'.

52 Anna Zajenkowska and Uri Levin

AZ: You have been involved in teaching, supervising and conducting in many countries in Europe, for many years now. Can you tell us what your latest innovations are?

RF: Maybe my main innovation has to do with the understanding that the relations are at the centre of our emotional life. The individual, and the group-as-a-whole influence relations, but it is through relations that we can understand and change the emotional world of individuals and groups. This perspective on human and social development can be best seen and applied in groups. Thus, our unconscious world is trans-personally influenced (Foulkes, 1948) and our pathology is created and may be cured by relations. Further, the permeable boundaries of individuals-in-relations in societies which look for glory or protection from existential threats make for Soldier's Matrices. These are more basic approaches, which sometimes create a technical innovation. One example would be 'social dreamtelling', which is different from Gordon Lawrence's 'social dreaming' (2000) because in my approach the group looks not only at a told dream, but at its relational context as well. It is often the relations in dreamtelling which help us to understand both the dreaming of a society and the dream's relational messages of containment and influence in the group.

UL: The way I understand the originality of your perspective is that you locate the dream not in the isolated psyche, but rather in the intersubjective space. What are the highlights of your perspective, and could you share with us some insights you might have gained from your long years of conducting 'Dream Workshops' all over Europe?

RF: I can talk about dreams for a week . . . the uniqueness that I found is that dreaming and telling dreams is just part of a process. It may not have started with the dreamer alone, but maybe a dream is shared by others. Then I also think that dreams have communicative functions (to me and/or others). The audience to the dream is told to listen as if it was his/her own dream. I also try to help the listener to re-dream the dream. This is the best way to help the dreamer, and usually, also oneself. I believe in the dream's unconscious communication: first, the dreamer has a demand for influencing the relation with the persons or group who listen to the dream. He wants to change feelings, to be loved or feared or touched by the dream. So, the main issue is a dream-in-a-relation. Dreams also carry a request for containment of excessively dreadful or glorious feelings.

Dreams are also social; I would love to work with a politician's dream, I would know his/her fears and we could start a dialogue that always brings something good. There are specific differences in dreams in different countries, like in Russia people dream more openly about sex and aggression, and it is all very open and strong. In Copenhagen, where I worked for fifteen years (twice a year), it is more about if I can show myself, how do I have to behave in order to be OK, a dialogue with shame and self exposure. I gave you here two extremes, so you can see the differences.

AZ: Dreams are a safe way to talk about desires, drives . . .

RF: And aggression. . . . We live now in a very extraordinary time, so many years in Europe without a war, and still you can find many personal and social aggressions in dreams, from childhood onwards. Maybe dreams tell us something about human proneness to aggression?

AZ: That brings us to our last question: Do you think human beings are able to overcome a mass murder trauma? Maybe a bit naïve but can people live in peace?

RF: I am optimistic about it, but I do not think we can ever live without suffering. I am sure we are progressing, maybe the EU is facing problems or even deteriorating, but still life in Europe is much quieter than here in Israel. One of the achievements of Europe, notwithstanding many political problems, is that war nations, like Germany, France, the UK etc. have developed first anti-Soldier's Matrices and then peaceful cultures. The first step seemed so important, because it meant that matrices work together in order to not threaten each other nor to achieve glory by defeating and humiliating one another. When international existence is secured, it also, with time, influences intra-national political developments. In a way, the EU is a (not perfect) model of development, worthy of copying. The quality of life of the individual, together with the growth of the civil society, help me even now to keep my natural optimism.

AZ and UL: Thank you Robi. We hope you enjoyed the interview at least as much as we did and wish you to continue contributing to so many people and organisations for many more years.

References

Foulkes, S. H. (1948). *Introduction to group analytic psychotherapy*. London: Heinemann. (Maresfield Reprint, London: Karnac, 1991.)

Friedman, R. (2013). Individual or group therapy? Indications for optimal therapy. *Group Analysis, 46*, 164–170.

Lawrence, G. (2000). *Tongued with fire: Groups in experience*. London: Karnac.

PART TWO

Particular understanding

5

THE IMAGE OF EUROPE IN THE SOCIAL UNCONSCIOUS OF ISRAELI JEWS

Haim Weinberg

Introduction

Europe is certainly not a unified continent, and European people differ in their behaviours, attitudes and communicational styles. A "cold-blooded" Scandinavian certainly reacts differently than a "hot-tempered" emotional Italian in response to an interpersonal conflict (and of course this is more of a stereotype and an over-generalization). However, it is interesting to note that regardless of those differences, "Europe" is perceived stereotypically by many Israelis as a polite, highly organized and well-mannered continent. European behaviour is associated with respect and dignity and seen as a model for civilized human interaction, perhaps in contrast to "Middle-Eastern" norms that are stereotypically perceived as vulgar, noisy, dirty, and inconsiderate. This image was internalized by Ashkenazi Jews (Jews who came from Europe and their descendants[1]) who considered themselves superior to Jews who came from Arab countries. These stereotypes influenced the structure of Israeli society from its inception (see Smooha, 1978). The Ashkenazi Jews usually looked upon "the Levant" (a popular term for eastern Mediterranean countries) as an inferior region compared to civilized Europe.

However, when we dig more deeply, the picture is much more complicated and the attitude towards Europe is much more ambivalent. For many Jews, Europe also symbolizes the birth of anti-Semitism and the origin of centuries of persecution and decrees against Jews. Since the 4th century, Christianity has been the dominant religion in Europe. Christian anti-Semitism (Levy, 2005) influenced the attitude of Europeans toward Jews, leading to blood libels (believing that Jewish rituals involve drinking the blood of a Christian baby), pogroms (massacres) and the frequent instances of slaughtering of Jews, and to decrees that discriminated against Jews, limiting their professional choices and minimizing their civil rights. Occasionally, Jews were exiled from towns and countries in which they had lived for centuries, adding to the myth and image of the Wandering Jew. Of course, the peak phenomenon of modern anti-Semitism is the Holocaust, which resulted in the extermination of one-third of the Jewish people and left its scar on modern history for Jews and non-Jews, and indirectly contributed to the establishment of the Israeli State.

We know that unelaborated social trauma can leave its unconscious impact on society many years later (Volkan, 2004). Social traumas compose an important part of the social unconscious (Hopper and Weinberg, 2011, 2015, 2017) and even become its building blocks (Weinberg, 2007). Thus, we can expect these traumatic events over hundreds of years to leave their mark on Israeli Jews. Indeed, Israel is a traumatized and traumatizing society (Nuttman-Shwartz & Weinberg, 2012; Weinberg, 2017a; Yair, 2015b). The long shadow of the Holocaust hovers above, and together with memories of centuries of persecution and existential threat exists in the Israelis' consciousness and unconsciousness. Volkan (2001) describes what he calls "chosen trauma" as the shared mental representation of a massive trauma from which the group's ancestors suffered. When a Large Group (such as a nation) regresses, its chosen trauma is reactivated in support of the group's threatened identity. Every time Israeli Jews are threatened by terror or war, their collective memories (Halbwachs, 1980) of previous disasters are unconsciously triggered, evoking existential threats in the national memory in order to ward off potential complacency. Small wonder that Israeli Jews can respond to what seems like a minor threat from the outside with exaggerated force, exposing it to repeated criticism from European countries. Because of the historical complicated relationships with Europe, this criticism is rarely considered on its face value and is usually brushed off as driven by anti-Semitic forces. From a relational perspective, the more Israel is labelled as aggressive by Europeans, the more it activates the paranoid feelings of Israelis as being persecuted for acting in self-defence. This is seen in the expression, "The world is entirely against us", a well-known Israeli slogan. In summary, unconscious forces and traumatic historical events leave their trace on Israeli politics and its relationship with the world, especially Europe.

In this chapter I want to address how the social unconscious of Israeli Jews and their European legacy is seen in clinical situations, so let's turn to some clinical examples.

The Wandering Jew and the shadow of the Holocaust

Jews were exiled from their motherland, Zion, more than 2,000 years ago, and had to wander all over the world to find a place in which they could live in peace. As mentioned above, living in peace did not last too long and they suffered expulsion again and again. Let me start with a very personal example that shows how annihilation anxieties and the "Wandering Jew" (Heym, 1999) syndrome are activated in times of war.

In 1967 Abdul Nasser, the Egyptian ruler at that time, blocked the Tiran Straits, which provide the only naval access to Southern Israel. This operation was defined by Israel as *casus belli* and was one of the main causes of the Six Day War. In the

The social unconscious of Israeli Jews 59

FIGURE 5.1   *The Wandering Jew* by Gustave Doré

period between this and other Egyptian acts (such as evacuating the UN forces from Sinai) and the outbreak of the war, known as the "Waiting Period", anxiety in Israel skyrocketed, resulting in panic shopping, evacuation of the southern city of Eilat and many people frantically trying to flee abroad. Here is my personal account and memories from that period:

> At that time, my parents decided to send my little brother (10 years old) to Europe until the situation cleared. I couldn't understand this decision. It felt irrational and cowardly to me (I was a teenager). Only when I grew up did I understand that they were sure that Israel was going to be exterminated and

wanted to save him in case our family perished (I assume that deeper family dynamics reveal themselves in this story as well, as my parents chose to save only the youngest child).

In retrospect, this fear that Israel would be destroyed was clearly overblown.

Apparently, oversensitivity to dangerous times due to historical traumas, and the need to be prepared for a possible catastrophe, affects Jews everywhere, even in places that are perceived as relatively free from overtly anti-Semitic history. Here is an example from my experience as a therapist in the USA:

> Immediately after Trump was elected for presidency in the USA in 2016, an American Jewish patient in California came to his regular therapy session with me, anxious and shocked: "I told my wife that we should sell all our shares and assets, buy gold or diamonds, and leave the US", he said. His grandparents emigrated from Russia at the beginning of the 20th century, fleeing pogroms by Cossacks. He told me that he was almost sure that right-wing racists would soon turn against Jews and that it already felt dangerous and unsafe. Although I could understand his point of view, I also saw this as an over-reaction, although it was not a rare reaction among my Jewish patients in the USA. It shows how quickly Jews feel insecure under political upheaval and how the "Wandering Jew" complex can easily be activated and triggered in times of uncertainty. This patient was sure that I would understand him, as he knew that I am Jewish myself. However, he also knew that I am an Israeli living in the States, which made me more resilient and less anxious in his eyes.

Although many people, including Christians, as well as Muslims, patients and non-patients, reacted with similar anxieties after Trump's triumph, and anxiety in the USA heightened, in my opinion the anxiety of this patient and his strong reaction was triggered also by unconscious or half-conscious prosecution anxiety, and not only by objective evaluation of the situation.

The unconscious impact of the Holocaust in literature and clinical practice

As we know, unconscious social processes can be understood through analysing art pieces, from poetry to books; from sculptures to movies (for an example see Weinberg (2017a)). The shadow of the Holocaust reveals itself in the Israeli literature again and again just as it appears in many clinical situations with Israeli Jews. In *See Under: Love* (1986), David Grossman, one of the most famous Israeli writers of the latest decades, tells the story of Momik, the son of two Holocaust survivors who are obsessed not to let him know anything about the atrocities they went through, in order to protect him and give him a "normal" childhood. However, at the beginning of the book, an old man (Momik's late grandmother's brother) joins the family after being released from a psychiatric hospital. He was probably hospitalized following what he had gone through during the Holocaust. The old man speaks in broken words and sentences and Momik tries to complete them and to create a coherent story out of what he hears. Momik, a sensitive and isolated kid, builds a fantastic narrative of his own about the Holocaust and his family's history. In his frightened imagination, "the Nazi beast" his mother whispers about, lives in the basement. He feels as if he must tame the beast that harmed them "over there", so that it no longer continues to torture and persecute the people he loves and allow the family to regain full lives.

In this wonderful story Grossman describes the psychological mechanisms involved in the transgenerational transmission of social trauma (Volkan, 2001) and the creation of "Second Generation" syndrome (Danieli, 1985), which explains how the memory of the Holocaust is embedded in the unconscious processes of Israeli Jews. As many Holocaust survivors were not able to talk about the atrocities they suffered from the Nazis, whether because they wanted to protect their children or because it was too painful to remember and to discuss, they left too many unanswered questions for the second generation. Even if they did not mention anything about what happened to them during the Holocaust, their children sensed something and could only imagine how terrible it was. In the fifties and sixties of the twentieth century, no public discourse about the Holocaust occurred in Israel. Those who could not repress or forget paid a high price either by recurrent nightmares or, worse than that, needing hospitalization for psychiatric symptoms. At any rate, the fact that these issues could not be elaborated in the public sphere is exactly what Volkan (2001) describes as the perfect conditions to create a "chosen trauma".

As said, Grossman is not the only Israeli author who tried to deal with the Holocaust in his writing. Another one is Amir Gutfreund, whose book *Our Holocaust* (2000) is populated by Holocaust survivors all living in a small neighbourhood in Northern Israel. The book is entirely about how two young children slowly reveal the story of the Holocaust. There is an unwritten agreement not to tell the children about the horrors of the Holocaust and when they ask about that period, they are told that "they have to reach the age". However, these horrors are unconsciously transmitted: for example, the kids are not allowed to throw away any food leftovers, and no explanation is given. Only later they find out that "people died for one potato" or that "people turned in their parents to the Nazis for some cabbage".

It is true that in many families around the world, throwing food away is condemned. Sometimes the background is social trauma from which previous generations suffered (I was shocked to hear similar sentences from a Singaporean student who participated in a process group I have led, explaining that her grandmother suffered famine during the Japanese occupation of Singapore in WWII). Some other times it has to do with a background of family poverty. However, for many Israeli Jewish children, this attitude towards food was not explained or discussed, and thus the origins of the behavior remained unconscious.

These books are not fiction at all and we can easily find similar stories in our patients' lives. Here is one example from a group patient:

> Rebecca, a single woman in her thirties, who had just finished her Medical Doctor studies and was about to become a physician, joined a therapy group.

Despite her professional achievements (her grades at the medical school were excellent) she was extremely anxious and unsure of herself. She was unsuccessful in finding an intimate male partner, attributing it to her being ugly (which was far from the impression of the group leaders and members). It seemed that she became repeatedly attracted to men who exploited and sometimes abused her. As the group progressed, more and more we heard about the strong influence of her mother on her life. This mother seemed to be very controlling, wanted to know everything about Rebecca's whereabouts, and criticized her for everything she did. Nothing Rebecca had done satisfied her mother, and especially every act of independence was severely condemned. She was unable to get angry with her mother and developed a silent submissive attitude towards her mom, and actually towards any abuse. The more she opened up in the group and talked about this relationship, the more group members became angry with her mother. It was clear that a process of projective identification was taking place, and that group members acted out the anger she suppressed.

In one painful memory from her childhood Rebecca told us that she brought home a small deserted dog she found in the street and gave him food and milk. When her mother found out about it she had a fit, shouting "throw this Nazi beast (!) out of my house", which she did. Rebecca could not understand this cruelty, but the group leaders thought that this event might give us a clue to understand the mother's behaviour. Indeed, we found out that Rebecca's mother was a Holocaust survivor. Rebecca did not know exactly what happened to her mother "over there", except that it was horrible and unspeakable. We could speculate on the deep reasons for her mother's need for control, that probably reflected her deep anxiety and need to protect her child. One of the group members finally wondered who was that "Nazi beast" and dared saying that sometimes she imagined Rebecca's mother as adopting a Nazi's behaviour. The psychological mechanism of identifying with the aggressor comes to mind. The group even speculated that Rebecca might give the men in her life the role of "the Nazis". It was a difficult and painful discussion, and at first Rebecca tried to protect her mother's reputation, but the discussion clearly had a big impact on her. In a few months she succeeded in leaving her mother's house, renting a small room of her own, despite her mother's dramatic scenes, blaming her for being an ungrateful daughter and for torturing her "more than *they* have tortured her over there".

It was interesting that following this "Nazi beast" story, more group members revealed untold family stories about surviving WWII. For example, suddenly one of the group members found hidden documents in her parents' bedroom showing that they were both married in the war and lost their partners in the concentration camps. This past was never discussed in the family, although this group member always felt that there are secrets in the family.

The social unconscious of Israeli Jews **63**

In short, the Holocaust casts its long shadow on the life of Israeli Jews, unconsciously influencing their behaviour in many hidden ways and also affecting their attitude towards Europe.

Unconscious anxiety from Christianity[2]

Another factor that unconsciously affects Israelis' attitude and perception of Europe and Europeans is the fact that Europe is perceived as a Christian continent, and Jews have a long problematic history with Christianity. The following example, taken from my clinical experience, shows how unconscious anxieties from Christians can be transmitted over generations and affect Jews' behaviours hundreds of years after the original trauma occurred.

An Israeli living in the USA for twenty-two years and married for eighteen years to a non-Jewish North American woman, came to therapy, due to difficulties in his marriage. He was aware of the cultural differences that might have caused some of the troubles but attributed the difficulties to his impatience and intolerance. Throughout his marriage, they became more distant and estranged, which he thought is the fate of any long-term relationship. They collaborated well but did not feel intimately connected. Although the couple never had an open fight, there was always some tension in their relationship, as if there is a continuous underlying conflict. The man observed the Shabbat and other Jewish religious commands, like some religious Jews do, and his wife was indifferent to it. The woman grew up as a Catholic but did not practice Christianity and did not visit church regularly. Usually, they did not have to deal with differences of religious rituals and traditions, until they were invited to participate in the confirmation ceremony of the wife's niece. During the ceremony, which my patient attended out of respect for his wife and her family, he felt inexplicable tension. He controlled himself until the priest started walking down the aisle, swinging the incense bowl, spreading its scent, and murmuring prayers. When the priest approached him, my patient felt intolerable anxiety, panicked, and ran out of church.

My patient did not have anxiety or panic attacks before and it was an enigma for him what caused it. His associations took him to his family of origin and to his parents vaguely warning him to be careful of associating with Christians while he was younger, living in Israel. Another association was about a poem they learned in school in Israel describing how dangerous it was for the Rabbi's daughter to fall in love with a non-Jew (which shows that it was not only a threat for him, but unconsciously transferred to Israeli Jews in general). It all pointed to a deep sense of danger when he got close to gentiles (non-Jews), but it was unclear where it was coming from. My usual experience with Israeli Jewish patients led me to think that perhaps his parents survived the Holocaust, and that this was the usual transgenerational transfer for the second generation. To my surprise he told me that his parents grew up among Muslims in Turkey, in a relatively peaceful environment, and were never persecuted. After a thorough exploration and research of his family history, we found out that his family was originally the descendants of the Jews who were expelled from Spain. It seems as if those events took their toll hundreds of years later as they remained an unelaborated trauma in the social unconscious of this man and his family. Working through these hidden issues, we understood more and more that the long-term unconscious social trauma contributed to his hidden conflict and distance from his wife.

The explanation of the patient's marriage difficulties on the background of the Social Unconscious does not mean that this is the only factor that determined his problems with his wife. Cultural differences and personality traits took their toll, of course. However, exploring the Social Unconscious and adding this factor to the other explanations contributed a dimension that this man had not thought about before, and according to his claim, added to his ability to work on the relationship with his wife.

Ambivalence towards Europe among Israelis

As mentioned in the introduction, the attitude of Israelis towards Europe is complicated, and can best be described as ambivalent. Influenced by annihilation anxieties described above, many Israelis, especially youngsters, are looking for a second citizenship, or a European passport, either in order to take advantage of free high educational opportunities or "just in case" they will have to escape from a future disaster in Israel. In recent years many young Israelis immigrated to European countries. The most perplexing phenomenon is the immigration of Israelis to Germany, especially to Berlin. One might expect that Berlin, the center of the Nazi regime, responsible for the extermination of six million Jews just a few decades ago, will not feel very attractive to Israelis. Strange enough, many of them find it a very pleasant place to live in (emphasizing economic advantages and other practical reasons) and seem to ignore the impact of the many memorials for WWII spread around the city. They seem to disassociate from the memories embedded in the social unconscious of Israeli Jews.

However, a closer examination reveals that there is more than the naked eye observes. Gad Yair, an Israeli sociologist, interviewed many Israelis living in Berlin and has written a book in Hebrew titled *Love Is Not Praktish: The Israeli Look at Germany* (2015a). Yair concludes that Israeli ears are sensitized to hearing German sounds that echo Nazi-associated memories; and Israeli eyes see beyond the here and now – as they gaze into past days and decipher traces of identities long gone. He uses the metaphors of the "wounded eye" and the "scratched ear". The eye observes German teachers marking kids who stay for lunch in school with color ink on their arm, making clear who gets to eat. Israelis are shocked, as their association for this act is the number engraved on the Jews' arms in the concentration camps. When they hear someone shouting "Achtung" ("attention" in German) their immediate association is to Nazi soldiers shouting this word while hurrying Jews to their deaths. As pointed out, Yair is not the only one to conclude that the trauma that the Holocaust inscribed in Israeli culture still exists even after half a century or more (Weinberg, 2017a; Zertal, 2005).

Conclusion, discussion and more thoughts

The attitude to Europe and Europeans by Israeli Jews is complicated and ambivalent. On the one hand Europe is perceived in positive terms and is idealized as a civilized place and a model for good manners and "high culture". However, the impact of anti-Semitism, the memories of the Holocaust and centuries of persecution and the fact that Europe is a Christian continent unconsciously negatively affect how Israeli Jews relate to Europe, associating this "civilized" place with deep, dark drives and threats. While examining the complicated attitude of Israeli Jews towards Europe and Europeans, some of its origins not totally known to them, we should also bear in mind the socio-political situation in the world and in Europe nowadays, as we hold the relational frame of reference and see any human situation as co-created by all participants. I believe that there is an interaction between political events in Europe and the ambivalent attitude of Israelis. The world in the 21st century feels more and more unsafe. The collapse of the Twin Towers in 2001 in New York symbolized the shatter of the illusion of security for Americans. Several years later, Europe joined that turmoil, as European countries suffer more and more terror attacks, leaving their citizens anxious and worried. France, Germany, the UK, Belgium and Spain all took their share in this bloody scene.

In addition, waves of immigrants from North Africa, Syria and even from Afghanistan flooded Europe, creating an immigration crisis and posing a dilemma for democratic countries how to balance between staying human and maintaining safety and national identities. All those processes pushed many European countries into right-wing populist parties, especially in Eastern Europe. Stretching from Poland to Macedonia, these parties have taken power in Bosnia, Bulgaria, the Czech Republic, Hungary, Poland, Serbia and Slovakia. Israelis hear the echoes of racism from WWII and are worried about the return of persecution against minorities, currently Muslims, but who knows where it will end. At the same time, similar processes occur in Israel itself, where right-wing government is in power and Palestinians' rights are violated daily in the name of security. This double standard that Israelis developed covers an unconscious identification with the aggressor and a deep confusion between victims and victimizers.

Notes

1 This is also an overgeneralization, as mostly these Jews came from Germany, France and Eastern Europe.
2 A version of this vignette appears in Weinberg (2017b).

Bibliography

Danieli, Y. (1985). The treatment and prevention of long-term effects and intergenerational transmission of victimization: A lesson from Holocaust survivors and their children. In C. R. Figley (Ed.). *Trauma and its wake* (pp. 295–312). New York: Brunner, Mazel.

Grossman, D. (1986). *See under: love*. Tel Aviv: Keter pub (in Hebrew).

Gutfreund, A. (2000). *Our Holocaust*. Tel Aviv: Zmora-Bitan publication (in Hebrew).

Halbwachs, M. (1980). *The collective memory*. New York: Harper & Row.

Heym, S. (1999). *The wandering Jew*. Evanston, IL: Northwestern University Press.

Hopper, E., & Weinberg, H. (Eds.). (2011). *The social unconscious in persons, groups and societies: Volume 1: Mainly theory*. London: Karnac.

Hopper, E., & Weinberg, H. (Eds.). (2015). *The social unconscious in persons, groups and societies: Volume 2: Mainly foundation matrices*. London: Karnac.

Hopper, E., & Weinberg, H. (Eds.). (2017). *The social unconscious in persons, groups and societies: Volume 3: The foundation matrix extended and reconfigured*. London: Karnac.

Levy, R. S. (Ed.). (2005). *Antisemitism: A historical encyclopedia of prejudice and persecution*. Santa Barbara, CA: ABC Clio.

Nuttman-Shwartz, O., & Weinberg, H. (2012). Organizations in traumatized societies: The Israeli case. In E. Hopper (Ed.), *Trauma and organizations* (pp. 215–231). London: Karnac.

Smooha, S. (1978). *Israel: Pluralism and conflict*. London: Routledge and Kegan Paul.

Volkan, V. D. (2001). Transgenerational transmissions and chosen traumas: An aspect of large-group identity. *Group Analysis, 34*(1), 79–97.

Volkan, V. D. (2004). *Blind trust: Large groups and their leaders in times of crisis and terror*. Charlottesville, VA: Pitchstone Publishing.

Weinberg, H. (2007). So what is this social unconscious anyway? *Group Analysis, 40*, 307–322.

Weinberg, H. (2017a). The social unconscious of Israeli Jews – described and analysed by an Israeli living in North America. In: E. Hopper & H. Weinberg (Eds.), *The social unconscious in persons, groups, and societies: Volume 3: The foundation matrix extended and re-configured* (pp. 129–150). London: Karnac.

Weinberg, H. (2017b). The social unconscious and issues of conflict & reconciliation in therapy. In G. Ofer (Ed.), *A bridge over troubled water: Conflicts & reconciliation in groups and society* (pp. 139–152). London: Karnac.

Yair, G. (2015a). *Love is not Praktish: The Israeli look at Germany*. Tel Aviv: Hakibbutz Hameuchad publication (in Hebrew).

Yair, G. (2015b). The Israeli existential anxiety: Cultural trauma and the constitution of national character. *Social Identities, 20*(4–5), 346–362.

Zertal, I. (2005). *Israel's Holocaust and the politics of nationhood*. Cambridge: Cambridge University Press.

6

POLAND AND THE OTHER – THE OTHER AND POLAND

A dialogue between a newcomer and a native

Ziad Abou Saleh and Bogdan de Barbaro

> *Motto*
> *"Why do you kill me?"*
> *"What! do you not live on the other side of*
> *the water? If you lived on this side, my friend, I should be an assassin, and it would be*
> *unjust to slay you in this manner. But since you live on the other side, I am a hero, and*
> *it is just."*
>
> —*Blaise Pascal*

Introduction

One of the most frequently discussed topics in public debates, in official statements by politicians, but also presumably among people interested in problems facing the contemporary world, is the mass influx of people from the Middle East and North Africa into Europe. We have to come to grips with migration movements unheard of for many decades. They involve several million people. This is thus an unusually important phenomenon for social, political, and economic reasons. The "demographic catastrophe" in the modern world is characterized by the ongoing population decline in Europe and other highly developed countries, including Japan in particular, with very strong demographic growth in countries of the Middle East and North Africa. For many years, Europe has had a negative birthrate, resulting in the aging of European societies, adversely affecting the economy. In demographic studies, such tendencies are considered irreversible. This problem is most visible in the Federal Republic of Germany, which is the most populous nation in the European Union.

The demographic forecasts for Poland are just as bad. According to the Central Statistical Office, there will be a decrease of 3.15 million people in the country's population by 2050, or as much as 8.3 percent. The birth rate will fall while, conversely, the death rate will increase. In 2050, as many as 174,000 more Poles will die than will be born, and people over 65 will make up more than 30 percent of the population.[1]

Certain laws govern a society. One of them is the law of progressive development of generative capacities, driven by an increase in social needs, which in turn leads to the transformation of quantitative changes into qualitative ones. If a society begins to die out in demographic terms, the scale of social needs will also start to shrink and thus, economic processes will begin to appear which will lead to the inhibition of economic development and then to the permanent regression of generative capacities. As a result, these societies will begin to regress in civilizational development.

Reflections on Poland in the second decade of the 21st century show that one of the most important challenges faced by the inhabitants of this country is the search for a mature relationship with the Other − with the Other in society, the Other in the family, and the Other as an individual. The last few years have shown a growing tension between those who are fearful, adopting a hostile attitude towards the Other, and those who are building relationships with the Other in the spirit of curiosity and kindness.

The situation calls for some reflection.

ZIAD ABOU SALEH: From the perspective of a Pole and also a psychotherapist, what is the current cultural context defining the relationship between Poles and Others?

BOGDAN DE BARBARO: The relationship of I-and-the-Other is fundamentally dependent on the cultural context in which I meet the Other. The rapid, sometimes even revolutionary changes that have taken place in Poland in recent decades have collectively determined the attitude of Poles towards the Other. Although the "revolutions" which I'll describe on later are universal in character (or at least they don't merely concern Poland), their impact on the individual is very conspicuous in countries of Central and Eastern Europe, i.e. in those societies that became sovereign after 1989.

First of all, there is a tension between a Catholic society's tradition and post-modernity. The turn of 21st century immersed Poles in postmodernity on a wide scale. In Poland, a collision occurred between, on the one hand, the postmodern uncertainty of the world, the dissolution of the search for objective truth, the multiplicity of cultural norms, and ethical relativism ("everything goes") with, on the other hand, the traditional, conservative norms that had existed for centuries − the strong position of the Catholic church, the tendency to respect the hierarchical social structure, and observing the dichotomy of "we" (citizens) versus "they" (the government).[2] Old signposts giving existential and moral support began to weaken: consumerism led to the transformation of the *sacrum* into the *profanum*, leading people out of churches and into shopping centers (or perhaps one should say it made temples out of supermarkets). Although the Catholic Church is still strong

A dialogue between a newcomer and a native **69**

and politicians must reckon with it, the presence of this institution in social life is increasingly expressed mainly at the level of ritual and "superficial" faith.[3]

From a political perspective, these two currents – the postmodern and conservative – are largely reflected in the division between "pro-European supporters" and "supporters of traditional Polish values", creating an ever deepening dichotomy. Among citizens, there's a growing emotional tension and an increasing reluctance between the supporters of these two currents to have anything to do with each other. This is reflected both in journalistic and parliamentary debates as well as in the growing avalanche of Internet hate.[4] Behavior and language that would have been deemed as unacceptable a dozen or so years ago are now the norm, no longer causing outrage.

At the same time, liquid modernity, as Polish philosopher and sociologist Zygmunt Bauman (2005) put it (liquid, because it cannot be ordered and clearly described), carries with it an extremely important element: openness to what is the Other. Postmodernity encourages resignation from the tribal reaction to the Other ("attack or run away"). Consequently, by opening up to the Other, there can be personal enrichment by assimilating those elements of otherness considered valuable.

In light of what I've mentioned above, it becomes clear that the 21st century has fated Poles to come into sudden contact with many different values and lifestyles: on the one hand, there's been an openness to what is different and foreign, and on the other, fear of what is different as well as aggression towards what is foreign.

ZAS: But there are some additional (technological, economic, historical) circumstances which impact the situation.

BdB: Of course. Another important factor that has been shaping the landscape of modern Poland, in tandem with other factors, is the technological revolution. It is not a coincidence that there are two eras: BI v. AI ("Before the Internet" versus "After the Internet" Era). In this way, an increasingly prominent division is forming between members of society from Before the Internet Era and those from After the Internet Era.

In 1989, after almost half a century of political and economic dependence on the Soviet Union and life in so-called *real socialism*, Poles regained national sovereignty and adapted to the rules of the capitalist market. For those who are adroit, strong, and creative, this has meant experiencing freedom, the possibility to move freely, using material and cultural goods formerly inaccessible, as well as new opportunities for self-fulfillment, enrichment, and expansion. Such a lifestyle creates a sense of belonging to the Western world and increasingly allows us not to feel worse or different from "those from the West". However, for the weak and helpless, seasoned in the art of learned helplessness (uniquely characteristic of societies from the so-called Eastern bloc), this change leads to a sense of grievance, anger, and longing for a welfare state.

70 Ziad Abou Saleh and Bogdan de Barbaro

In the case of Poland, this change collides with a particular historical context. Poland, as a country located between Germany and Russia, has long been fated to the role of being a "bulwark" (to use the term willingly employed by Polish historians), and consequently often placed in the position of being an entity that is attacked and abused (at the level of the state, society, and citizen). Poland's national mythology is dominated by the myth of sacrifice, and the thesis, authored by Polish messianists and romantics, that Poland is the "Christ of nations" entails extraordinariness and a suffering for others experienced at the hands of foreign oppressors.[5]

ZAS: It can create a relationship between Poles and the Other.
BdB: You are right. Thus the role of the hero who's been wronged is the basis of Poland's national mythology. It is worth emphasizing here that the role of the person who has suffered wrong brings with it clear emotional advantages, in particular the sense of moral superiority. And yet, it's not any one of "Us", but "Others" who commit this wrong. This Other can be someone from another country, from another generation, someone who's of a different gender, who has different political views, who's from a different religion, hails from somewhere else, has a "non-normative" sexual preference, or has other ethnic or racial roots. The Other could be a Russian, a German, a representative of the European Union, a Jew, a Muslim, a homosexual,[6] a black person, etc. So we are constantly fated to fight this "dangerous Other". This readiness to fight the Other sometimes takes on (at the level of politics) nationalistic shades, while simultaneously and paradoxically combining Christian (or in any case Catholic) symbolism with aggression directed against Others.

It should be emphasized, however, that among Poles there are many who are open (sometimes uncritically) to Western Europe, indifferent to Polish history and historical tradition. As mentioned above, the opening up of borders – literally and figuratively – has made some Poles (especially the young generation – educated people who have been learning English since the start of primary school – who do not remember what it was like before 1989) consider multiculturalism, liberalism, and democracy to be something natural and, with regard to socio-political issues, often adopt an attitude of distance or indifference.[7]

In public discourse, it's rare to combine these two opposing points of view, according to which Poles know and respect their roots, history, and healthy traditions, and at the same time are able to see and critically examine the dark aspects of their past and present (xenophobia, anti-Semitism, homophobia). Two hostile political camps fight by means of two narratives: the narrative of harm and uncritical pride, as well as hostile insularity which is at times jealous, collides with a narrative dominated by revealing the dark pages in the latest chapter of Polish history (in particular its anti-Semitism) and affirming – sometimes uncritically – Western European liberalism.

ZAS: How would you describe the emotional consequences of this situation?

BdB: For some people, what is new presents an opportunity, a source of strength and satisfaction in life; the Other can be a source of interest and personal enrichment. However, for those who accept the new with fear, the world becomes less understandable, more threatening, less transparent, as the boundaries between good and evil become ambiguous and the structure of power (whether inner-psychological or familial or social) illegible. The need to be "looked after" is greater the greater the threat is from what's new and what's Other, and if there is a politician giving a sense of security (even one that is illusory), his followers ("the children of this leader") will hide under his wings, because he (or maybe *He*) promises care and protection from others. And if the Father relishes in this authority, he will demonize the Other so that the "children will be afraid" and would be increasingly in need of him and obey him. In this way, anxiety and aggression in anxious and aggressive individuals are strengthened and transmitted from the leader: "It's scary, but I will defend you". Under these conditions, the temptation to return to an anti-democratic model may grow stronger; with reluctance, suspicion, fear, and even aggression towards the Other, a strong patriarchal father (whether at the level of the family or state) promises security for the price of freedom. From the psychotherapist's point of view, it would be an instance of regression to a paranoid position.

I think that now is the appropriate moment to move onto describing the relationship between Poles and Arab residents in Poland.

ZAS: In Poland, the Muslim community, including its portion of Arabs, is relatively small. In July 2015, it numbered just 5,584 people, which is only 0.015 percent of the population of Poland (Czyż & Polakowska, 2015). An interesting phenomenon is the fact that Poles cannot properly determine the size of this national minority, exaggerating their numbers and implication. In the survey conducted by Ipsos MORI, Polish respondents in Poland expressed the view that Muslims constitute as much as 7 percent of the country's population which, easily calculable, would mean that there are around 2.6 million people living here (Arabs and other nationalities). This fact testifies to the citizens' total ignorance of problems concerning the population as well as religion persuasion in contemporary Poland;[8] it also seems to reveal the emotional attitude held by many Poles towards the Muslim minority.

BdB: Can you describe the empirical research you conducted with representatives of the Arab community living here in 1994 and – with the same group – in 2015/2016? Present at least some of the results.

ZAS: OK.[9] I tried to evaluate the process of integration, acculturation, education, and presence of Arabs living in Poland. They were at the time breaking new ground both in terms of their scale (almost the entire population of Arabs who were studying in Poland at the time was examined) and the issues dealt with. The focus was not only on topics related to the cultural assimilation of the

Arab community, but also on the problem of perception held by Arab students and PhD candidates concerning Poles.

The primary purpose of these studies was to describe the relationships that arose between representatives of both cultures; the interactions between different behavioral norms and value systems, as well as the possibility of integration and what that looks like. That involved looking at the attitude of Arabs towards the society in which they lived and the attitude of Poles towards the former, as well as assessing the effectiveness of cultural integration after more than twenty years of living in Poland. Mindful of an important problem calling for an assessment of the mutual relations between Poles and Arabs (the "Others"), the following question was raised: Have the Arabs, who have been living in Poland for over twenty years, adopted a new (Polish) way of life? Or do they cultivate and stick to the traditions and values taken from where they came from? Do Poles have a real basis for fearing the Arab population living here?

It was, therefore, an attempt to indirectly answer the question whether Poland is a "good" or "bad" country to integrate the Arab population (the "Others"). The information contained in these studies was designed to capture an image of Poland and Poles, as it were, through "the eyes" of Arabs living here.

Most of the work was based on in-depth surveys involving interviews with representatives of all the nationalities of the Arab world who were studying in Poland in the academic year 1993/94 or had completed at least the first year of studies and had taken a Polish language course for foreigners. Among the group of Arab students and doctoral candidates to be examined, these conditions were met by 945 people. They constituted 65 percent of the total number of people of Arabic origin studying at that time in all years and fields of study. The study distributed 945 questionnaires and answers from 610 people (64.5% of the target population) were obtained. In the group covered by the study, there were 436 students and 174 doctoral candidates. Individual demographic data on this group is presented in Table 6.1.

The decreasing number of respondents resulted mainly from changes in people's places of residence (some returning to their homeland), which significantly impeded contact. Many of them refused to participate in the study again in 2016, justifying this with weariness, in a relatively short period, of discussing similar topics.

BdB: How would you describe the Arab community in Poland and its attitude to the problems of religion?

ZAS: An extremely important problem for Arabs is their attitude to religion, and thus also their attitude towards the legal right of criticizing religion and the clergy. This is why the Arab respondents were asked a question about the right to criticize the standing of religious institutions – Christian churches and mosques. The following question was asked respondents in 1994: Should people who criticize the church/mosque be allowed to voice their views?

A dialogue between a newcomer and a native 73

TABLE 6.1 Characteristics of the respondent population

Socio-demographic features	Year 1994 610 persons	2015 132 persons	2016 38 persons
Country of origin	Algeria 26 Egypt 3 Iraq 8 Yemen 86 Jordan 31 Lebanon 11 Libya 52 Morocco 33 Palestine 82 Tunisia 31 Sudan 51 Syria 194 UAE 2	Algeria 7 Egypt 2 Iraq 5 Yemen 21 Jordan 11 Lebanon 3 Libya 5 Morocco 5 Palestine 18 Tunisia 7 Sudan 7 Syria 41	Iraq 3 Yemen 2 Jordan 1 Lebanon 2 Palestine 5 Tunisia 2 Sudan 1 Syria 22
Gender	600 male 10 female	131 male 1 female	37 male 1 female
Average age	27.6	49.5	51.6
Unmarried respondents	475 persons	2 persons	1 person
Married (to a Polish wife)	17 persons	43 persons	26 persons
Married (to an Arab wife)	112 persons	86 persons	10 persons
Married (to a wife of other origin)	6 persons	1 person	1 person
Length of time spent in Poland (average time in years)	5.29	30.8	32.1
Living in a place of one's own	11 persons	108 persons	34 persons
Polish citizenship	7 persons	57 persons	37 persons

Source: Independent study (studies from 1994, 2015, and 2016).

TABLE 6.2 Respondents' answers about church and mosque criticism

Should people who criticize the church/mosque be allowed to voice their views?

	Year 1994	2015	2016
The church	67.7 %	90.2 %	92.5 %
The mosque	51 %	84.1 %	89.5 %

Thus, there is a visibly steady increase in attitudes tolerant of criticizing religious institutions, both Christian and Muslim, although to a lesser extent with Islam. A phenomenon similar to the increase in religious tolerance was observed in answers to questions about people going to churches and mosques: *Are Poles who*

74 Ziad Abou Saleh and Bogdan de Barbaro

don't go to church just as good as Poles who do? Are people who don't go to mosques just as good people as those who do?

As evident, morally condemning people who do not practice religion diminishes over time. The results of this study at the same time confirm the thesis that people with deep faith regard people who do not practice religious as bad, regardless of the religion they profess. It should be mentioned that religious tolerance is understood as the right to accept or reject beliefs and practices postulated by various religions, beliefs, and religious trends. It is one of the basic values of culture in contemporary society. The principles of religious tolerance and freedom of conscience are important elements in the constitution of many countries. This principle is based on the full separation of the state from the church and unfettered freedom of religion and conscience, constitutionally guaranteed in Poland, but not found in most Arab countries.

BdB: Nowadays in Poland, this principle is criticized by some politicians with a nationalist-clerical attitude who are beginning to openly proclaim their desire to create a religious state which they intend to be a "Catholic Republic". It is not a large group, but it is characterized by much activity and marketing skills. The opinions expressed by the Arab respondents when it comes to criticizing religious institutions not only testify to their views, but to a certain cultural assimilation, which consists in adopting from Poles a critical attitude towards the church. For the last twenty years, the Catholic Church has been criticized by wide circles of society, including a large proportion of believers. Pedophile scandals, the profligacy of the clergy, and their tendency to live in luxury and wealth, combined with a noticeably arrogant and frequent disregard for social criticism give rise to unfavorable views of the church and distance many people from religion and its values.

ZAS: Such circumstances obviously have an impact on the attitude of the Arab community towards similar issues and promote views that are critical of the clergy, not only of Catholicism but Islam as well. However, it should be emphasized that in some Muslim and especially Arab countries, such views that are critical of the clergy and religion are unacceptable.

BdB: And now's a moment for "gender issues".

ZAS: OK. The following traits were taken into account in Polish men: hospitality, cordiality, not imposing on others their customs and culture, diligence, willingness to help, adherence to tradition and culture.

TABLE 6.3 The distribution of people based on whether they go to church/mosque or not

Are people who don't go to church/mosque just as good people who do?

	Year 1994	2015	2016
To church	78.5 %	92.5 %	94.7 %
To mosque	61.3 %	90.2 %	92.5 %

The following question was also asked: Are Polish women industrious, devoted, cheerful, lazy, beautiful, loyal, easy, proud, passionate, obedient, demanding, or stubborn? The respondents were of similar opinion in all research periods as to the most characteristic features of Polish women. The vast majority of respondents think that they are: happy, beautiful, proud, demanding, passionate, and hard-working. As can be seen from this picture, in the eyes of Arab students and PhD candidates, they consist primarily of traits regarding appearance and behavior. Almost half of respondents believe that Polish women are rather loyal. The vast majority claimed that they are disobedient (disobedience is understood here as disregarding the opinion of a man). This opinion was expressed by as much as 83.2 percent of respondents in 1994 and 89.4 percent in 2016.

BdB: Provide a few more interesting results.

ZAS: The respondents unanimously recognized the lack of respect for elders as a negative character trait in Polish men. In Arab culture, the elderly enjoy great

TABLE 6.4 Respondents' opinions on some character traits of Polish men

In your opinion, what traits best characterize Polish men?

	Year 1994	2015	2016
Not imposing on others their customs and culture	63.8 %	53.1 %	50 %
Cordiality	67.3 %	54.5 %	52.6 %
Attachment to tradition and culture	67.5 %	75.9 %	79 %
No respect for older people	99.8 %	90.2 %	89.5 %
Tendency to drink alcohol	41.1 %	59.9 %	63.9 %
Craftiness	57.2 %	44 %	42.1 %
Complaining	43.3 %	72 %	79.2 %

TABLE 6.5 Comparison of Polish women's traits in the eyes of Arabs in 1994, 2015, and 2016

	Year 1994	2015	2016
Diligent	94 %	85.6 %	84.1 %
Devoted	76.5 %	70.5 %	71.1 %
Cheerful	96.3 %	94 %	89.5 %
Lazy	17.9 %	25 %	21.1 %
Faithful	47.1 %	57.6 %	60.6 %
Attractive	97.9 %	98.5 %	97.5 %
Proud	85.4 %	78.1 %	79.2 %
Obedient	16.8 %	12.1 %	10.6 %
Demanding	80.3 %	19 %	21.1 %
Stubborn	67.7 %	30.3 %	31.6 %

authority. In 1994 99.8% believe that in Poland, older people are not treated with appropriate respect, and in 2016 there were 10% fewer (89.5%). Placing parents in nursing homes, as well as the lack of family ties, were likewise negatively evaluated. Another trait the respondents pointed out was an excessive tendency to drink alcohol. In 1994, 41.1% made mention of it, and in 2016, as much as 63.9%. Also, respondents recognized craftiness as a negative trait in Polish men, which is, however, increasingly rarely assessed as something negative. In 1994, 57.2% of respondents thought of it as a shortcoming, while in 2016, 42.1% thought that way. Another negative trait is complaining: in 1994, 43.3% of respondents negatively assessed Poles for excessive complaining, and almost twice as much in 2016 (79.2%). On the basis of this research, it can be seen that Poles at the beginning of the transformation period complained a lot less despite more difficult living conditions than at present which is seeing high, constant economic growth. Could the reason for this phenomenon be disappointment with life in the new social and political system?

The respondents most often chose such aspects that could not be found in their native culture. One of them was the adoption of children, which in Arab countries is prohibited by a religious ban. Another thing that's significant is the standing of husband and wife. In Arab culture, it is widely believed that in the history of mankind, women haven't invented anything, haven't improved anything, haven't invented any work tools, haven't formulated any philosophical system, and haven't created any masterpieces of art without supervision and help from men. Women, however, are not considered contemptible as Arabs affirm that women's bio-social role is different. A man cannot be a mother after all. Feminine eloquence is associated with the functions of motherhood and the education of young children. Her mind cannot be compared in any respect with the masculine mind that's creative and logical, created for domination, research, and struggle for survival. The woman's mind is in fact imitative, capable of imitating, and helping in a world that is dominated by masculine strength. The woman's mind is in the sphere of feelings.

The biggest problem faced by Arabs living in Polish society is the failure to deal with complex socio-religious problems. It's well known that the everyday conditions of Polish life are not conducive to strengthening cultural values which Islam requires from every true Arab Muslim. According to Islam, he should bring his achievements to a fulfilling, responsible citizenship, pursuing universal coexistence through mutual understanding and tolerance of others, human brotherhood, freedom of thought, and the preservation of human dignity (Hammudach, 1993, pp. 16–17). The respondents want to adhere to the moral values mentioned above, but their thoughts on the following issues do not corroborate this, indicating the respondents' rapid adaptation, acculturation, and even assimilation in the new environment.

BdB: Try to compare the models of Polish and Arab families.

ZAS: In Arab societies, the difference between the patriarchal and the matriarchal systems is very visible and important. In Arab families, the father, who is the "head", has always had the final word (Al Achras, 1996, p. 68). This is emphasized by Saudi sociologist Al-Samaloty, who defines the father's tasks towards the family as follows: he influences the choice of spouse for his children; he takes care of the biological continuity of the family; he takes care of raising children in accordance with the moral and religious principles of society; he is responsible not only for underage children, but also for adults and independents and he provides mental stability to members of his family (Al Samaloty, 1996, p. 68). The position of the husband and father in the Polish family differs in a fundamental way from the Arab model. This is confirmed by the respondents' answers to the question: *Do you think that the position of husband and wife in Polish families is the same?* The vast majority, more than 95% in 1994, 2015, and in 2016, believed that it was equal. There was a follow-up question: *What is your opinion about it? Do you like it or not?* Analyzing the opinions of respondents, we can observe that the model of a democratic-partner marriage made sense to 53.1% of the respondents in 1994. However, a clear change occurred in their opinions by 2016, where 92.6% of respondents noted that the democratic-partner model suited them. It can be assumed that such a significant change in attitude, such a loosening of value judgement, resulted from the weakening of moral pressures prevalent in traditional Arab communities. The decision to live in a culturally different reality would, in part, be associated with freeing oneself from the influence of this form of morality, but would also consequently lead, under the influence of new experiences, to a natural verification of its durability. As is known in the Arab family, the patriarchal model is dominant, in which authority and leadership belong to men, or in which men overwhelmingly exercise dominant power. This was confirmed by how the respondents listed traits which they think define the image of the average Polish man. According to the collected data, the feature that most of the respondents first associated with Polish men was obedience, or submissiveness. In 1994, this opinion was held by 90.5% of respondents, and in further research, by 76.4% (2016).

BdB: Which conclusions have resulted from your research?

ZAS: The results of the study shows that the vast majority of the Arabic population sees the coexistence between the Arab and Polish worlds as possible, as well as building closer relations with each other both in the cultural dimension and at the level of direct interpersonal relations.

The research partially shows that the Arab population in Poland already follows similar patterns of life as most Poles. It seems that at least some Polish Arabs have accepted local lifestyles including the kinds of social relations that are common in this country, and have adopted Polish customs. Undoubtedly, it can also be said that in practice they manage to co-create, despite obvious differences, a society based on diversity and equality. They are positive, contributing hope for a future that confirms that there doesn't have to be a contradiction between being an Arab and a Pole or a European.

It is obvious that the social consciousness and mentality of Arabs living in Poland differ from the mindset of their forebears and relatives who've never been to Poland. The research participants, who have lived here for over 25 years, see their fellow citizens through a Polish-Arab prism, making it in some sense a lot easier for them to perceive Polish realities, making use of knowledge about local customs and culture.

The opinions of Poland's Arab minority affirm the positive aspects of living in Poland – this is what the results of the research seem to indicate, and the more detailed analysis presented above leads to the conclusion that Polish Arabs, due to long-term, everyday, and often close contacts with Poles, have become different than their relatives and friends who lack similar experiences. Arabic respondents expressing their views on Poles were based on experiences gained from their own family home as well as those acquired during their stay in Poland. Their knowledge about the Polish way of life is understandably changing while extending their stay in Poland. Many answers given by the respondents testify to their effective adaptation in Polish society as well as knowledge of the problems of the Polish family. The study shows that there is a real chance of understanding both cultures thanks to mutual education – "learning about oneself" and becoming acquainted with what is unfamiliar.

It can be said with certainty that by 2015, relations between the Polish and Arab communities were nearly predictable, characterized by a mutual desire to learn and understand each other – no areas of conflict were created between them. Unfortunately, after 2015, a rapid increase in racist and xenophobic moods could be observed in Poland, influenced by the acceptance of such attitudes by many politicians of the ruling party. The current prospects for mutual good relations are getting worse. It is sad to say that in Poland, there are attacks on the Muslim minority by the racist segment of society. Until a few years ago, that seemed unrealistic.

I told you about my sociological research. How do these results correspond with your perspective as a psychotherapist?

BdB: The feeling of being rejected, unwanted, and excluded is a deeply traumatic experience. Anyone who does not believe it, let them remember a situation from childhood when their younger siblings got more attention from their parents (or in any case had the impression that they got less attention); or a situation when they asked a friend to borrow a book and was refused; or a situation when they wanted to sign up for a youth club and it turned out that for some reason they weren't deemed suitable and acceptable. This injury can be multiplied a thousand times and approximate to the experience had by someone who's been socially rejected. This is a situation similar to what a person who undergoes psychiatric treatment experiences, who after staying in a psychiatric hospital, returns to his or her environment and experiences what we call stigmatization. People turn away, or look with unhealthy curiosity and reluctance, and loudly protest when informed that this person will be returning to their former professional or student responsibilities. And there's no substantive reason not to accept the person, and yet one hears a firm "go away".

A dialogue between a newcomer and a native **79**

This "go away" is heard from people who are calm and gentle. But from those who are aggressive, harboring anger (which anyway has some other source) the Other wouldn't hear "go away", but simply experience an aggressive rejection, and thus active violence.

Does this view of Otherness somehow correspond with your experience? What was the main value of assimilation in Poland for you, and what do you consider a threat to your identity?

ZAS: In my case, there were no obstacles to being an Arab and at the same time a good citizen of the Polish state as a foreigner living here. After experiencing both worlds, I do not see any significant contradictions and problems that arise between my Arab values and the system of values in Poland on a daily basis. Knowledge of the language, readiness to learn about Polish culture, and cultural codes helped me. By choice, I consider myself a fellow citizen, and I'm not indifferent to the fate of Poland and of Poles – as well as of Arabs. I have become and I want to continue to be part of Polish reality no matter where our common ship is steered by present/past/future Polish politicians.

The success of cultural assimilation depends on, among other things, cultural competence. Deepening knowledge of Polish and Arab cultures can lead to mutual understanding and can make tolerance not merely theory – mutual respect can thus become more prevalent in social relations. The real key for both cultures to exist in symbiosis is to enjoy positive aspects of their respective achievements, to implement what is good for their own lives, and not inclining towards ills, shortcomings, and neglect. It is particularly harmful to generalize negative traits on a whole population and to fuel hatred towards ordinary people.

The conflict of cultures in Polish-Arab relations, despite obvious cultural differences, does not appear by itself. We create it ourselves (on both sides) when we succumb to stereotypes, when we hastily rely on reckless opinions. Regardless of whether we live on the other side of the street or on the other side of the world, we're just two steps away from turning on the computer or getting on the plane. If we are to live in harmony, we must get to know each other well. And above all, we must want this. Such connections can only be ensured by culture, in particular, knowledge of a foreign language and literature in which the most intimate matters of nations are recorded.

BdB: In that case, share your experiences and tell me if today a Syrian were to come to Poland and he didn't know the country, what advice and warning would you give him?

ZAS: As an "Other", I was at one point the head of the Committee of Foreign Students (of those "Others") in Wrocław. About 1,500–2,000 foreigners were educated at Wrocław's universities, and from 25,000 to 30,000 in Poland. Most of them were Muslims – Iraqis, Syrians, Tunisians, Algerians, Moroccans, and Palestinians. Many of them assimilated, started families here, and still live and work in Poland. I had the feeling that contacts with a previously unknown culture, mentality, and customs were interesting and beneficial for both parties. We were mutually attracted to each other, and the kindness was especially worth noting. There were, of course, misunderstandings, but they concerned individual relationships. In everyday life, it was difficult to see signs of negative attitudes towards foreigners or narrow-mindedness towards Muslims.

Like most of us, like all people, I have witnessed or been part of difficult, traumatic, and sometimes incomprehensible events, but I have not experienced the situation that we are currently seeing in Poland. After over thirty-five years of learning about Poland and Poles, I'm surprised by some of the statements and actions of my European compatriots. I did not expect such an unfavorable attitude towards refugees, nor its intensity nor extent. I even see a bizarre alliance bringing together a significant part of society against an enemy (this time a very hypothetical one). A unique alliance that's overcoming divisions: an alliance of dislike.

Contemporary Poles in everyday relations do not have the opportunity to really encounter cultural differences. The appearance of something foreign is treated as a curiosity, more often as a departure from a socially accepted norm, and usually evokes some kind of anxiety. Hence, from the get-go, there seems to be a tendency to recognize it is as unknown, strange, and above all, Other/Alien. After several generations of living in a mentally, morally, and religiously cohesive culture, we are often at a loss as a nation in such situations.

In present-day reality, when society is divided into those who are "wrong" and those who are "noble", how do people with different opinions engage in dialogue with each other? Can such a society be called a community? Is the identity of "us" based on the fact that we are not "them"? Can such an identity be stable, or is it uncertain and fragile? We tend to complain and feel defeated, and this automatically reduces the level of positive self-esteem. It also decreases respect for other people. Currently, a significant part of the Polish population cannot tolerate themselves, so it is natural that they aren't favorably disposed towards foreigners. For the reasons mentioned above, I think that the arrival of a Syrian to a world in which he isn't kindly viewed could be associated with risk to himself, but also to society. Both the Syrian and Pole can become victims of wrong-headed politicians, clergy, and businesses of one and the other world. I would advise him to think deeply about it.

A key related question is: In your opinion, is it possible to familiarize the Other in Poland? And why is it so difficult?

BdB: I think it's more a question for you as a sociologist than for me. But if I look for some psychological or psychiatric factors, I would draw attention to what we call our national mythology. It is a set of ideas, attitudes, and prejudices, the sources of which could be found in the history of a given society. And here's the challenge: How do we overcome this myth that we've been harmed and exposed to hostile activities of foreigners? How do we overcome this national mythology, whose message that "the Other-Alien wants to hurt you" and is in its essence a warning and cautionary tale concerning the Other? In this context, the year 1989 was an opportunity for Poles with the Schengen Agreement and the symbolic and literal OPENING OF BORDERS, and consequently opening up to people who had different points of view, looked differently, and held different beliefs. Unfortunately, I have to use the past tense – "was" – because the populist-nationalist wave spreading throughout Europe (and how painfully present it is in Poland) is putting the brakes on "becoming acquainted with the Other". And, in my opinion, this wave is surging off of emotions held by people who remain anonymous. It seems that in Poland, the idea of multiculturalism (both as *melting pot* and *salad bowl*) is losing to the fear of Otherness.

ZAS: We deal with various forms of multiculti – the coexistence of many cultures in a specific social space. This term is extremely simplistic and therefore does not reflect the diversity and complexity of this phenomenon, both at the level of definition as well as political and social practice. We can, therefore, speak of a political doctrine proposing a social order based on the recognition of identity and specially distinguished laws reflecting the diversity of minority groups. There are also proponents of the model calling for the equivalence of cultures in ethnically, culturally, and religiously diverse societies. An important element here is the process of co-existing traditions and customs to come into contact with each other while protecting individuality at the same time. There are also concepts according to which, as in the idea of multi-ethnicity, one regards, above all, breaking society into different groups, foreign to each other, as a threat, internally destabilizing the functioning of society.

BdB: As an argument against accepting refugees, sometimes Poles use the thesis that the acceptance of Others threatens national and cultural identity. What would you say to them?

ZAS: In one sentence, I'm not convinced by such arguments, because in my opinion, it is an apparent explanation of real, albeit exaggerated, fears Poles have for the Other. For years I have been observing the extraordinary economic and political transformations that have been taking place in Poland, freeing itself from the pressures of more powerful neighbors and the dramatic burdens of history. It was not uncommon to face the repercussions from decisions made by unpredictable politicians who, unable to think in terms of the interests of their country and countrymen, led many great initiatives to failure – in recent years and many, many years before as well.

At one time, the enemy was a system imposed by force and upheld by the authorities; now the enemy is a neighbor, colleague, brother. In this respect, things aren't looking well in Poland today. In the media, on the streets, and in houses, in private and public discussions, the wraiths of emotions, half-truths, and simplifications are evident. This also applies to how foreigners are imagined (including the specific group of immigrants/refugees). We've become disturbingly selfish. There are signs of rising nationalist attitudes. At the public level, all the while, we can speak of how identifying as human-citizen is weakening.

Poles feel (or observe) in their own country a lack of mutual trust, craftiness, social anomie, and various forms of state dysfunction: low level of health care, earnings not in line with expectations, the inadequate role of the Church, and a lack of objectivity in state media. Added to this is the difficult – and often incomprehensible – situation of Poland in Europe. It lowers self-esteem, but it also decreases respect for other people. One of the elements accompanying this process is anxiety and fear of Otherness, appearing as a threat to national and cultural identity. We do not have, on a daily basis, direct contact with refugees, with Arab culture, or with Islam in Poland. Our fears are therefore built around an imaginary picture of the Foreigner, unfortunately propped up by little knowledge about the cultures of other nationalities.

The saturation in Polish, Arab, and international media about death, killing, and cruelty undoubtedly influences the change in social awareness. Information, films, and entertainment, with their short, hasty messages, use a certain pattern in which terrorism is placed in the context of Islam, with the refugee visible in the background. In the media world, an Arab refugee is associated with danger. The presence of Muslim immigrants – as implied in this fashion – therefore threatens the lives of Polish citizens, and in the best case scenario, means that Islam will intrude on people's private spheres. Our contacts with real Arabs, however, are sporadic and superficial. Apart from tourist trips, we have practically no opportunity to get to know or understand their customs and mentality. Instead, there are stereotypes and arbitrary ideas about the so-called Global Muslim/refugee wandering outside the borders of our country.

I think that in as much as Poles are experiencing difficult times today, they're facing their own issue of maturity. There is something beautiful and intriguing about it. On the one hand, there's fear, a sense of loneliness, and loss in a world that is guided by difficult, often incomprehensible principles, and on the other, a huge desire to enforce the right to realize their own needs, to manifest objections to progressive globalization. Existing norms are weakening, values are redefined, and there are changes to the hierarchy. Perhaps that is why radical ideas are gaining traction as there is a desire to build a sense of security in isolation. The presence of people with different views, and from different ethnicities or customs becomes a problem to be faced with, not to mention supporters of an open society.

Behind complex socio-cultural processes, there often lie countless frustrations held by those who are part of such processes as they face the pressures of transformation. In my opinion, Polish reluctance and distrust of refugees and of the Muslim minority result from experiencing those very tensions. They aren't clear-cut signs of hostility, but rather testify to the intensity of experience.

Research shows that social unrest in Poland may be caused by the purely theoretical possibility of the arrival of several thousand Muslim immigrants (from the perspective of a ethnically homogeneous nation numbering in many millions, a truly negligible amount). Sociologically speaking, the main problem is not so much the issues related to the immigrant population as it is the mindset of the local population, and more to the point, what gives rises to such a mindset. Anxiety and

A dialogue between a newcomer and a native **83**

reluctance can be interpreted as signs of weakness and insecurity, and little faith in the durability and validity of one's own views. Hatred or hostility are then forms of expressing internal anxiety. We can – more simply put to express our thoughts better – recognize that when we talk about refugees, in reality we sometimes are talking about ourselves above all. A negative attitude towards foreigners would not be a problem for refugees (because they are not coming to this country anyway), but mainly for Polish society. It collectively reveals very important clues about Poles: about their sense of sovereignty and identity, approach to tradition and culture, and idea of nationhood which they identify with.

In mature societies, all the elements essential for their proper functioning and development are strengthened in the encounter with Otherness – creative modification subsequently occurs. Communities and nations, which remain separated for a long period of time, affecting many spheres of life, lose their natural vigor, become deformed, and die away. A serious discussion about refugees/Muslims is for Europe – and, of course, Poland – a form of self-reflection, an opportunity to possibly redefine needs while estimating the possibilities of implementing them, and to define their true place in the world today. The issue of the influx of Muslims and their presence in Europe affects Poland today, above all, in that manner.

BdB: I don't know if this will be too personal, but in order to wrap up, I suggest that we quote a fragment from a letter you wrote – holiday wishes I got from you. By referring to the existential and ethical dimensions, you exposed problems which in our texts and conversation were described in cultural, political, and psychological terms. Perhaps this is the core of the problem?

ZAS: In this letter, I wrote: " [. . .] I wish you and me the willingness and determination to think about ourselves. [. . .] Let's look at our works. Our world is changing; we also are changing. Our consumeristic lives create new identities and memories in us. May it not lack space for our struggles with our own weaknesses, so that we can appreciate the silence midst the noise of life. Holidays come [. . .] to encourage us to make a life journey into our tired interior, to help create a good and humble community in a cordial world. Perhaps listening to the meaning of our own lives will revive our memory and imagination, and bring us closer to the truth about ourselves and others. I wish that in these days we would enjoy beautiful, tasty food in our homes, but felt, above all, the atmosphere of accord and love, not the smog of division, hostility, and fear. Remembering the power and timelessness of our actions, gestures, and words, I wish you and myself that we would not be easy prey to the tyrants of the world."

Notes

1 Who will live in Poland in 2050? *Agata Wosik*. Retrieved March 10, 2017, from http://wiadomosci.onet.pl/kraj/kto-bedzie-mieszkal-w-polsce-w-2050-roku/q31y1de
2 The division into "us" and "them" is a remnant of the period when power belonged to the communist party and there was limited state sovereignty.

84 Ziad Abou Saleh and Bogdan de Barbaro

3 The category of "True Pole" is used (by some with pride, by others ironically) as a synonym for a conservative-minded Catholic.
4 In May 2018, a group of lay Catholics (with the participation of a Catholic priest) organized the ceremonial "Enthronement of Christ as King of Poland". This was met with insults on the Internet and some participants of this assembly were sent to a psychiatric hospital.
5 The nun Maria Faustyna Kowalska, a saint of the Catholic Church, a mystic, describing her spiritual and mystical experience in her *Diary*, states that in 1938 Jesus said to her: "I especially loved Poland".
6 Poland occupies the last but one place in the European Union and 38th (out of 49 countries) in Europe in terms of rights and situations of LGBT persons – according to the Rainbow Europe ranking of the ILGA (International Lesbian and Gay Association). More: http://wiadomosci.gazeta.pl/wiadomosci/7,114883,23400077,polska-na-dnie-rankingu-homofobii-w-krajach-europy-przed-nami.html
7 During the last parliamentary elections (2015), the lowest turnout came from the 18–21 age group (less than 48% entitled to vote).
8 Muslims in Europe – their numbers and percentage figure in the European population. Source: www.ideologia.pl/muzulmanie-w-europie/
9 For the needs of the doctoral thesis from the beginning of the 1990s, I [ZAD] began a large-scale research on social problems faced by Arabs in Poland. At that time, I examined almost the entire population of Arabs studying in Poland, undertaking a number of research problems focused not only on issues related to their cultural integration, but also on the perception of Poles in the opinion of Arabs. In order to perform a comparative analysis after twenty-one years (in 2015), the research was again carried out on a sample of 132 people from 610 respondents from 1994. In 2016, research was repeated on a group of 38 people from the same respondents. The comparative research was based on the same questionnaire as in 1994. This was aimed at making a comparative analysis of the change in Arab attitudes towards Poles and the assessment of the effectiveness of integration and cultural assimilation after twenty-one years of living in Poland and after socio-political changes that took place in the world, affecting Europe and Poland.

Bibliography

Abou Saleh, Z. (1997). *Picture of Poland and Poles in the eyes of Arab students and PhD candidates studying in Poland* (Doctoral thesis), University of Wrocław, Wrocław.
Al Achras, M. (1980). *Sociology of the family* (p. 186). Syria – Damascus: Taraben Publishers. In Abou Salah, J., *Image of Poland and poles in the eyes of Arab students and PhD candidates studying in Poland* (Typewritten thesis), Wrocław 1996, p. 68.
Al Samaloty, N. (1990). *Sociology of Islam* (pp. 7–8). Saudi Arabia: Dar al Charek Publishing House. In Abou Salah, J., *Image of Poland and poles in the eyes of Arab students and PhD candidates studying in Poland* (Typewritten thesis), Wrocław 1996, p. 68.
Bauman, Z. (2005). *Liquid life*. Cambridge: Polity Press.
Czyż, B., & Polakowska, K. (2015, September 15). *Arabs and Muslims in Poland: We checked how many of them live among us*. Source: UdSC, data as at 1 July 2015.
Hammudach, A. (1993). *A look at Islam* (pp. 16–17). Bogdan Ataullah Kopański, Łódź: Association of Muslim Students in Poland.
Odie, M. (1995). *Basics of sociology*. Lebanon- Beirut: Dar al Nahda Publishing House. In Abou Salah, J., *Image of Poland and poles in the eyes of Arab students and PhD candidates studying in Poland* (Typewritten thesis), Wrocław, 1996, p. 69.
Ryszewska, M. (2011). Why Europe (doesn't) needs Euroislam? In A. Śliza & M. S. Szczepański (Eds.), *Multiculturalism: Conflicts or co-existence?* (p. 127). Warsaw: IFiS PAN.

7

THE GERMAN "WELCOMING CULTURE" – SOME THOUGHTS ABOUT ITS PSYCHODYNAMICS

Regine Scholz

Introduction

In the following chapter the reader will find some thoughts concerning the psychic backgrounds and dynamics of the so-called and much discussed summer fairy tale of August/September 2015, when the German government decided to leave its borders open to the refugees that were stuck on the Balkan after Hungary closed its borders.

Just as a reminder: In 2015 Germany took in ca 1 million refugees. On 31st August chancellor Merkel spoke the meanwhile world-famous words: "Wir schaffen das (We'll make it)." The complete quote was: "Deutschland ist ein starkes Land. Das Motiv, mit dem wir an diese Dinge herangehen, muss sein: Wir haben so vieles geschafft – wir schaffen das! (Germany is a strong country. The motivation to approach these things has to be: We already managed so many things – we'll make it.)"

What happened then, meanwhile is known as "German welcoming culture": the unscheduled and unforeseeable wave of helpfulness by German people – volunteers as well as officials – to accommodate these huge numbers of people.

The picture below is taken in Munich main station on 9th September 2015. Not only there, but all over the country thousands of people wanted to help, they volunteered to go to the stations where the trains with refugees arrived, welcoming them, providing them with food, warm tea and clothes, toys for the children etc. That was the real summer fairy tale – completely unexpected inside as well as outside the country. Everybody knew it wouldn't last forever – for a moment though, people were united in that nearly euphoric atmosphere, in a warm feeling of fusion.

Of course this surprising wave of readiness to help soon called for explanations. Interesting enough, these came more from outside the country. The main theoretical figure in this context is also to be found in Vamik Volkan's recent book "Immigrants and Refugees", where in the preface he writes, referring to a situation he

PICTURE 7.1 Arrival of refugees at Munich central station

Source: Photo Sven Hoppe, copyright: picture alliance/dpa

experienced 2015 in Berlin "the Germans . . ., especially the younger ones, wanted nothing to prevent them from taking care of the suffering of Others and reverse their Holocaust related guilt feelings" (Volkan, 2017, p. XIV). Similar arguments were discussed in many European and overseas journals, e.g. *National Geographic* in France (Kunzig, 2016), *20minutes* from Switzerland (Gabriel, 2015), *The Washington Post* (Stanley-Becker, 2017) and *The Guardian* (Freedland, 2015).

This argument contains a more or less subtle turn, and says that the actions are not aimed at the refugees, but at the emotional well-being of the helper – in that context the refugees serve the function of a remedy for the trans-generationally wounded soul of the helpers, who thus becomes the patients. It is a turn that tries to regain the moral authority by implying that the helper's altruism just covers up their selfish motivation.

Every argument has a content and implies at the same time a statement about the sender. Let us start with the content of this argument: It hurts and it is shaming – because in the moment of joy and satisfaction in doing something good and meaningful, the helper is told to be a hypocrite, an egoist by hiding their own wounds and using the misery of the refugees to heal – at least to mitigate – their own pain.

The problem is – there is some truth in that. The argument hints to a deep-rooted pain and shame. Volkan explicitly refers to the younger ones. For them – additionally to guilt and shame – a profound helplessness is part of the package to carry, to carry something that you had no influence on (see Bernhard Schlink, in *The Guardian* 16th Sept 2012). Being identified with and identifying oneself as German results in an emotional impasse, feeling guilty for something you didn't do. That is the moment, where "the Other", other persons as members of the formerly attacked groups come in – the opponents in war, the victims of the Holocaust and their offspring – and become important. Their acceptance of the now good deeds "look, I'm not bad (anymore)" is urgently wanted/needed to calm down the inner drama. Because all this goes in a disguised – mainly unconscious – manner, it always carries a somehow false tone.

Identification with the refugees I

Sharing and underlining the argument of Holocaust- and WWII-related guilt feelings playing a crucial role in the psychodynamics of the great helpfulness of summer 2015 and thereafter, does not exclude considering additional psychic dispositions to explain the 2015 mass movement in helping refugees. Some other factors, covered by this first layer, should be taken into consideration too.

First there is a deep identification with the refugees – on more than one dimension, e.g. the experiences of being bombed, generally living through the horrors of war, the sufferings from traumatic flights with its accompanying violence, the shock of being displaced, the pains of not being welcomed – and much more.

PICTURE 7.2   Migrants walk to the border with Hungary after arriving by train at Botovo, Croatia

Source: *Photo*: Laszlo Balogh, copyright: picture alliance/Reuters

For example, look at Picture 7.2, of the long lines of people on their way through the Balkans in 2015. The next picture shows people after WWII on their way towards the West. According to the Bundeszentrale fuer Politische Bildung, 12 million people (other sources mention 14 million) came between 1945 and 1950 to the Western parts (including later GDR) of former Germany – an estimated 2 million didn't survive the treks (Zeidler, 2012). They came from formerly German territories in the East (East-Prussia, West Prussia, Pomerania, Silesia etc.) fleeing from the approaching Russian army – but also from areas in the Baltic States, Soviet Union/Russia, Hungary, Rumania, Czechoslovakia, Slovenia etc. – the whole German diaspora. The incredible crimes committed by Germany before and during the war secured the broad international support for the geopolitical decisions made at the Potsdam Conference in summer 1945 to expel ethnic Germans from their traditional areas of living (Oltmer, 2005). Though: before these treks there was the Holocaust and there was the war. There was Coventry and Rotterdam, Oradour and Lidice, Auschwitz and Treblinka.

PICTURE 7.3 Displacement

Source: Photographer unknown. Repro: Ahles (private)

In Germany, not much is spoken about war, bombing, flight and expulsion. Building up a new life in the devastated country absorbed everybody's energies and helped to split off the mourning of the lost innocence and the grandiose aspirations connected to the "Führer", it hindered the ability to emotionally realize the amount of guilt connected to the crimes committed by Germans (Mitscherlich, & Mitscherlich, 1967) – and it also blocked feelings of the physical and emotional wounds of war, flight and displacement.

To bear in mind and heart just one of these mass crimes and horrors is already too much – two or three of them are simply unbearable. Consequently and for various

The German "Welcoming Culture" **89**

reasons, most of the traumatic material had to be split off. Nonetheless, the pictures of the war in Syria also brought back memories of some of the horrors. Picture 7.4 was taken on 22nd March 2015 in Kobane, Syria. It might resemble for many elderly Germans the situation shown in Picture 7.5, taken in 1952 in West Berlin.

PICTURE 7.4   Syrian Kurds in Kobane

Source: Photo Cagdas Erdogan, Depo, copyright: picture alliance/abaka

PICTURE 7.5   Boys on ruins

Source: Photo Herbert Maschke, copyright: Cornelius Maschke

If you let yourself be touched by these photos, the idea might not be so far-fetched that many Germans – though the generation that lived through fascism and the war is mainly not alive anymore – from their own childhood experiences and by intergeneration transmissions have a deep connection to these scenes of bombed cities, ruins, flights and refugee treks. These memories were reactivated by pictures of recent events leading more to identification and compassion than to fear of "the other".

What are also transferred in families are the experiences of an unfriendly (to say the least) welcome to those coming to the West. At that time they were not simply considered as Germans (belonging to us) but as foreigners with different accents, habits and sometimes religions. Moreover, they came into a destroyed and bitterly poor country – there was not much to share. Mostly the original population remained hostile, displaying all the well-known stereotypes to be heard again nowadays: the newcomers are dirty, they stink, steal and they rape. Sometimes they also were accused to be Nazis. Of course, that often was true – though not more or less as for the autochthonous population. To defame the newcomers as Nazis was an unfair attempt to whitewash their own guilt by projection.

It is always said that the integration of these millions of people went without problems – that's not true (Kossert, 2008). What is true is that in the end, it worked out. The cities were rebuilt, and today Germans of all origins are considered as one nation and consider themselves as such. To preserve peace and allow integration into the Western world, the whole complex of war, flight and expulsion was more or less excluded from public discourse – only taken up and exploited by the far right. The world-famous German memory culture – born in decades of post-war fights originally imposed by the allied forces and then taken on inside the (divided) country – refers mainly to German war crimes and the Holocaust (about its developmental process, see Frölich, Jureit, & Schneider, 2012). The intertwined though mainly split off complex of own direct traumatization then in 2015 also showed up indirectly in the compassion for current refugees, which allowed some expression of the old pains whilst circumventing the intractable moral conflicts around war crimes and the Holocaust.

Identification with the refugees II

Another split that became visible on the issue of welcoming and integration is a clear gap between the Western and Eastern parts of Germany, mirroring the division of Europe by the Iron Curtain, which caused different developments. The West is usually friendlier than the East, though nearly no foreigners live in the East (Bertelsmann-Stiftung, 2017). One reason might be that former West Germany has a longer tradition of taking in people from far away countries and therefore could adapt emotionally to these changes over a longer period of time. Reacting to a lack of workers, West Germany from the mid-1950s made treaties with Italy, Spain, Portugal, former Yugoslavia and Turkey and asked for "guest workers". Until 1973, 14 million followed this call; 11 million of them went back, the others brought their families. For comparison: In 1989 only 93,000 foreigners lived on the territories of GDR – mainly as contract workers. Picture 7.6 shows Italian workers at Wolfsburg station leaving for a Christmas holiday.

PICTURE 7.6 Italian "guest workers" at VW – 1970

Source: Photo Fritz Rust, copyright: picture alliance/Fritz Rust

There are more groups that settled in (mainly West) Germany: refugees from East Germany (1949–1961: 2.7 million, later 700,000 until 1989), re-settlers from formerly German settlements in the nearer (Poland) and further away (Kazakhstan) Eastern parts of the European and Asian continent (3.2 million since 1953), refugees of the Balkan war in the 1990s (440,000, part of them returned), Jews from the former Soviet Union (1989–2009: 219,000), asylum seekers from different countries, e.g. from Hungary after 1956 (ca. 16,000), Czechoslovakia after 1968 (ca 4,000), after 1973 from Chile (ca 2,500) and after 1979 from Vietnam (38,000). In the 1980s the largest groups came from Iran, Poland and Turkey, but also from Sri Lanka, Pakistan, Ghana and other countries (see Mediendienst Integration 14.10.2015).

Many of these people – and meanwhile their children and grandchildren – also volunteered in welcoming refugees in 2015. Picture 7.7 from 8th September 2015 shows on the right a 73-year-old man originally from Egypt, at that time living for decades in Germany. Here he is answering questions of men just arrived from Syria.

PICTURE 7.7 A former immigrant who came to Germany in the 1970s answering questions of refugees at Munich main station

Source: Photo and copyright: Karim El-Gawhary

In 2016 of the population living in Germany, 22.5% have what is called a "migration background", i.e. either they themselves or at least one of the parents was not born in Germany, and nearly half of them (48.2%) have a German passport (Bundeszentrale fuer Politische Bildung 4.4.2018).

When volunteering and helping the refugees, members of this group have a different agenda than those who have longer and therefore deeper family ties in Germany, resulting in more dense psychic connections with German history. For them it is more about telling indirectly their own, somewhat different stories: They demonstrate their success – that they made it in Germany – thus reassuring themselves about the difficult road they went, and at the same time encouraging the newcomers by their example. But – whilst volunteering – they also show to the

The German "Welcoming Culture" **93**

wider German public "look, that's how people in need have to be welcomed", thus telling something about the hardships of their own way into this society and what they would have wished for. In that respect, they resemble those coming after the war from the East – they differ in their connection to German history though.

One might say that this group has a lesser part in the "German neurosis" mentioned in the beginning of this paper. Though it might occur that there are persons belonging to both groups: one parent is originally from abroad, the other parent is a descendent of somebody who came after the war from Eastern parts of Germany.

A complementary perspective

Let us return to the issue of German guilt feelings being a (main) motivation for the "welcoming culture" in 2015. As said before: that is true – for large parts of the population. Though on a conscious level, which can be accessed when conducting telephone surveys, guilt feelings are not the first layer that shows up. A study from MEMO (Multidimensionaler Erinnerungsmonitor) indicates that only 10% admit guilt feelings, though a great majority (84.3%) feel a high responsibility for the future, hindering the return of national socialism (MEMO February 2018) – which appears to me (at least in parts) as the classical turnaround of time sequence often observed in trauma contexts: instead of confronting the painful and unchangeable past, the problem is located in the future, where it can be fought.

In contrast to the low number of people reporting guilt feelings in this survey, clinical experience shows a different picture and gives us ample evidence of the transformation of real guilt denied by the perpetrator generation into guilt feelings in the unconscious life of their children and grandchildren (Bar-On, 1993; Bergmann, Jucovy, & Kestenberg, 1982; Hirsch, 1997; Jokl, 1997; Lohl & Moré, 2014). I can confirm these findings from my personal perspective – personal as second generation from the perpetrator's side and clinical, especially as one of the organizer' of the conferences "Voices after Auschwitz" where offspring from both sides meet.

Now – in a second step – a change of perspective is suggested, asking what this argument tells us about the conscious or unconscious motivation of those who use it. The question in this context might be dangerous and seen solely as a defense – and concerning the immense guilt connected to the war and the Holocaust, defense always is lingering. Nonetheless – that doesn't change the well-known fact that each communication does not only have a content, but also gives some information about the sender/speaker.

What first is striking is this intensity of psychological argument, otherwise not so often heard in political debates, even if it could be helpful. And of course, if you go for psychological explanations you are close to labeling somebody being neurotic: s/he is ill, but perhaps can be cured. It does not allow for the possibility that there could be some rationale in the behavior.

Second it implies that the one who is diagnosing is not ill, is healthy. That implies that their opinions and actions – e.g. not taking in refugees – are the correct ones and out of debate. It's a power play, who is allowed to define whom. Third it is a confusing argument, as for a long time German guilt feelings were demanded – sometimes exploited. Who would have dared to say the Germans should leave their guilt feelings behind?

A question could be which psychic function the Germans and German mass crimes fulfilled for the allied nations. For years and partly still today these crimes were the reason to identify the Germans as the international "bad guy", i.e. the others as the good ones. Splitting creates order and here allows for a veil, e.g. their own collaboration with the Nazis or to face their own crimes in colonisation and slavery. France had the Vichy government, Great Britain had Oswald Mosley and Lord Londonderry with their followers, the US had a flourishing Nazi scene recruited mainly from German immigrants after WWI (Diamond, 1974). Nonetheless it is not before 1995 that the then-president of France Jacques Chirac finally acknowledged the French responsibility in the deportation of the French Jews in July 1942 (wikisource), which was confirmed by his successor Emmanuel Macron in July 2017 (Le Monde, 2017). For the UK and the US one might say – though not immune against Nazi ideas – that the crimes connected to colonisation and slavery predominate their involvement with the Nazis and were outweighed by their contribution to free Germany and the Nazi-occupied countries. Nonetheless, neither the connections during the 30s and 40s nor the crimes of the British Empire nor the disgrace of slavery found much attention by governments and people of these countries. It took, e.g. until September 2016, for the US to recognize the history of African Americans and their contributions to their country by dedicating to them a museum (Official Guide to the Smithsonian National Museum of African American History and Culture 2017). The British are still waiting for a comparable museum dedicated to the history (which often means crimes) of the British Empire (Hirsch, 2017). It took until 2012 for the British government to give victims of colonialism the right to claim compensation (Wessely, 2017). For this special case (and only for this – trying to avoid making it a precedent) in 2013 followed an official apology by the then–foreign secretary William Hague.

The monstrosity of the Nazi/German crimes – incredible in amount and executed not far away but in the heart of Europe – covered all this for a long time and allowed people of the allied nations to feel: We may have our shortcomings, but we are the good ones as we suffered ourselves. The possibility that also Germans could be nice, warm-hearted and friendly people did not exist in this picture (see the English and American movies/fictions until today; for detailed analysis see Scholz, 2004 and Bredella, Gast, & Quandt, 1994; and for fun the gorgeous John Cleese in "Don't mention the war", 2009). Given this construction, the pictures and TV news from Germany in summer 2015 must have been at least confusing, challenging the split and thus threatening to the ego-balance of people abroad. To declare these Germans to be ill – they are crazy these Germans – also helps to re-establish the old order. And when the first terror attacks occurred, everybody felt justified.

Summary

In a way, this whole article is about splitting, denial, disavowal of inner and outer realities – inside and outside the country. It is not about the rational of how best to deal with the challenges of mass migration. It is about some historical facts and the largely unconscious reactions to these facts that shape personal and collective mentalities, the inner lives of thousands of people when dealing with modern situations in Europe – here focused on the summer 2015 in Germany.

As main factors for the overwhelming willingness to help, additionally to the attempt to mitigate feelings of guilt and shame related to war crimes and the Holocaust, two long-time neglected complexes were identified: The first is the long-lasting disavowal of war-related traumas in Germany. This is slowly changing due to an aging society. The children (see Bode, 2004) who lived through war and experienced heavy trauma during the times around 1944/1945 now are elderly people – their defenses weaken and sometimes they come into therapy (Peters, 2018). The now slowly opening discourse about the psychic impact also of this part of German history could help to disentangle some psychic knots in dealing with the challenges of the current international situation. There still is much work to do bringing together opposing, even antagonistic experiences: the memories of the Holocaust, of the persecution of all those who opposed the regime (though not enough in number), of the war crimes and on the other hand the memories of war, flight and displacement.

The second is the long-time denied fact that Germany is an immigration country. There was not any kind of immigration law until June 2019, when the parliament eventually agreed on a "Fachkräfte-Zuwanderungsgesetz" (skilled personnel immigration law), which critics consider to be far from meeting the requirements of this aging society (Geuther, 2019). The experiences of all the immigrants that came into the country over the last decades were mainly disregarded by the wider public – their contributions and their pains, their aspirations and their dreams, their success and their problems of belonging also constitute an important background of the situation. Integrating these experiences and emotions into a larger narrative of "being German" still is a task that at best just began. In summer 2015 both complexes found a somewhat displaced and disguised expression, which went largely on unconscious levels.

Visible was the enormous splitting as a central element in Germany in summer 2015 and later. The good ones helped the refugees that bad ones warned against – or worse (in 2015, 1,031 attacks on asylum shelters were counted – mostly committed by the far right). The ambivalences of the whole situation were put aside for the moment (and came back later), feeling an urgent need to help – and a strong optimism that all problems could be and would be solved. This quasi erotic fusion went along with an intense split between the good and the bad ones; there was not much space for sober contemplation of the situation, looking for longer-lasting solutions. The next wave of high emotions came with the infamous New Year's night in Cologne, when all the suppressed anxieties seemingly found

96 Regine Scholz

their justification (about some realities see *The Correspondent* 2nd May 2016), soon exploited by a well-organized right-wing/neo-Nazi scene, playing on the old topos of the black man, who rapes white women. Tracing these counter-movements would entail another book chapter though; this one limited itself to the welcoming culture.

Despite some sobering and rather complicated realities to deal with, there is still much solidarity with the refugees. Following research carried out by the Institut for Demoskopie Allensbach (Institut for public opinion polls Allensbach) in summer 2017, from 2015–2017, 55% of the population in Germany had been involved in voluntary work, while 19% still were active in 2017 and ongoing. Much former voluntary work was also taken over by official institutions – with good results in housing, language skills and bringing people into jobs.

This ongoing support for refugees – in spite of even terror attacks – is not much mirrored in TV and print media, who meanwhile focus more on the problems and on the radical opposers to the intake of refugees, thus mirroring more the split than the actual situation and attitudes towards migrants. According to research carried out by Ipsos on behalf of More in Common, you could find in Germany not just two but five major groups of attitudes towards immigration and refugees: humanitarian sceptics (23%), liberal cosmopolitans (22%), economic pragmatists (20%), moderate opposers (18%) and radical opposers (17%). Humanitarian sceptics are in favor of offering shelter to people in need, fleeing from war and warlike situations, though having some concerns about the possibilities of long-term integration; economic pragmatists welcome refugees as help to the aging German workforce whilst being very much aware of the complexities of the situation.

The tasks are enormous as well as the social and psychic energies needed to deal with these challenges. The world order that was established after WWII is changing not only in Germany, and the topic of this chapter – the overwhelming willingness to help and its psychic backgrounds – is only a minor part of it. The future has giant tasks for every community, nation, person to face. Let us be prepared, there is no way back. Much courage will be needed, also the courage to look into the mirror facing the multifaceted, often contradictory realities – the good, the bad and the ugly ones.

References

Bar-On, D. (1989). *Legacy of silence: Encounters with children of the Third Reich*. Cambridge, MA: Harvard University Press.

Bergmann, M. S., Jucovy, M. E., & Kestenberg, J. (Eds). (1982). *Generations of the Holocaust*. New York: Basic Books.

Bertelsmann-Stiftung. (2017). *Willkommenskultur im "Stresstest". Einstellungen in der Bevölkerung 2017 und Entwicklungen und Trends seit 2011/2012*. Ergebnisse einer repräsentativen Bevölkerungsumfrage, Gütersloh.

Bredella, L., Gast, W., & Quandt, S. (1994). *Deutschlandbilder in amerikanischen Fernsehen*. Tübingen: Gunter Narr Verlag.

Bode, S. (2004). *Die vergessene Generation – Die Kriegskinder brechen ihr Schweigen*. Stuttgart: Klett-Cotta.

Bundeszentrale für Politische Bildung. (2018). Bevölkerung mit Migrationshintergrund I – In absoluten Zahlen, Anteile an der Gesamtbevölkerung in Prozent, vom 04.04.2018. Retrieved from http://www.bpb.de/nachschlagen/zahlen-und-fakten/soziale-situation-in-deutschland/61646/migrationshintergrund-i

Brenner, Y., & Ohlendorf, K. (2016, May 2). Time for the facts. What do we know about Cologne four months later? *The Correspondent.* Retrieved from https://thecorrespondent.com/4401/time-for-the-facts-what-do-we-know-about-cologne-four-months-later/740617958817-a498b7c3

Chirac, J. (1995). Discours prononcé lors des commémorations de la Rafle du Vel'd'Hiv' – 16 juillet 1995. Retrieved from https://fr.wikisource.org/wiki/Discours_prononc%C3%A9_lors_des_comm%C3%A9morations_de_la_Rafle_du_Vel%E2%80%99_d%E2%80%99Hiv%E2%80%99

Connolly,K.(2012,September16).BernhardSchlink–BeingGermanisahugeburden.*TheGuardian.* https://www.theguardian.com/world/2012/sep/16/bernhard-schlink-germany-burden-euro-crisis

Diamond, S. (1974). *The Nazi Movement in the United States, 1924–1941.* Ithaca, NY: Cornell University Press.

Fawlty Towers – BBC. (2009). Don't mention the war. Retrieved from https://www.youtube.com/watch?v=yfl6Lu3xQW0

Frölich, M., Jureit, U., & Schneider, C. (Eds.). (2012). *Das Unbehagen an der Erinnerung – Wandlungsprozesse im Gedenken an den Holocaust.* Frankfurt am Main: Brandes & Apsel.

Gabriel, O. (2015). Migrants: Pourquoi l'Allemagne accueille à bras ouverts les migrants. *20 minutes* (CH). Retrieved from https://www.20minutes.fr/economie/1681419-20150907-migrants-pourquoi-allemagne-accueille-bras-ouverts-migrants

Garschagen, T., & Lindner, J. (2015). Welche Migrationsbewegungen haben Deutschland geprägt. Retrieved from https://mediendienst-integration.de/artikel/fluechtlinge-asyl-migrationsbewegungen-geschichte-einwanderung-auswanderung-deu

Geuther, G. (2019, June 7). Fachkräfte-Zuwanderungsgesetz: Zwischen Bremsen und Werben. *Deutschlandfunk.* Retrieved from https://www.deutschlandfunk.de/fachkraefte-zuwanderungsgesetz-zwischen-bremsen-und-werben.769.de.html?dram:article_id=450871

Hirsch, A. (2017, November 22). Britain's colonial crimes deserve a lasting memorial. Here's why. *The Guardian.* https://www.theguardian.com/commentisfree/2017/nov/22/british-empire-museum-

Hirsch, M. (1997). *Schuld und Schuldgefühl – Zur Psychoanalyse von Trauma und Introjekt.* Göttingen: Vandenhoeck und Ruprecht.

Hopper, E. (2003). *Traumatic Experience in the Unconscious Life of Groups – The Fourth Basic Assumption: Incohesion: Aggregation/Massification or (ba) I:A/M.* London: Jessica Kingsley.

IfD Allensbach. (2018). Engagement in der Flüchtlingshilfe Ergebnisbericht einer Untersuchung des Instituts für Demoskopie Allensbach im Auftrag des Bundesministeriums für Familie, Senioren, Frauen und Jugend. Retrieved from https://www.bmfsfj.de/bmfsfj/service/publikationen/engagement-in-der-fluechtlingshilfe/122012

Jokl. A. (1997). *Zwei Fälle zum Thema "Bewältigung der Vergangenheit".* Frankfurt am Main: Jüdischer Verlag.

Kellerhoff, S. (2017). so viele Freunde hatte Hitler in Großbritannien. Retrieved from https://www.welt.de/geschichte/zweiter-weltkrieg/article144397997/So-viele-Freunde-hatte-Hitler-in-Grossbritannien.html?wtrid=socialmedia.email.sharebutton

Kendrick, K. M. (2017). *Official guide to the Smithsonian National Museum of African American History and Culture.* Washington, DC: Smithsonian books.

Kossert, A. (2008). *Kalte Heimat: Die Geschichte der deutschen Vertriebenen nach 1945.* München: Siedler.

Kunzig, R. (2016, November). Comment l'Allemagne accueille-t-elle les réfugiés? *National Georgrafic France*. Retrieved from https://www.nationalgeographic.fr/histoire/2016/11/comment-lallemagne-accueille-t-elle-les-refugies

Le Monde. (2017, July 16). Macron réaffirme la responsabilité de la France dans la rafle du Vél' d'Hiv. Retrieved from https://www.lemonde.fr/societe/article/2017/07/16/macron-reaffirme-la-responsabilite-de-la-france-dans-le-vel-d-hiv_5161159_3224.html

Lohl, J., & Moré, A. (Eds.). (2014). *Unbewusste Erbschaften des Nationalsozialismus. Psychoanalytische, sozialpsychologische und historische Studien*. Gießen: Psychosozial-Verlag.

MEMO Deutschland. (2018). *Trügerische Erinnerungen – Wie sich Deutschland an die Zeit des Nationalsozialismus erinnert*. Institut für interdisziplinäre Konflikt- und Gewaltforschung der Universität Bielefeld und Stiftung "Erinnerung, Verantwortung und Zukunft".

Migazin vom. (2017, November 7). Immer noch täglich ein Anschlag auf Asylbewerberheim Immer noch täglich ein Anschlag auf Asylbewerberheim. Retrieved from http://www.migazin.de/2017/11/07/bka-statistik-immer-anschlag-asylbewerberheim/

Mitscherlich, A., & Mitscherlich, M. (1967). *Die Unfähigkeit zu trauern*. München: Piper.

Oltmer, J. (2005). *Zwangswanderungen nach dem 2. Weltkrieg*. Bundeszentrale für Politische Bildung. Retrieved from http://www.bpb.de/gesellschaft/migration/dossier-migration-ALT/56359/nach-dem-2-weltkrieg

Peters, M. (2018). Das Trauma von Flucht und Vertreibung – Psychotherapie älterer Menschen und der nachfolgenden Generationen. Stuttgart: Klett-Cotta.

Purpose Europe Ltd | More in Common. (2017). Attitudes towards National Identity, Immigration, and Refugees in Germany. Retrieved from https://static1.squarespace.com/static/5a70a7c3010027736a22740f/t/5aec61741ae6cff5ed8d8bb3/1525440898162/More+in+Common

Scholz, R. (2017). The fluid and the solid – or the dynamic and the static: some further thoughts about the conceptualisation of foundation matrices, processes of the social unconscious, and/or large group identities. In Hopper, E., & Weinberg, H. (Eds.), *The social unconscious in persons, groups, and societies, Vol. 3: The foundation matrix extended and reconfigured* (pp. 27–46). London: Karnac.

Scholz, W. (2004). *Formen und Funktionen der narrativen Inszenierung nationaler Selbst- und Fremdbilder in zeitgenössischen englischen Romanen*. München: GRIN.

Stanley-Becker, I. (2017). In Germany, Merkel welcomed hundreds and thousands of refugees. Now many are suing the government. *Washington Post*. Retrieved from https://www.washingtonpost.com/world/europe/merkel-welcomed-hundreds-of-thousands-of-refugees-now-some-are-suing-her-government/2017/07/20/2d9e13aa-68a7-11e7-94ab-5b1f0ff459df_story.html?utm_term=.a1efbb722bda

Vernet, D. (2015). Épouvantail ou modèle : l'Allemagne instrumentalisée sur la scène politique française. *Allemagne d'aujourd'hui, 214*(4), 107–117.

Volkan, V. (2017). *Immigrants and refugees: Trauma, perennial mourning, prejudice, and border psychology*. London: Routledge.

Wessely, A. (2017). The Mau Mau case – five years on. Retrieved from https://www.leighday.co.uk/Blog/October-2017/Kenyan-colonial-abuses-apology-five-years-on

Zeidler, M. (2012). Flucht und Vertreibung der Deutschen aus Ostpreußen, Westpreußen, Danzig, dem Warthegau und Hinterpommern. In Surminski, A. (Ed.), *Flucht und Vertreibung, Europa zwischen 1939 und 1948* (pp. 66–100). Hamburg: Ellert & Richter.

8

NORWAY

Between grandiosity and inferiority

Thor Kristian Island

> "It is typically Norwegian to be good!"
> —*Former Prime Minister Gro Harlem Brundtland (1992)*[1]

Introduction

This statement, originally referring to Norwegian winter sport successes, was reframed by the prime minister as a new slogan for Norway. This seeming grandiose self-image drew a lot of ridicule and laughter from the Norwegian public.

Traditionally, Norway has been a very homogenous country: demographically, culturally and with minor differences in economic status. It is considered a "high-trust society": high trust between people, high trust in the political system, high trust in the welfare and health systems and high trust in the police and justice systems. Gender equality and human rights are highly valued. Political and religious extremism are minor problems. According to the United Nations Development Report, Norway is "the best country in the world to live in" (UNDP, 2018).

Internationally, Norway wishes to play a significant role in peace negotiations, international aid, environmental preservation and climate change prevention. However, no matter how much we achieve, and no matter how much international recognition we gain, the feelings of being insignificant, inferior or of lesser value seem embedded in our national memory and social unconscious. How do we understand these contradictions? What can our history tell us?

Europe in transition

Europe has faced major challenges in recent years. The surge in immigration has led to increased polarisation among the population, with the related emergence of xenophobia and an increased emphasis on national values and populist politics. Traditional political parties have seen a decline in favour while new populist and nationalist parties – Alternative für Deutschland in Germany, and the Sweden Democrats in Sweden, to name a few – have gained increased support. This has forced the traditional and "responsible" parties toward the right. This has been the case, albeit to a lesser degree, in Norway. Norway is still perceived as a small, homogeneous country. The truth is, however, that we are not so homogeneous anymore. Fifty years ago, Norway was one of the most ethnically and culturally homogenous countries in the world. Almost all (99.9%) of its inhabitants were ethnic Norwegians (Tvedt, 2017). Increased immigration due to humanitarian crises and wars around the world has led to a significant demographic change. As of early 2018 there were 750,000 immigrants with an additional 170,000 born in Norway to immigrant parents. Now 17.3% of the inhabitants have immigrant backgrounds (Statistics Norway, 2018a) Norwegian society has changed radically during these years. The change has happened rapidly; since 2000, it has occurred faster than in any other European country.

This development reflects social-democratic Norwegian values and humanitarian ideals, a society in which all peoples, regardless of ethnic background or religious conviction, should have the same right to claim the country as their own. In a public speech on 1 September 2016, King Harald stated: "Home is where our hearts are . . . It does not matter if your heart is in Pakistan, Afghanistan or Norway, whether you believe in Jesus or Allah or nothing . . . It does not matter. It's everyone's state as well." The speech gained international attention.

In a recently published book, Professor Terje Tvedt (2017) argues that this development has been guided by a political leadership in partnership with a cultural elite of academics, intellectuals and journalists who hold multiculturalism as an ideal. According to him, there have been conscious choices ruled by ideology, not by coincidence and circumstance. This view, however, ignores the possible influence of unconscious forces embedded in our history and the social unconscious, which I will reflect upon later in this chapter.

Norway is now a multicultural society. Increased immigration – migrants, refugees and asylum seekers from non-Western countries, and their descendants – represents cultures that are significantly different from that of Norway. What does this imply for our society, our Norwegian values, culture and identity, and not least our welfare state? Is there a limit to how open the national identity can be, and still be an ethnic identity? Many people fear that customs, habits, traditions and values from other countries will lead to a deconstruction of Norwegian identity (Andresen, 2012). It represents major challenges, especially in certain areas of the capital, Oslo, where the majority have ethnic backgrounds other than Norwegian. There is an open debate on whether this multiculturalism represents an enrichment or a threat to our values and our identity. Nevertheless, despite this uncertainty, the overall attitude towards "strangers" is still positive among Norwegians (Statistics Norway, 2017).

After World War II, there was a consensus among Norwegian governmental and voluntary organisations to assist refugees in Europe. The Norwegian Refugee Council (NRC), an independent, private foundation, has played a significant role since 1956, when refugees from the Hungarian uprising came to Norway. In 1968, many fled from Czechoslovakia, and many refugees arrived during the Balkan Wars. Helping people in need has been an important aspect of Norwegian self-image, from the missionary women who knitted stockings for children in Madagascar, to the more extensive development aid projects in which the country has been involved. An unconscious identification with the poor and oppressed seems deeply rooted in the Norwegian mentality, originating from the time Norway was itself a poor and oppressed country. Solidarity with the poor and a commitment to sharing prosperity through aid is a value in Norwegian society. However, the recent surge in migration challenges these traditional Norwegian values, with a divide between those who benevolently welcome refugees, those who are more sceptical towards immigration and those who are openly hostile to immigrants. Our tolerance of and solidarity with the poor is being put to the test. Are we willing to share, after all, if our own welfare is threatened?

National identity and the social unconscious

National identity is a sense of a nation as a cohesive whole, as represented by distinctive traditions, culture, language and politics (Oxford Dictionary, 2015). It refers to the subjective feeling one shares with a group of people about a nation; the shared narrative about the past that includes national symbols, traditions, memories of national experiences and achievements rooted in the nation's history (Kelman, 1997). It incorporates a system of beliefs, values, assumptions and expectations that are transmitted from generation to generation (Smith, 1991).

In recent years there has been a growing interest in how these narratives are embedded in the social unconscious (Hopper, 2003; Hopper & Weinberg, 2011). According to Haim Weinberg, "The social unconscious is the co-constructed shared unconscious of members of a certain social system such as a community, society, nation or culture. It includes shared anxieties, fantasies, defences, myths, and memories" (Weinberg, 2007, p. 312). Its building blocks are chosen traumas and chosen glories (Vokan, 2001); that is, stories of shared trauma and loss or stories of heroism and honour:

> The idea of the social unconscious assumes that some specific hidden myths and motives guide the behaviour of a certain society or culture. It also assumes that a large group or society might use some shared defences. In the same manner that unconscious forces drive an individual without knowing it, a group, an organization or the entire society can act upon unconscious forces too.
>
> *(Weinberg, 2007, pp. 309–310)*

What is the history of Norway?

Norway as we know it today is a rather young nation. But Norway's history goes back more than a thousand years. The Viking era, which ended a thousand years ago, still remains in our national memory, reminding us of the time when the nation was powerful, respected, even feared. The Vikings were explorers and voyagers. Though the Vikings were known abroad as ruthless pirates, at home they lived in a well-ordered society based on the rule of law and democracy. They were craftsmen and poets. Women held strong positions in society. Today, the Viking Museum is an attraction. Viking costumes are sold as souvenirs for tourists. At international sports events, the Norwegian public often show up with Viking helmets.

Later, Norway was subjugated to Denmark in a union lasting more than 400 years, or as it has been called, "the 400-year-night" (Ibsen, 1867). Norway played a subordinate role in the union. All political and economic power was focused in Denmark. Copenhagen, the king's city, was the cultural and economic centre. There lived the upper class and the nobility. Norway was a poor, looted nation. People lived as peasants, smallholders, crofters and fishermen. Life was very hard and poverty was rife. Austerity was a necessity and a virtue. The Norwegians had to pay taxes to the Danish king. The official language was Danish. Civil servants wrote and spoke Danish. Norwegian identity and culture were mainly absent. A strong sense of insignificance and inferiority prevailed. Norwegian artists, painters, sculptors and musicians had to travel to Copenhagen to gain recognition.

However, not least due to the Danish defeat in the Napoleonic wars, a strong desire for the country to separate from the union and become independent emerged. That culminated on 17 May 1814, when a National Assembly declared secession from the union and independence from Denmark. Norway got its own constitution, among the most modern in Europe – a proud moment that we still celebrate on 17 May each year. All over the country, people dress in traditional Norwegian folk costumes and march in parades – not military, but happy and excited schoolchildren waving the Norwegian flag: a sign of national pride, of freedom and independence.

However, due to defeat in the Napoleonic Wars, Norway was ceded to Sweden under the terms of the Kiel Treaty in 1814, a few months after the declaration of independence from Denmark. The new union with Sweden was less oppressive than the subordination at the hands of Denmark. We had our own Norwegian parliament with a high degree of domestic self-government. We had our constitution, a national anthem and a university in Oslo, but in foreign affairs we were subject to Swedish policy. Norway was still not independent. However, from the early 1880s there was a growing interest in Norwegian life among officials and the intellectual elite (Glenthøj, 2008). Influenced by romantic and national romantic ideas from Europe, a romanticised idealisation of the peasants and rural life took place.

They collected cultural artefacts that were defined as typical Norwegian: national symbols, myths, idioms and handicrafts that could create a resounding basis for a Norwegian culture. National-romantic paintings and music also played a significant role. A Norwegian identity emerged. Norwegians became more and more aware of their own national identity, of a pride in being Norwegian and a strong desire for the country to separate from the union and become independent resulted. With increasing national self-esteem and Norwegian identity-building, a demand for independence grew stronger. In 1905, Norway unilaterally declared independence from Sweden, and after a peaceful process Sweden agreed without a shot being fired.

Today we talk less about the unions, as though we need to repress our insignificance during "the 400-years-night". We emphasise the glorious moments in our history: the magnificent Viking era, the struggle for freedom from oppression during the union, the liberation from Denmark and Sweden, our independence – our "Chosen Glory" (Vokan, 2001). However, a subtle feeling of inferiority associated with being the insignificant, underprivileged, less cultivated partner in the unions seems embedded in our national fabric, our national memory and social unconscious. A sense of inferiority that has been difficult to shake off, despite our wealth and success, as though our grandiose pride is a narcissistic defence against subservience, or an unpleasant recognition that we are not *that* great. Though the centuries of union get little attention in daily life, it emerges when "dangers threaten". During the fierce fight against membership of the European Union, it was argued that Norway would once more be engulfed by a union. We would be exploited and experience destitution and poverty.

Norway and the European Union (EU)

The relationship to the European integration process has been one of the most controversial issues in Norwegian foreign policy since World War II. While big business and some members of the political elite have been positive, the wider Norwegian population has been sceptical from the start. Resistance to the EU has many motives based on a multitude of attitudes and interests. Loss of sovereignty has always been central.

In 1972 and 1994 there were two referendums regarding application to membership of the EEC/EU. A very polarised discussion ensued, almost splitting the nation in two. The slogans against membership had clear reference to our history: "Say no to selling Norway!" "Fight against EEC and destitution". The European Union unconsciously symbolised associations to the previous union with Denmark, when Norway was poor, exploited and dominated. As a small nation we would play a subordinate role in the EU – not be heard, not respected, treated as insignificant: all fears that are deeply embedded in our social unconscious. The population voted no at both referendums, admittedly with a slender majority. Since 1994, full membership of the EU has not been part of the political discourse. However, as a member of the European Economic Area (EEA) agreement, Norway is closely connected to the EU, and we have to adapt to developments in the EU in ever-expanding areas – from economics and trade to social issues, the labour market, immigration, police cooperation and security policy.

A new concern has now arisen due to Brexit. Will the United Kingdom become a member of the European Free Trade Association (EFTA)? In relation to other members Iceland and Liechtenstein, Norway has been the dominant nation in EFTA for many years. If the UK enters the association, Norway will once again become a little sibling.

The Norwegian self-image

In her book *The Origins of the Regime of Goodness*, Nina Witoszek (2011) writes that Norwegians at the beginning of the 21st century have created one of the most amazing countries on our planet. Norway is a country of welfare, equality, justice, concern for the environment and charitable activities. Norway is still perceived in many ways as a stable, culturally and socially homogeneous society with a high level of interpersonal and social trust (Delhey & Newton, 2005). We trust our political system, the police and law enforcement. We rely on the provision of welfare, the tax system and the community. Society is characterised by equality and minor differences (Statistics Norway, 2018b). We have no nobility or aristocracy. We advanced from poverty to prosperity, and prosperity should be shared. That is a fundamental solidarity perspective that is maintained through a widely accepted tax and distribution policy: "The self-image is about equality, relationships to our surrounding nature, simplicity and austerity, and other Protestant virtues. They exist as ideals. 'Dugnad' (voluntary work) is a national virtue" (Hylland Eriksen, 2013). Thereby, values, norms and social practices that promote democracy and economic efficiency are achieved (Stoltenberg, 2009).

We are proud of our country; prouder, in fact, than most other Western European countries. More than half of Norwegians believe that Norwegian culture is better than others (Pew Research Center, 2018). We cherish our national heroes: the polar explorers Nansen and Amundsen, our artists and authors like Munch and Ibsen, our winter sports athletes. Norway has never been a colonial power, and we have never initiated war or committed war crimes. Norwegians perceive Norway as a small but influential country that promotes international standards for ethical conduct. Norwegians score higher than other countries in terms of tolerance (PEW Report, 2018). They have an inclusive understanding of national identity. Pride and tolerance go hand-in-hand. Ethno-nationalism, where national pride is combined with dangerous intolerance and xenophobia, has no place in Norway (Taraku, 2018).

However, despite the national pride, Norwegians have a need to be acknowledged. We are concerned about the judgement of others. We are like small children who yearn for confirmation – "Look at me! Look at me!" – although with all our wealth, we should be less concerned about others' opinions of us. It is a need that has to be continually replenished due to a fundamental lack of self-belief, no matter what we achieve. "The Norwegian self-image oscillates between subservience and megalomania" (my translation), said Gudmund Hernes (1990) in connection with the Olympic games at Lillehammer. "We believe we are important players on the world stage, while hardly anyone knows what Norway is". Our sense of self fluctuates between grandiosity and inferiority.

Norwegian values

Norway is an egalitarian society (Østerud, 2005). Everyone has equal rights and it is important that everyone is given equal opportunities – "the quality of equality", as Hernes (1990) phrased it. The people have a basic democratic sense of mind, with a high degree of trust in societal institutions, as I described earlier, perhaps with a naïve belief that our democracy can be transmitted to countries lacking these traditions and values. We have a robust welfare state and a strong economy, not least due to the oil industry. Norwegian policy has shown great stability and has been largely consensus-oriented. The Norwegian public is less polarised than most other countries. There are relatively small differences between poor and rich. Both the OECD and the World Inequality Report (2018) show that Norway is among the countries with the least difference between poor and rich, though this is gradually changing with globalisation. We also score very highly on international happiness scales (UN World Happiness Report, 2017).

Traditionally, women have had a strong position in society, ever since the Viking age. Viking women were responsible for the farm when the men were abroad. They kept the key to the property. No women were forced into marriage, unlike most other cultures at that time. Later, the wives of fishermen had to take care of the household while their husbands were away for months during the fishing season. Gender equality has been an essential aspect of Norwegian politics for many years. Women play a central role in most areas of politics and cultural life. Gro Harlem Brundtland became our first female prime minister in 1981. In 1986 her government consisted of eight women and ten men, which gained international attention. Today, the leaders of the three government parties are women. We have a female prime minister, finance minister, foreign minister and several other female ministers. Our former minister of defence was a woman. The Norwegian Confederation of Trade Unions (LO) and the Confederation of Norwegian Enterprises (NHO), as well as other major organisations, are led by women. At work as well as in family life, there is a high degree of gender equality. Parental leave after birth is generous, with a total of 49 weeks to be shared between the parents; the paternal quota is at least 15 weeks. In 2011, however, Norwegian values and ideals were seriously tested.

When Norway lost its innocence

In the afternoon of 22 July 2011, a car bomb exploded in the Government Quarter in Oslo. Eight people were killed, and the buildings totally destroyed. Later that day, 69 adolescents were killed in a mass shooting at Utøya, the summer camp of the youth organisation of the Labour Party. The terrorist was a white ethnic Norwegian, Anders Behring Breivik. According to Breivik's manifesto (2011), there is an imminent danger that Europe, Norway included, will be transformed to a "Eurabia" where Muslim norms and traditions will wipe out the Christian heritage and way of life. According to him, this "grand narrative" has been under preparation for centuries, and intellectuals and Marxists have been in conspiracy with Muslims to create this caliphate. Because of the danger to Western civilisation, radical and extraordinary "security measures" had to be taken, and it was his (and others) responsibility to act. The youths at Utøya, the summer camp, represented the next generation of the social democratic elite, which, in Breivik's opinion, is responsible for the increasing "multiculturalism", "cultural Marxism" and "Islamisation" that threaten Norwegian society and Christian conservative values. They are traitors and should be treated as such, he argued. His terror attack was directed towards the ruling Labour Party, but it was also an attack on fundamental Norwegian values and ideals.

When the terrorist was arrested he was convinced that he would be executed immediately, which he perceived as martyrdom. For Norway, it was important to treat him within the values and laws of the Norwegian civil society, with the rights and responsibilities that this implied, and not to act on his perception of being outside and above Norwegian society and laws. During the court trial, it was important to deal with Breivik within the framework of existing laws, and not under martial law.

Though Behring Breivik was a sole terrorist with a severely pathological personality (Lovdata, 2012), we also learned that his extreme views resonated with the opinions of a sub-culture of European far-right nationalists and anti-Islamists who met online at blogospheres such as Gates of Vienna. This was a sub-culture that had previously received little attention from the Norwegian public.

The immediate responses proposed by the prime minister and political parties after the terror attack were to uphold the values of the open democratic society with dignity and respect, and not to revert to retaliation and mob justice. The Norwegian public responded to the terror attack with a parade of roses. Hundreds of thousands of people gathered in the streets of Oslo carrying roses, marching and singing the national anthem, thereby demonstrating the values of respect and dignity – not hatred and retaliation. A statement from one of the survivors of Utøya went viral: "If one man can create so much hatred, imagine how much love we together can create". The political leadership, the emphasis on Norwegian values and the strong belief in openness and democratic processes prevented the nation from reacting to the national trauma with fear and social fragmentation.

Norway in the international arena

Christian missionary organisations have been dedicated to helping the poor through missionary projects in Africa and Asia for more than a century. Since 1963, Norwegian development aid has been a government-organised project. Norwegians

Norway: between grandiosity and inferiority **107**

engaged in this endeavour with great energy and enthusiasm. There was strong optimism and belief in development projects. Soon developmental aid became an institutionalised and professionalised growth industry. In 1982, the expenditure goal (1% of GDP) was achieved (NORAD, 2010).

By 2016 Norway had become the "world champion" in development aid, with projects in more than one hundred countries (Tvedt, 2017). Norway has become internationally recognised, not for wars, but for identification and solidarity with the poor and oppressed. Norwegian politicians believe in dialogue and cooperation across party lines and political differences. Resolution of conflicts and opposites must be solved through dialogue, rather than war and abuse of power. Development aid, initially aimed at helping desperate people in need, has become increasingly geared towards promoting good governance, democracy and a vital society of civil rights in developing countries. This is a political project that focuses more and more on international peace and reconciliation processes. Being a world champion in aid does not seem to be enough. Norway wishes to be a humanitarian superpower; a peace-negotiator and respected actor that will play a major role in the international peacekeeping arena.

Norway played a central role in the process of creating peace between Israel and Palestine. Through secret diplomacy, representatives from the two parties met at the negotiation table. A dialogue was achieved that led to mutual recognition between the Palestine Liberation Organisation (PLO) and Israel. Expectations for the Oslo Accords were great when Yitzhak Rabin, Yasir Arafat and President Bill Clinton met on the lawn in front of the White House in Washington in 1993. It was a proud moment for Norway. The accords did not lead to any lasting peace between Israel and Palestine. For Norway, however, this Middle East diplomacy represented fame and prestige. Peace negotiations became a Norwegian "export product" after the Oslo Accords (Waage, 2009, 2013). Peace diplomacy became an important tool for Norwegian foreign policy, ensuring that the superpowers would still be interested in Norway (Selmer, 2016). The world's eyes were on Norway, and not only when the Nobel Peace Prize was announced.

Nevertheless, Norway's attempt to create peace during the civil war in Sri Lanka was a complete failure. The Norwegians tried to act as negotiators without sufficient knowledge of the political complexity of the conflict (Salter, 2015). They were too naïve and grandiose in their perceptions of themselves as peace negotiators.

The Norwegian authorities also played a key role in the peace process in Sudan and the establishment of South Sudan as an independent state. The celebration of this new state was a magnificent moment for the Norwegian peacekeepers, with representatives from government and the royal family on the stage. They seemed fascinated by the grandiose idea that democracy, based on experience from Norway, could be transmitted to a country on the verge of collapse. They neglected the serious warnings and concerns regarding the creation of a state led by corrupt leaders; leaders who seemed more concerned with defeating each other than the interests of the country's population (Tvedt, 2017). Regardless of these defeats,

Norway's involvement in the peace negotiations in Colombia between the government and FARC guerrillas seems to have been successful.

Despite disappointments, the image of Norway as a typical peacekeeper remains strongly rooted in our self-image. Our perception is that Norway is an exceptionally peaceful country, unlike other European countries. The fact that since 1990 Norway has almost continuously been involved in a series of wars – in the Balkans, Afghanistan, Iraq, and last but not least, the bombing in Libya – has not altered that impression.

Mark Curtis (2010) labels this "doublethink" in his report to the Forum for Development and the Environment:

> Government officials and ordinary Norwegians tend to see Norway as a small but influential country that often sets international standards for ethical behaviour and that does, and overtly seeks to do, good in the world. Norway is widely known as a large aid donor and promoter of international development, a strong supporter of UN peace processes, and along with other Scandinavian countries, as committed to clean environmental policy. But how real is this benign image and how ethical is Norway's foreign and developmental policy in practice, both compared to its declared policy and to other countries?
>
> *(Curtis, 2010, p. 6)*

Curtis, as well as others (Tvedt, 2017), questions the background and motives for Norway's international engagement. They maintain that international recognition bolsters Norway's self-esteem as an important international actor (Leira, 2015). Why is that so important? Why do we, as a small country, have this constant need for international recognition? Are there unconscious driving forces? On the one hand, Norway's involvement internationally reflects a feeling of responsibility and a sincere desire to assist those in need, based on humanitarian values and solidarity with the suffering and oppressed people. Norway's engagement in peace processes is also due to a genuine wish – and even an obligation – to contribute to peace, perhaps with a naïve belief that today's international challenges can be solved in line with Norwegian values, attitudes and tradition. However, beneath these noble causes we should consider other, conscious and unconscious, driving forces. Today's Norway is a rich country, but unconsciously we identify with the poor and oppressed, an identification that is rooted in our own history, when we were the poor and oppressed. At the same time, international recognition and respect might give us a feeling of moral supremacy – that we are better than the people we should be helping (Engh, 2015; Simensen, 2003). Unconsciously this might represent a grandiose, narcissistic compensation and defence against the inherent feeling of national inferiority. A feeling of inferiority, rooted in our history, when for hundreds of years Norway was the insignificant, neglected, oppressed and exploited small country. Those memories are embedded in our social unconscious, along with the prouder and more glorious moments in our history, and thereby shape our self-image: between grandiosity and inferiority.

Summary

In this paper I have tried to illustrate some aspects of Norwegian society, its values and ideals, norms and attitudes. I have also discussed our relationship to Europe and the world at large. We have a strong desire to play a significant role in the international arena. We are strong supporters of supranational cooperation, but with scepticism towards supranational dominance. Norway is a European country, but we are not member of the EU. National autonomy seems important, though we have to adapt to EU regulations. We want to be influential, but simultaneously there is a feeling of insecurity and scepticism towards the stranger. Do we have an inferiority complex, no matter how much we achieve? Is our contradictory self-understanding a grandiose defence against inferiority? I have looked at our history and tried to illustrate how historical events, memories and myths seem embedded in our social unconscious. To what extent do these unconscious processes shape and influence our actions today? These are the questions I have tried to address.

Note

1 New Year's television address, 1 January 1992.

References

Andresen, N.A. (2012, November 18). Hvor norsk kan man bli? *Minerva*. Editorial. Retrieved from www.minervanett.no/hvor-norsk-kan-man-bli/

Behring Breivik, A. (2011). *2083: A European declaration of independence*. Retrieved from https://publicintelligence.net/anders-behring-breiviks-complete-manifesto-2083-a-european-declaration-of-independence/

Curtis, M. (2010). Doublethink: The two faces of Norway's Foreign and development policy. *Forum for Utvikling og Miljø*. Retrieved from www.forumfor.no/assets/docs/Double think-by-Mark-Curtis_jan2010.pdf

Delhey, J., & Newton, K. (2005). Predicting cross-national levels of social trust: Global pattern or Nordic exceptionalism? *European Sociological Review, 21*(4), 311–327.

Engh, S. (2015). *Norsk utviklingshjelp 1945–1970. UiO 2015*. Retrieved from www.norges historie.no/velferdsstat-og-vestvending/artikler/1856-norsk-utviklingshjelp-1945-1970.html

Glenthøj, R. (2008). *En moderne nations fødsel – Norsk national identifikation hos embedsmænd og borgere 1807–1815. (The inception of a modern nation – Norwegian national identification of assets and citizen 1807–1815)*. Odense: Syddansk Universitetsforlag.

Hernes, G. (1990). Mellom husmannsånd og storslagenhet. *Samtiden, 2*, 77–86.

Hopper, E. (2003). *The social unconscious: Selected papers*. London: Jessica Kingsley.

Hopper, E., & Weinberg, H. (Eds.). (2011). *The social unconscious in persons, groups and societies, vol 1: Mainly theory*. London: Karnac.

Hylland Eriksen, T. (2013). Typisk Norsk. *Samfunnsviter'n, 20*(1), 4–5.

110 Thor Kristian Island

Ibsen, H. (1867). *Per Gynt*. København: Gyldendal.

Kelman, H. C. (1997). Nationalism, patriotism, and national identity: Social-psychological dimensions. In D. Bar-Tal & E. Staub (Eds.), *Patriotism in the life of individuals and nations* (pp. 165–189). Chicago: Nelson-Hall.

Leira, H. (2015). The formative years: Norway as an obsessive status seeker. In B. de Carvalho & I. B. Neuman (Eds.), *Small state status seeking: Norway's quest for international standing* (pp. 22–41). New York: Routledge.

Lovdata. (2012). *Oslo District Court (Oslo tingrett) – Judgment*. Retrieved from https://lovdata. no/static/file/1282/toslo-2011-188627-24-eng.pdf

NORAD. (2010). *Milepæler i norsk bistandsarbeid*. Retrieved from www.norad.no/om-norad/ historie/milepaler-i-norsk-bistandsarbeid/

Østerud, Ø. (2005). Introduction: The peculiarities of Norway. *West European Politics*, *28*(4), 705–772.

Oxford Dictionary. (2015). *National identity*. Retrieved from https://en.oxforddictionaries. com/definition/national_identity

Pew Research Center. (2018, May 29). *"Being Christian in Western Europe" nationalism, immigration and minorities*. Retrieved from www.pewforum.org/2018/05/29/being-christian-in-western-europe/

Salter, M. (2015). *To end a civil war: Norway's peace engagement in Sri Lanka*. London: Hurst & Co.

Selmer, E. (2016). *Sri Lanka: Norsk fredsmekling slo feil (Sri Lanka: How Norwegian peace negotiations failed)*. Retrieved from www.bistandsaktuelt.no/arkiv-kommentarer/2016/ sri-lanka-megling-slo-feil/

Simensen, J. (2003). 1952–1975: Norge møter den tredje verden. In *Norsk utviklingshjelps historie 1*. Bergen: Fagbokforlaget.

Smith, A. D. (1991). *National identity*. London: Penguin.

Statistics Norway. (2017). *Attitudes towards immigrants and immigration*. Retrieved from www. ssb.no/en/befolkning/statistikker/innvhold

Statistics Norway. (2018a). *Immigrants and Norwegian-born to immigrant parents*. Retrieved from www.ssb.no/en/befolkning/artikler-og-publikasjoner/immigrants-and-norwegian-born-to-immigrant-parents-archive

Statistics Norway. (2018b). *Income and wealth statistics for households*. Retrieved from www.ssb. no/en/statbank/table/07756/

Stoltenberg, J. (2009, January 1). *The prime minister's new year's televised address*.

Taraku, S. (2018). Den inkluderende nasjonalismen kommer ikke av seg selv. *Morgenbladet*, *199*(22).

Tvedt, T. (2017). *Det internasjonale gjennombruddet (The international break-through)*. Oslo: Dreyer.

United Nations Development Program. (2018). *Human development indices and indicators: 2018 statistical update*. Retrieved from www.hdr.undp.org/sites/default/files/2018_human_ development_statistical_update.pdf

Vokan, V. D. (2001). Transgenerational transmissions and chosen traumas: An aspect of large group identity. *Group Analysis*, *34*(1), 79–97.

Waage, H. H. (2009). Fredspolitikk i Midtøsten (Peace politics in the Middle East). In E. Lange, H. Pharo, & Ø. Østerud (Eds.), *Vendepunkter i norsk utenrikspolitikk: nye internasjonale vilkår etter den kalde krigen*. Oslo: Unipub.

Waage, H. H. (2013). *Konflikt og stormaktspolitikk i Midtøsten (Conflicts and Super-power Politics in the Middle East)*. Kristiansand: Cappelen Damm Akademisk.

Weinberg, H. (2007). So what is this social unconscious anyway? *Group Analysis, 40*(3), 307–322.

Witoszek, N. (2011). *The origins of the regime of goodness.* Oslo: Universitetsforlaget.

World Happiness Report. (2017). Retrieved from http://worldhappiness.report/ed/2017/

World Inequality Report. (2018). Retrieved from https://wir2018.wid.world/

9

FAR FROM THE MADDING CROWD

Pre to post Brexit Britain

Halina Brunning and Olya Khaleelee

Introduction

The heading of this paper is inspired by Thomas Hardy's fourth novel written in 1874. Hardy places *Far from the Madding Crowd*[1] in rural southwest England. The novel deals with themes of love, honour and betrayal set against a backdrop of the seemingly idyllic, but often harsh reality of a farming community in Victorian England. We selected this as a fitting metaphor for Brexit because it seems to encapsulate the wish to escape into a peaceful imagined place evocative of a past idyllic habitat, where love, honour and betrayal come to a heady explosive mix. Furthermore, the strongest support for leaving the European Union was expressed by the rural communities of Britain in 2016.

In this chapter we consider the conscious and unconscious reasons for calling the Referendum and the uneasy result that it brought: a split country, the Leave vs. the Remain camps hostile to each, the resignation of the Prime Minister who called the Referendum, the ongoing political upheaval within the UK and the implications for the European Union as a whole in the wake of Great Britain's decision to give up its membership.

In order for this chapter to be more than just a rehash of information readily available in the press we have included our own narrative, hypotheses and interpretations. We do so from our roles as psychodynamic psychologists but also as citizens of Great Britain.

Pre Brexit Britain

Britain joined the EEC (later renamed the EU) in 1973 as 'the sick man of Europe' because it was failing economically. Membership of the EU, to which the British people recommitted themselves in the referendum of 1975, led over the following

Pre to post Brexit Britain **113**

40 years to growth and prosperity. Eventually, Britain prospered more than its European neighbours and until 2017, the UK was the fifth largest world economy. However, as the EU countries within the eurozone became increasingly centralised, this generated anxiety over loss of boundary control which threatened national identity and autonomy. This anxiety might also have been heightened given that Great Britain is an island nation benefitting from a clear physical boundary provided by the sea. Loss of boundary control could be felt as a particularly intrusive 'invasion'.

During the 2015 general election campaign, the Prime Minister, David Cameron, promised to renegotiate the terms of the UK's EU membership and later to hold a referendum on the subject if a Conservative majority government were to be elected. The promise was that after a Conservative win, the government would try to negotiate more favourable arrangements for continuing British membership of the EU, particularly in relation to migration and control of its own borders.

Yet, according to d'Ancona writing in *The Guardian* 'the intellectual ancestry of the leave cause has much more interesting and coherent roots' than those about immigration expressed by a new right-wing party, UKIP, under the leadership of Nigel Farage. 'The argument of the more thoughtful Brexiteers is that post-war, post-Thatcher Britain has reached a point of economic strength, cultural maturity and confidence that enables it to be weaned from the unreformable EU' (D'Ancona, 2016).

When David Cameron failed to renegotiate more favourable terms of membership, he was compelled to fulfill his referendum promise. What was not realised at that time was that the splits in the Conservative Party between what came to be known as 'Remainers' and 'Leavers' mirrored the splits in the country (Khaleelee, 2016). This was partly because politicians and indeed most other people do not tend to think from a psychological, systemic or a global perspective. Therefore, what is missed are the 'macro' movements of which the UK's splits and behaviours are a representative 'microcosm'. As we work our way through the Brexit process, these elements have been becoming more visible.

Brunning and Khaleelee (2018) recently wrote about the various independence movements that have emerged over the last three years.

> Catalonia has had an 'illegal' referendum confirming a wish to separate from Spain, resulting in its proposed leader finding himself in self imposed exile, and with Catalonia experiencing the full might of the Spanish Government's authority. It has not so far delivered the hoped for result for those Catalonians who wish to separate. Meanwhile, Kurds are renewing their efforts to separate from three host countries, Syria, Iraq and Turkey in order to form their own nation state, Kurdistan. One can predict the turbulence and bloodshed ahead, since the host countries will resist these efforts to separate and build a new nation.
>
> There are other examples of more or less peaceful strivings for independence. Such signs of individuation but also of fragmentation suggest that the

world is regressing to the tribal level and the politics of identity are emerging strongly once more. There is a concurrent growth in the anti-globalism movement.

These are examples of identity being

> played out at different levels e.g. the level of nation state (UK), country (Scotland), community (students and youth in general), race (Black Lives Matter), single issue (campaigners and eco-warriors), gender (women speak out against male abuse and Saudi Arabian women allowed to drive from 2018), religion (attempts to modernise Islam in some liberal mosques in Germany and Denmark), or sexuality (transgender movement growing stronger). We can be optimistic about some of these developments. However, such changes are never easy to achieve nor tranquil whilst in the process of becoming.
>
> *(p. 134)[2]*

These changes also impact on other countries in Europe and on the EU itself, and we have seen in recent years with the influx of refugees how that pressure continues to affect boundary management within the Schengen zone differently for different countries: Greece and Italy have clearly taken the brunt of many thousands of refugees but Hungary and Austria have responded quite differently to the lead given by Germany, by building robust physical boundaries, and Poland for instance, by refusing to accept migrants who are ethnically or religiously different from their own indigenous population. It is not just the UK that is experiencing threats to identity and autonomy, but perhaps because it is an island, it has been the first to break off from the containing boundary of the EU.

Why has Brexit occurred?

One implication of this argument is that Brexit is inextricably linked with the drive to maintain and to avoid any threats to national identity.

> From a system psychodynamic perspective, this decision could be seen in the context of our understanding of large groups, which, being dominated by primitive impulses, are prone to splitting and fragmentation. Twenty-eight members of the EU is in group dynamic terms too large a number to engage in effective government and decision-making under a centralised bureaucratic organisation.
>
> *(op.cit 2018)*

The idea of a European Army – the Permanent Structured Cooperation Pact (PESCO) – involving greater defence expenditure and more centralised policy-making – was felt to be unacceptable by several countries, including the UK, partly because it overlaps with membership of NATO, creating new complexities and rivalries.

Bion (1961) refers to the tension that always exists between the individual's desire for autonomy on the one hand and the desire to belong to the group on the other: independence vs. interdependence. This tension can also be seen to exist at country level and, we hypothesise, is being expressed – even enacted – by the UK on behalf of other members of the EU. Additionally, the anxiety generated by an influx of refugees from Syria and other European ex-colonies, who were perceived even at governmental level as threatening to 'invade' the UK from the 'Calais Jungle', was one of the triggers that generated this 'calving' of 'iceberg UK' from the landmass of the EU.

An internal perspective, however, was that, despite hefty EU subsidies, swathes of UK citizens experienced themselves as forgotten and abandoned in this era of globalisation and therefore they opted for the fantasy of 'taking back control of our borders'. Whilst the feeling of being forgotten was possibly more to do with how the population felt about the remoteness of their representatives in Westminster, it has been displaced onto the wider EU system. Perhaps the referendum outcome was a protest vote?

There is a parallel here with how Westminster seems to view the representation offered by members in the European Parliament (MEPs) in Brussels, so remote as seemingly non-existent, certainly rarely referred to in the media. We have little awareness that our MEP representatives help to make the laws that are experienced as impositions by Brussels. It is as though the experience is of larger entity (the EU) having swallowed up the smaller entity (the UK), a view perhaps shared by other European countries.

The decision to leave the EU can thus be interpreted as a protectionist response to the threat of annihilation of national identity (Bion, 1961), but the electorate was not aware that without the labour flexibility provided by immigration, and without a good understanding of the benefits of belonging to a single market, the UK economy and standard of living could suffer hugely. Every decision has its price. One price is that the UK's economic status is predicted to decline once Brexit has come to fruition.

The widening gap between rich and poor – whereby the rich increased their wealth by 64% whilst the poor became poorer by 54% over the last decade (Wikipedia) – is likely to remain or increase, which will continue to fuel national resentment and the class divide. The government, unable through austerity/moral bankruptcy to deal directly with some of these issues, tends to use displacement techniques. One example is the attack on the Windrush generation.[3] With their British-born descendants, they have had their citizenship and presence in the UK threatened, instead of the government developing a system to enable real illegal immigrants to be found and deported. This scandal has resulted in the recent resignation of the Home Secretary.

Splits are therefore partly to do with a widening disparity between rich and poor, whereby some parts of the population, particularly in London (virtually a city state) have benefitted from globalisation and membership of the EU; and others, in Middle England and the North, feel that they have not. These less cosmopolitan and diverse swathes of the country, which particularly represent English identity, are those that have voted to protect their sense of nationhood, unaware at that time of the significant national costs of this decision. Omnipotent fantasies of future greatness, with Britain, the great seafaring nation, making independent deals with far-flung parts of the world, probably also fed into the outcome of this referendum. Finally,

> the outcome of the 2017 US election had parallels to Brexit in three ways: firstly, by the sudden mobilisation of those left behind by the power of globalisation; secondly, as a way of expressing loss of respect for the ruling elite; and thirdly, through probable interference by the Russians in both electoral processes via weaponisation of the internet.
>
> *(Gilligan, 2017) (op cit.)*

Societal processes before and after the referendum

Since the referendum the positions taken by politicians have been characterised by splitting, wishful thinking and the impossibility of agreeing how to proceed. No-one had thought about the border between Northern Ireland and Eire, nor about the fact that most of the 2 million residents in Northern Ireland had voted Remain, leading to a case of the tail wagging the dog. This became more complex when the government without a clear majority became reliant on a Northern Irish political party (the Democratic Unionist Party – more pro 'Leave' than 'Remain' in attitude) to get its agenda through parliament.

The desire for a 'harder' or 'softer' Brexit can be seen as a battle between ideology and reality. In addition to the fact that the government is in such a perilous position, arising from the Prime Minister deciding in June 2017 to go to the country for an endorsement that did not happen, there is also the other significant factor of the Russians manipulating the electorate through bots, fake news and opinions circulated through social media.

According to research by *The Sunday Times* in conjunction with Swansea University (April 29th, 2018 front page), 6,500 Russian Twitter accounts rallied behind Labour in the weeks before last year's election, helping supportive messages to reach millions of voters and denigrating its Conservative rivals. Many of the Russian accounts have been identified as internet robots (bots) that masqueraded under female English names but were in fact mass-produced to bombard the public with orchestrated political messages. This was hypothesised to have increased electoral support for Jeremy Corbyn, Leader of the opposition Labour Party, from 25% to 40% during the election campaign. How far does such fake news impact on the ideological positions taken by some of our politicians on both sides of the main parties? Furthermore, various promises were made by both sides in the run up to the Referendum. According to Infacts (2016), the Leave Campaign promised unrealistic monetary advantages, particularly for that most important 'maternal' institution in the UK, the National Health Service (NHS): Vote Leave's battle bus

Pre to post Brexit Britain **117**

said: 'We send the EU £350 million a week. Let's fund our NHS instead'. More financial support was also offered to other groups, such as farmers and scientists. In summary,

> those who are dealing with Brexit operate in a VUCA environment (Volatile, Uncertain, Complex, Ambiguous).[4] Some of the decisions will be made without all the facts and with ambiguous information, the challenges and opportunities are complex and often unclear and, of course, the situation is ever-changing due to world events and the vagaries of politics.
>
> *(Rennie, 2018)*

As we write in May 2018, the 'Hard' and 'Soft' Brexiteers continue to battle it out in the Cabinet with a weakened leader in Theresa May. Meanwhile the younger, more outward-looking, European-oriented generation, which was not of an age to vote in the referendum but would now be eligible to do so, are pushing

STRENGTHS	WEAKNESSES

• Link and trade with the rest of the world including the Commonwealth
• Build upon our own values:
  – Parliamentary democracy
  – Autonomy
  – Freedom
  – Self determination
  – Creativity, entrepreneurial spirit
  Innovative arts and sciences
• Export our franchised educational model
	• Loss of growth
	• Loss of jobs and investments
	• EU subsidies dry out
	• Greater gap between rich and poor
	• Lower economic prosperity
	• City [UK financial hub] being undermined by rival financial centres in Paris and Frankfurt due to the loss of "passporting rights"

OPPORTUNITIES	THREATS
• Forging new role on the world stage linking with the 'Five Eyes' countries re: national security considerations • Forging temporary opportunistic needs-led alliances with different political powers • Initiating new trading agreements • Setting up own space research • Re-establishing our own judicial supremacy	• Lesser role on the world stage leads to lesser influence • Loss of special relationship with USA, France • Being isolated with no immediate allies • Loss of tariff-free trade • Loss of security and higher vulnerability • Loss of role in the Galileo Space programme • Higher unemployment • Inability to recruit to key areas • Civic disturbances if Brexit fails to deliver on promises

FIGURE 9.1 The SWOT table (Strength, Weakness Opportunities and Threats) presents a picture of the UK in a post-Brexit world

for a further referendum to agree the terms once they have been negotiated with Brussels.

It is probable that the Leave campaign succeeded in capturing the imagination of the electorate because the loss of trust in government and the splits in society are so profound. This decision is the most important that the UK has made in the last 50 years and it is really interesting that it has been based on so little factual information. It is an *emotional* decision.

Our own reflections and concluding remarks

We will now conclude this chapter by sharing some of our own reflections on the reasons, processes and outcomes of Brexit.

Firstly, we need to differentiate between the current position occupied by the UK as we write this chapter in the middle of 2018, which may well be different from the final position the UK will find itself occupying in 2020 when this book will be published. Whilst it is possible to predict some outcomes with a degree of certainty, other outcomes may well be unknown and unknowable at the present time.

A summary and analysis of our reflections:

David Cameron, the UK Prime Minister, went to Brussels to renegotiate the UK's role within the European Union. This attempt to influence the EU failed. Poised between the pro-European and anti-European factions of his government and the Conservative party, whilst also concerned about unexpected advances made by the new anti-European United Kingdom Independence Party (UKIP), Cameron called for a National Referendum. This was held in June 2016 with the voters split 52/48% in favour of leaving the EU.

Two new camps emerged: 'Remainers' in favour of staying in the EU and the 'Leavers', later called the Brexiteers. The country was split at all levels and across all layers: geographically, generationally, city/rural communities, in relation to class and income, educationally and between the 'urban elite' and the apparently less well-educated 'shires'. Support of a main political party did not correlate with how people voted in the Referendum, since both Conservatives and Labour supported and rejected both positions. The outcome was a surprise and, with no contingency plan for dealing with it, Cameron resigned and disappeared from public view.

The role of the Prime Minister was given to Theresa May, who was 'crowned' rather than elected, being the second woman ever to hold this office in Britain and the second woman leader within the Conservative party. May was a 'Remainer', but upon accepting the role, she promised to implement Brexit.

Her cabinet was split evenly between the two positions when negotiations with Brussels began. For a short time May appeared as if she believed this was a do-able job and as if she was the only 'strong and stable' element on the political stage. However, this process soon unravelled when continual internal fights and a further general election meant that instead of increasing her majority, it was reduced even further. In fact the Conservatives lost their majority, resulting in a hung parliament.

Theresa May then negotiated with the DUP of Northern Ireland to get their 10 votes which enabled her to get legislation passed if all Conservative and DUP MPs voted with the government.

This ushered in a period of leadership impasse, which is still with us as we write in May 2018. The cabinet shows the lowest collective capacity for dealing with the greatest of challenges the country faces since the outbreak of the World War II. Their negotiating position is weak, uncertain, frequently changing and regularly out-maneuvered by representatives of Brussels.

This strand of our political landscape was made additionally complicated in June 2017 by a tragic fire engulfing the residents of a high-rise block housing the poorest people living in the richest borough of London. This literally provided fuel for a class and party war, with Corbyn leading the Labour Party's attacks on the government for being callous. This was the point at which feelings became openly used as weapons fanned to an inferno via social media.

Interestingly, in keeping with the nostalgic fantasies mentioned at the start of this chapter, we see a new phenomenon – that of a surprising level of support for a particular public-school-educated, Conservative MP, not even a cabinet member, called Jacob Rees-Mogg, whose old-fashioned values and presentation seem to some in the population to symbolise the lost yet strangely recoverable riches of our past. Onto him they project the Messianic rescue of Great Britain! The signs are that he is preparing to challenge the current Prime Minister for her role.

This dynamic was set within a most complex set of international conditions, with a newly appointed President Trump, an ongoing Syrian war and an emboldened Russia. Referring to this, the Conservative MP Tom Tugendhat, said, 'Over the years Moscow has turned from being a corrupt state to an exporter of instability' (Sunday Times, 2018).

The cabinet has often looked weak, dogged by in-fighting and unable to plan. Furthermore, it has suffered from a lack of expertise to predict events and define trends with which to appraise the best options for future negotiations. There were a number of unanticipated challenges, still unresolved in spring 2018. The main issue was the Customs Union's impact on the border between Northern Ireland and Eire, and how it might affect the Good Friday agreement, which maintains an uneasy peace within the province.

Another issue is the actual shape of the United Kingdom resulting from the first Scottish referendum in 2014 which brought results favouring the Union with England – 55% in favour and 45% against – but with ambivalence about the value of staying connected. This issue has been shelved temporarily rather than resolved. The theme of territorial definition and British identity within a country comprising a multiplicity of ethnically diverse populations and different geographical regions is important. Are we in danger of becoming a Dis/United Kingdom or a Little England? As though to emphasise this, a best-selling book has just been published entitled *Brit(ish): On Race, Identity and Belonging*, by Afua Hirsch (2018).

Adding to the deepening of the original 52/48% split, we have the entrenched camp mentality which rules the narrative, the ease with which foreigners, be they newcomers, European immigrants, illegal immigrants or the settled immigrants from decades ago (the Windrush generation) and the Jewish population, become an easy target for projected hatred which could lead to violence.

In the meantime, Brussels exerts steady pressure. The UK through its mandated negotiators appears regularly less prepared to manage these difficult talks, exacerbated by the internal differences of opinion within the Cabinet. It is impossible not to conclude that Brussels is trying to make an example of the UK as a warning for other European countries should they ever dare to attempt withdrawing themselves.

Anxiety about Brexit not coming to fulfillment has never been higher. Given that the Remainers and the Leavers have been unable to come to an agreement about what is best for the country, there is a likelihood of settling on a classically British 'fudge'[5] solution to Brexit: a compromise between the two warring factions of the Conservative party. This might bring Brexit 'in name only' as the UK would remain in the customs union, allowing EU migration to continue, the European Court of Justice would continue its jurisdiction etc. without the UK having any influence or voice in the Union.

Unfinished as these negotiations are at the present time, a question should be asked: What price are we, the citizens of the United Kingdom, likely to pay for our decision to leave the European Union? We can predict that paradoxically, those who voted most vociferously to leave who were already the less well-off within our society, those who were less educated, less travelled, less exposed to European workers, i.e. UK citizens living in smaller, more homogeneous communities, rather than in great metropolitan enclaves, will not do well. These are the most likely victims of a financial downturn which might come about after we leave the EU. Having said that, for a sovereign country with its legendary parliamentary democracy, the United Kingdom may well feel imprisoned and resentful that EU negotiators seem to make it impossible to leave a 'club' which the UK willingly joined in 1972, the membership of which it has now democratically voted to terminate.

As long as uncertainty prevails regarding the/a Customs Union/partnership and the role of the City of London, which is the financial hub of both the UK and the EU, the UK's economic prospects are not guaranteed. It is already visible that security in the UK, despite being a member of NATO, may well depend on a range of temporary opportunistic alliances forged afresh with every new set of circumstances. This has already occurred when the Prime Minister successfully galvanized 28 countries to support her condemnation of Russia in relation to the Novichok poisoning of the Skripal father and daughter. One cannot escape the symbolism in these numbers!

In no time at all, there was a knock on the UK's door when Trump asked the UK, France and Germany to form a temporary coalition with the USA to bomb a Syrian chemical factory. Immediately, we see another coalition being forged to support the Iranian nuclear agreement after Trump's departure from the deal.

What nimble, agile and clever politicians the UK needs in government to be able continually to appraise and re-calibrate our response to these fast-changing threats.

Could Corbyn take such an initiative were the mantle of government to fall upon him and the Labour Party? These are the challenges of post Brexit UK that we already have the capacity to predict. The other predictable danger is the increased likelihood of the UK courting morally dubious regimes in order to attract future trading agreements.

Looking at the SWOT analysis we see the United Kingdom as a country that until now has been centrally positioned in the world and still is potentially capable of playing an important role, but the threats and weaknesses tend to cancel out the identified opportunities and strengths. One cannot be surprised that the calculus of gains and losses is neutral. What are we fighting for if at the end of the process we are neither much better off, nor much worse off but in a neutral space? Lost in space is a good metaphor here given the loss of our role in the European Galileo Space programme . . .

Even if the UK holds onto its position, rebuilds the economy, is once more a vibrant, thriving modern nation, it is likely to take a long time to re-establish the UK independently on the world stage. In the meantime what can be offered to citizens who opted for 'Leave', if their status suffers more than the rest of the population? Is the government equipped to consider a future within the United Kingdom with a possibly tumultuous mixture of heightened racial tension and angry identity-based politics, together with the Millennials' ongoing intergenerational disappointment with the 'baby boomers' (those born after World War II), not to mention economic worries and disparities in the wealth and health of the UK population? None of the political parties seem equipped to deal with these complexities and as time goes on Brexit appears more like an unresolvable Rubik's Cube.

What about the capacity of the United Kingdom to remain united? With Northern Ireland and Scotland (whose leader is asking for a second Scottish referendum) both strong 'Remainers' with deep connections to Europe, the Union is likely to be strained. Furthermore, the resurgence of the Irish paramilitary movement could use Brexit as an excuse to 'kick the British out of Ireland' (BBC Newsnight 15th May 2018).

These are some of the negative predictions we can make at present. On the more positive side there are other questions:

Does our fate as a country depend on the future of the European Union?

What if the European Union were also to change: for instance by becoming a smaller more exclusive club accessible only to the Eurozone countries? Given the difficulty of holding together 28 countries in a highly centralised bureaucracy, what if the EU fragmented further? Were that to happen, the EU might eventually fall back on the rump group comprising the six countries that originally formed the EEC.

Alternatively, is it possible that this European coalition might evolve into a more decentralised federal structure, or perhaps even disappear altogether in years to come? If that were to happen, what would happen to Germany and European stability once the corset of European unity is undone?

These centrifugal forces giving rise to fragmentation are dancing to the tune of a greater power. Which nations will decline and which will then emerge as more powerful given such profound tectonic shifts?

In the meantime, the skin of our split and wounded country has been temporarily soothed by the spectacle of a royal wedding when Prince Harry, the sixth in line to the throne, recently married a mixed-race American divorcee. This act of love and union jointly indicated to the UK and to the world that in the 21st century nothing is impossible and all assumptions can be revisited, if not revised.

Under these circumstances might the UK fragment into its constituent nations of Scotland, Wales, Northern Ireland and England or eventually even into geographical regions?

Or, would it eventually end up in the best position as the country that started the process of European fragmentation by seeking autonomy earlier and was then able to re-build its sovereign identity well ahead of other countries?

In other words: Far from the madding crowd . . . ?

Post scriptum

The manuscript was sent to the Editors 29th May 2018. As we prepare to send this chapter to the printers in July 2019, Britain remains the fifth largest economy for the moment. Brexit has not yet been delivered and may never happen. This results from the country being split, the Leave vs. the Remain camps' hostility to each other, the resignation of another Prime Minister and Parliament still unable to come to an agreement, resulting in ongoing political upheaval within the UK.

Acknowledgements

The SWOT Analysis table copyright by Halina Brunning
  Image by Kristof Bien

Notes

1 'Far from the madding crowd' is a place where few people go: many people like the idea of escaping to somewhere that is truly far from the madding crowd (Definition from the *Cambridge Advanced Learner's Dictionary & Thesaurus* © Cambridge University Press).
2 Reprinted with permission of the publisher Taylor & Francis.
3 The Windrush generation represents those Caribbeans who started to arrive from the Caribbean colonies from 1948 following the British Nationality Act which gave citizens of the United Kingdom and colonies status with the right to settle in the UK.
4 VUCA is a concept first developed in the 1990s by the US Army War College. Since then it has become a mainstay of US military doctrine and in recent years emerged into British military thinking (Rennie, op cit.).
5 Fudge – a fake solution which aims to obfuscate the real truth.

References

Ashworth-Hayes, S. (2016, August 31). Your cut-out-and-keep list of top 19 Brexiteer promises. *Infacts*. https://infacts.org/cut-keep-list-top-19-brexiteer-promises/

Bion, W. (1961). *Experiences in groups*. London: Tavistock.

Brunning, H., & Khaleelee, O. (2018). Danse Macabre spinning faster. *Journal of Organisational and Social Dynamics, 18*(1), 131–153.

D'Ancona, M. (2016, June 15). Brexit: How a fringe idea took hold of the Tory party. *Guardian,* front page.

Gilligan, A. (2017, November 5). Revealed: How Russia invaded the heart of the British power. *Sunday Times,* pp. 24–25.

Hirsch, A. (2018). *Brit(ish): On race, identity and belonging*. Jonathan Cape.

Khaleelee, O. (2016). Boarding school, Brexit, and our leaders' judgement. *Organisational & Social Dynamics, 16*(2), 271–276.

Rennie, M. (2018, June). Volatile uncertain complex and ambiguous in "Overlapping interests in a complex and ambiguous world". *The Psychologist, Journal of the British Psychological Society, 31*, 10–13.

The Sunday Times. (2018, April 29). Exposed: Russians tried to swing election for Corbyn by Insight team, in conjunction with Swansea University, front page.

10

WILL BREXIT BRAKE THE EU?

Shmuel Bernstein

Prologue

The gist of Erich Neumann's development theory, in his words, is "Away from the Mother-world! Forward to the Father-world!" ([1949] 1970, p. 402) – from the matriarchate to the patriarchate. At the beginning there is only small masculine germ in the Maternal Uroboros. It is a spark of consciousness slowly developing and separating itself from the symbiotic matrix, becoming the ego of the individual, and patriarchal culture, in the collective society. According to Neumann, culture is created through a process of cultivation of the masculine aspects of both individual and society. As he put it in *The Fear of the Feminine* (1994, p. 28):

> Sociologically and politically it is expressed in the development of a patriarchal culture . . . The patriarchal line of the development of consciousness leads to a condition where patriarchal-masculine values are dominant, values that are often conceived in direct opposition to those of the archetypal Feminine and of the unconscious. This development, directed by the archetypally conditioned cultural canon . . . leads to the separation of consciousness from the unconscious, to the evolution of the independent conscious system with a masculine ego as the centre, to a suppression of the unconscious, and to its greatest possible repression from the ego's field of vision.

When I mention male and female aspects, or masculinity and femininity, or father and mother realms or worlds, I refer to these aspects in the collective (culture, community), or in the individual aspects of the psyche of both men and women.

David Cameron gave up his authority in June 2016, when under the pressure of MPs of his party, he agreed to hold an in-out referendum in the UK. Immediately after the 'Leave' results, he resigned from his leading post. By this act he missed a second chance to take authority and ignore the unexpected results.

David Cameron was not the only male authority that withdrew from his leading position: also Boris Johnson and Nigel Farage, the leaders of the 'Leave' movement, ran away from leading the process of separation from the EU. Theresa May took the PM position and Diane James became the UKIP's first woman leader (though for a very short while). Since men represent the masculine aspect (of the individual and the collective), and women, the feminine aspect, my working assumption for the moment is that the male aspect in the UK, together with that of Europe and of the Western World as a whole, is weakening. In another paper of mine (Bernstein, 2016), I have referred to it as "The Western World has become Salmacis fountain". Just to summarise it to those not acquainted with the mythological story: The naiad Salmacis forced herself on the young Hermaphroditus while swimming in the fountain, and prayed to the gods to turn them into one person. When Hermaphroditus came out of the water and realised that he had become a hermaphrodite, he asked his parents to curse the fountain so that every man who touched its water would weaken suddenly and become half a man.

The project of the EU is a brave step towards a better organised community in Europe. The expectations from such a superstructure were for an improved economic situation, less national and local tensions and better cultural integration and productivity.

Culture according to C.G. Jung (1952, 1956) and E. Neumann (1949, 1970) is a creation of the patriarchate – the masculine aspect of community, which is parallel to the ego – the masculine aspect of the individual. The better organised the ego and the culture – the more developed they are. The course of development is always away from the matriarchate – the mother's realm (unconsciousness, domestic and safe, materialistic) and towards the patriarchate – the father's realm (consciousness, demanding and competitive reality, mission-oriented, rational and even spiritual), but it is always ambivalent – the challenging and curiosity evoking of father's realm is also discouraging frightening and infuriating, and the abandoned mother's realm, is always alluring to a passive and pleasurable state of regression.

Development from the Kleinian point of view (M. Klein, 1959) is the movement from the paranoid-schizoid position to the depressive position. In the European realm this stepping forward involves loss and mourning of idealistic wishes concerning the EU. Practically, it means the loosening of local national identity, of loosening control on local national governance and economies, accepting changes in lifestyle and in the composition of the population, in other words, being ready for major changes without losing confidence in the EU authorities and mutual trust.

Keeping mutual trust and confidence in the EU elected authorities, is trusting the father, or the male aspect, while keeping away from the deluded safety of the mother's domain. However there is a problem: The male aspect in Europe, as part of the Western World has been weakening for several decades. This is in line with Kant's (1720, para 28) words when writing about the sublimity of war: "a long peace generally brings about a predominant commercial spirit, and along with it, low selfishness, cowardice and effeminacy, and debases the disposition of the people".

126 Shmuel Bernstein

Here are some expressions of the weakening of the male aspect in actual segments of Western society:

1) The sperm count has declined over the last decades. Some scientists even warn of a sperm-count crisis, but there is an undecided debate about this issue (Fisch, 2008; Merzenich, 2010).

2) The LGBTQIA+ (Lesbian, Gay, Bisexual, Transgender, Queer, Intersex and Asexual) community is growing and becoming politically influential. On the one hand, this sector of the population represents the advanced relation of Western society to the various combinations of masculinity and femininity, and it can be assumed that only a firm patriarchate can contain femininity without fear. On the other hand, it symbolises a decline in virility – the symptomatic result of bathing in Salmacis fountain.

3) Single parenting is a growing phenomenon, again it expresses the tolerance of Western society to nontraditional relations between genders, though research findings (Weitoft, Hjern, Hauglund, & Rosen, 2003) suggest an increase of all sort of pathologies in children reared with no father, especially among male children.

4) There is rise of the 'mammone': Two-thirds of young Italian adults (18–34) live at home with their parents. In 2010, a minister in the last Berlusconi government called for laws to encourage youths to leave home by 18. The then–Innovation Minister, Renato Brunetta, said it was needed to "deal with the culture of mummy's boys and big babies". Mr. Brunetta added: "All these young people think they're living in a free hotel, and actually there's a price they pay. It allows their parents to keep control of them, emotionally, socially and financially" (Independent.co.uk, 9.2.2015). This rise is prominent in Italy but not limited to Italian society alone.

5) Man in the Western world is no more a begetter of progeny – the birth rate (Total fertility rate 2015) in most countries of the West is lower than 1.8 – the red line of survival of a community. This brings us straight to the immigration problem: the ambivalence towards immigrants in Western countries is rising. On the one hand, as Angela Merkel said when she supported large-scale immigrant absorption in Germany, there is a growing need for workers, especially unskilled labourers in the developed countries. On the other hand, masses of immigrants threaten the identity of local communities, which confront difficulties in assimilating the newcomers. This process creates a new situation that requires a determined strategy to contain large new and different populations in local ones.

6) There are allegations about Barack Obama, that under his presidency there has been a decrease in the status and authority of the USA, as the first world super-power. Governance barriers in democratic regimes of Western states bring authorities to a helpless stance against anti-democratic ideologies and movements, and against terrorism. Radical agents can preach against secular democracy and recruit young European citizens to radical Islamic terror organisations with no interference.

7) Democratic regimes refrain from setting a clear decisive policy of which migrants to accept.

8) Politically correct censorship in the West is relentless, sometimes almost as tyrannical as the Religion Police in some theocracies. The human need for aggression and obscene words is suppressed and channeled to shadowy courses.

9) The Islamic world, in a pre-patriarchal stage (Bernstein, 2015), exposed to Western affluence and hedonism, is frightened and challenged by the hermaphroditic stance of Western culture. It reacts with radical fanaticism and terror, as if in a desperate attempt to put the effeminate West under a burqa, allowing the world to develop into a spiritual patriarchate, from its point of view – an Islamic caliphate.

10) Leaders of undemocratic regimes, like that of Kim Jong-un of North Korea, Ali Khamenei and Mahmoud Ahmadinejad (until August 2013) of Iran, Vladimir Putin of Russia and others allow themselves to challenge international law, regulations and agreements, taking advantage of the weakening processes in the Western super-powers and the Western leaders' reluctance to engage in aggressive confrontations.

As a compensatory dynamic, nationalism and extreme right-wing parties in Europe gain growing support, citizens of the UK voted for leaving the EU and Donald Trump scorns PC trends and claims he will make America great again, thus gaining more support for his presidency.

11) If we look at the dynamics of the last British vote to leave the EU, it is another, new example for the weakening of the masculine aspect in the Western world: A political leader, ex-PM David Cameron, decides to hold a referendum – to follow the people who voted for his party instead of leading them in his course with such a critical question as whether to leave or to remain in the EU. This act is a metaphorical bathing in Salmacis pond instead of taking the father role.

Giving up the father position is undermining the male aspect, impairing the ego, for the collective as well as for the individual. It summons up danger to society, to law and order, to security and a threat of disintegration, loss of identity and even chaos.

The continent Europe was named after Europa, the beautiful Phoenician princess seduced and abducted to Crete by Zeus in the form of white bull (Ovid). In this mythological story, Europa is in a traditional state of passive and devoted woman. This is an ancient Cretan story, and Crete was the centre of the Minoan culture. The Minoans seem to have worshipped primarily goddesses, and their culture has been described as being based on a "matriarchal religion" (Marinatos, 2004) in which the bull was one of the major symbols. According to some scholars royal succession in Minoan Crete descended matrilineally – from the queen to her firstborn daughter – and the queen's husband would have become the Minos, or war chief. It is probable that the mythological Minos, king of Crete represents the turning point from pre-patriarchal to patriarchal civilisation in Europe. This assumption gains support from evident connections and reciprocal influences with the old Egyptian

128 Shmuel Bernstein

kingdom of Pharaohs Amenhotep. Amenhotep IV, who later changed his name to Akhenaton (Echnaton) died perhaps in 1336 BC or 1334 BC – at the last century of the Minoan culture in Crete. He is especially noted for abandoning traditional Egyptian polytheism and introducing worship centred on the solar deities and giving them a status above mere gods. He is considered to be half-monotheistic and this solar monotheism is an advanced step toward patriarchate.

Europa gave Zeus three children and got three presents from him: Talos, the bronze giant whose mission was to guard the shores of Europe in Crete; Laelaps, the swift dog; and the Javelin, both never missed a hunting, three powerful phallic symbols. It is not clear whether Europa made any use of these presents, but they all were lost or abused by others: Talos permitted the witch Medea to take off his golden blood and collapsed, Laelaps and the Javelin were given by Minos (son of Zeus and Europa) to Procris to seduce her to betray her husband and lie with him. Later, Procris gave them to Cephalus, her husband, as an appeasing present. Cephalus sent out the hound Laelaps against the uncatchable Teumessian fox, so they have been caught in a paradoxical chase and Zeus has turned them both into a constellation in the sky. The Javelin was tragically used by Cephalus to kill Procris taking her for a wild animal when she sneaked up on to see if he was betraying her with another lover. So, we can say that Europa was left unarmed – as a symbol of the mature feminine (positive) aspect, the Anima (the contra-sexual archetype in man's psyche – the feminine aspect of his psyche), in contrast with the more archaic Great Mother who can be also powerful and relentless. The Anima needs the ego – the mature male aspect, in a good conjunction – fertile intercourse, to promote development.

Europe seems, symbolically of course, to suffer from a Father Complex, like Europa with Zeus. This continent had been invaded and conquered and possessed along its history by external and internal forces: by the Greek and Roman Empires, the Frankish Empire, the Vikings and Normans, the Mongols and other wild tribes, the Ottomans, the Habsburg house and Austro-Hungarian Empire, the Nazis and the Russian communists, and was redeemed by the USA and USSR armies. NATO, the European defence treaty, was established and resourced, until this day, by the United States and not by an autonomic strong European collaboration. It came out from the unconscious that NATO motto is "Animus in consulendo liber" translated inaccurately to English as "A mind unfettered in deliberation". It was chosen to reflect the spirit of consultation in NATO, quoted from Sallust, who cited Cato the Younger's address to the Roman senate: "But there were other qualities which made them [our forefathers] great, which we do not possess at all". Here he mentions several qualities (efficiency at home, a just rule abroad), and ends with: "in counsel an independent spirit free from guilt or passion". The Animus (spirit) is the concept used by Jung when referring to the male aspect of the woman (in a more modern way I would say that it parallels with the Ego which is the male aspect in both man and woman). It can be said that NATO was founded to be a European phallus but . . . in deliberation, and with no passion or guilt. So Europe is still waiting for the inner spouse – for her male aspect to develop, for Talos revival.

As mentioned above, the EU project is a brave step toward a better organised community, meant to be a "quest of the hero" that will further advance the male aspect of Europe – to develop a continental Ego which will bring Europe to a higher stage of organisation and functioning.

Since there are developmental gaps among European states and societies, the process of development towards one united super-state, such as the USA, is slow and cautious. Nevertheless, one can clearly see the expressions of the antagonistic aspect of the ambivalence in the refraining of several European countries from membership in the EU, and in regressive tendencies, as in Greek society which was accused as lazy and underproductive, to abuse the money of the rich members of the EU.

The British vote for 'leave' in the last referendum, Brexit, is a real threat to brake the EU from further development. Symbolically, it is an assault on father – on the masculine aspect. But this attack on development is also a product of the former weakness of the masculine aspect in European and Western society in general. The leadership of the EU project was too hesitant and fragile (the undetermined ways in which it coped with the economic crisis in Greece, with the invasion of Putin into the Ukraine and with refraining from decisive migration policy) to such an extent that the elder generation of British citizens might interpret 'Remain' as a regression into a collective unity or rather into Basic Assumption Oneness, as described by P. M. Turquet (1974, p. 357): "members seek to join in a powerful union with an omnipotent force, unobtainably high, to surrender self for passive participation, and thereby feel existence, well-being and wholeness". They support 'Leave' as if it is a step towards autonomic development, in the same way as other European citizens are afraid to give up the safety of traditional identity and belonging, so much as growing numbers of them react by strengthening the right-wing and nationalistic parties even in the most advanced countries in Europe. It seems 'Leave' voters in England, EU opponents and nationalists in Europe consider themselves as daring to take an autonomous step, but this is probably more a defensive macho act, or falling into the opposite pole – the Basic Assumption Me-ness which Lawrence, Bain, and Gould (1996, p. 33) describe as hold on a well-worn niche like "'man's home is his castle' . . . because the changing reality of the real environment and real experience of external reality is denied". This is a fluctuation between two opposite basic assumptions and not the real work group opus of "Away from the Mother-world! Forward to the Father-world!" (Neumann, 1949, p. 402) needed for building the Collective Ego, the male aspect, the culture. Just to remind us here the above-mentioned withdrawal of the three male leaders after Brexit results as symbolising the shrinking male aspect. These regressive tendencies might pull Europe into nationalistic reserve and to all the potential implications of economic crisis and worse – political unrest and conflicts.

A different way to look at the dynamics of European culture is by using the Jungian Archetypes of Senex and Puer (Hillman, 1983). The Senex, old man in Latin, is wisdom, experience, reflection and connection to original sources of heritage and tradition on the positive side, and conservatism, rigidity and luck of energy

130 Shmuel Bernstein

and enthusiasm on the negative side. The Puer, a youth in Latin, is energy, curiosity, innovations, adventures and flexibility on the positive side, and lack of experience, recklessness, ignorance and radicalism on the negative side of the archetype. Any individual or collective needs a balance on the spectrum between these two archetypal principles, or as James Hillman (1983, p. 122) put it: "The archetype of old and new can't really be separated". The European fear of development toward an EU ultra-structure is activating the Senex archetype and oppressing the Puer archetype. Strengthening traditional-local-national entities and identities and resisting innovation might bring Europe to stagnation, and damages its political status in the whole world as well as mutilates the ability to cope with inner European problems.

So, one of the major European problems of the present time is how to revive the Puer principle — how to restore libidinal energy, to be an entrepreneurial culture again, to encourage innovations which are so important in the process of globalisation. The desire to revive Europe by absorbing masses of motivated migrants was disappointed by the unexpected problems of resistance to assimilation to the European lifestyle and worse than that — the antagonism, hostility and even acts of terror against the welcoming countries.

It seems that a key point was touched for a moment by Andrea Leadsom when she contested with Theresa May for the Conservatives leadership after Cameron's leave (resignation). Mrs. Leadsom put herself forward as the 'real world' candidate, and in an interview with *The Times* she suggested that being a mother, unlike Mrs. May, meant she had a particularly strong 'stake' in the future of the country, because her children and grandchildren will "directly be part of what happens next". This comment was not just un-politically-correct, but it also touched on a common denial of an essential problem in Europe — the low rate of childbirth. Symbolically, a child means renewal, hope, fertility and creativity, and lack of children is sterility and stagnation.

The Puer archetype is shrinking in Europe also because the young generations do not have collective initiation ceremonies and are not challenged by any collective missions. That makes them confused, disorientated and immature. Maybe this is one of the causes for turning to religion, sometimes to other religions, the most extreme case here, is those European Christians by origin, that convert themselves to Islam and volunteer to fight with ISIS.

In conclusion, the main danger to the EU is the Western World's weakening male aspect, or better said assault on father. It is expressed in the decreasing birth rate, in an absence of cultural initiation and rites of passage and in resistance to collaborative efforts to erect a European super-state.

The younger generation in the UK supported the movement to 'Remain' with the EU. They were defeated by the elder generation's support for 'Leave', yet there is still hope in Hillman's (1989, p. 227) characterisation of the Puer:

> (But) the parental complex is not alone responsible for the crippling, laming, or castration of the archetypal Puer figures. This laming refers to especial

weakness and helplessness at the beginning of any enterprise. This is inherent in the one-sided vertical direction, its Icarus-Ganymede propensity of flying and falling. It must be weak on earth, because it is not at home on earth . . . there is difficulty at the beginning; the child is in danger, easily gives up. The horizontal world, the space-time continuum which we call 'reality', is not its world . . . Death [of an idea or enterprise. s.b.] does not matter because the Puer gives the feeling that it can come again another time, make another start.

It is in line with C. G. Jung's (1930–1931, para 767) words on initiation and the development of masculinity:

> Whoever protects himself against what is new and strange and regresses to the past falls into the same neurotic condition as the man who identifies himself with the new and runs away from the past . . . In principle both are doing the same thing: they are reinforcing their narrow range of consciousness instead of shattering it in the tension of opposites and building up a state of wider and higher consciousness.

I would say that building the EU could be "building up a state of wider and higher consciousness".

In line with these reflections, Martin Schulz, the EU parliament chief, warned British negotiators against "playing one country against another hoping that by a split within the European Union you would get a better result". And in his meeting with PM May, he added that "Brexit would be a disaster for Britain and the EU". He also said "The best possible deal with the EU is membership with the EU" and stated that "the union is a community with a shared destiny, a model of society and not an accountants club" (*Express* 23 September 2016).

Lately (*The Telegraph*, 14 October 2016), Donald Tusk, the president of the European Council, warned: "Britain may decide against Brexit when they realise just how painful it will be". And he added: "The only real alternative to a hard Brexit is no Brexit".

So, it seems that the UK and the EU states in their present crisis need desperately to make place for the Puer principle, but it should be Hillman's expanded and more inclusive concept of this archetype including "the Hero, the Divine Child, the figures of Eros, the King's son, the Son of the Great Mother, the Psychopompos, Mercury-Hermes, Trickster, and the Messiah. In him we see a mercurial range of these 'personalities': narcissistic, inspired, effeminate, phallic, inquisitive, inventive, pensive, passive, fiery, and capricious" (1983, p. 227). This energy is needed to redeem Europe from her old 'La Belle et La Bette' complex (it is surprising to find how many versions this story has in Europe), of Europa abducted by the Bull-Great Father, and to make place for a prince charming – her own Animus to rise, an Animus with passion and guilt!

References

Bernstein, S. (2015). Globalisation versus clash of civilisations, facing developmental gaps. In S. Carta, A. Adorisio, & R. Mercurio (Eds.), *The analyst in the Polis* (Vol. I). Amazon e-book.

Bernstein, S. (2016, August). *The Western world as Salmacis fountain.* A paper read in The XX International Congress for Analytical Psychology: Anima Mundi in Transition, Kyoto. Available English text.

Fisch, H. (2008). Declining worldwide sperm counts: Disproving a myth. *Urologic Clinics of North America, 35,* 137–146.

Hillman, J. (1983). *Inter-views* (pp. 114–123). New York: Harper & Row.

Hillman, J. (1989). *A blue fire.* New York: Harper & Row.

Jung, C. G. (1930–1931). *The stages of life.* CW, Vol. 8, para 767.

Jung, C. G. (1952, 1956). *Symbols of transformation.* CW, Vol. 5.

Kant, E. (1720). *Critique of judgement.*

Klein, M. (1959). Our adult world and its roots in infancy. In *Envy and gratitude & other works* (pp. 247–263). New York: Delta Books, 1975.

Lawrence, W. G., Bain, A., & Gould, L. (1996). The fifth basic assumption. *Free Associations, 6*(37), part I, 28–55.

Marinatos, N. (2004). Minoan and Mycenaean civilisations. In S. I. Johnston (Ed.), *Religions of the ancient world: A guide* (pp. 206–207). Cambridge, MA: Harvard University Press.

Merzenich, H., Zeeb, H., & Blettner, M. (2010). Decreasing sperm quality: A global problem? *BioMed Central Public Health, 10,* 24.

Neumann, E. (1949, 1970). *The origins and history of consciousness.* Bollingen Series XLII. Princeton, NJ: Princeton University Press.

Neumann, E. (1994). *The fear of the feminine.* Bollingen Series LXI-4. Princeton, NJ: Princeton University Press.

Ovid. (1986). *Metamorphoses,* ii.833–iii.2, vi.103–107. trans. A.D. Melville.

Turquet, P. M. (1974). Ch. 5: Leadership: The individual and the group. In G. S. Gibbard, J. J. Hartman, & R. D. Mann (Eds.), *Analysis of group* (pp. 71–87). San Francisco, CA: Jossey-Bass.

Weitoft, G. R., Hjern, A., Hauglund, B., & Rosen, M. (2003, January 25). Mortality, sever morbidity, and injury in children living with single parents in Sweden: A population-based study. *The Lancet, 361*(9354).

PART THREE

Practical interventions

11

NATIONAL NIGHTMARE

Thoughts on the genesis and legacy of perpetrator trauma

M. Gerard Fromm

In the last footnote to the Introduction of his magnificent *A German Generation* (2012), Thomas Kohut quotes his psychoanalyst father:

> If the depth psychologist (or the historian, for that matter) is to make a contribution to the understanding of man's role in history and his control over his destiny, then he must try to extend his empathic observation not only to the victims but also to the persecutors, not only to the martyrs but also to the torturers. He must discover the human, the all-too-human, whether in the normal . . . or in the psychopathological, in the good and in the evil.
>
> *(Kohut, 1969–70, p. 119)*

Thomas Kohut is a psychoanalytically trained historian but he is also a son who learned deeply from his father. Taking up the latter's encouragement to find the all-to-human within the horrific, Kohut proposed that the Austen Riggs Center's Erikson Institute – of which I was the director and he a Board member – convene an interdisciplinary conference, which came to be called "The Legacy of Perpetrator Trauma in Groups and Families". With the help of a number of German colleagues, Kohut invited the key participants – Alexandra Senfft, Gerhard Wilke and Marcus Carney (Carney, 2007) – and I directed what turned out to be a profound, intellectually stimulating and emotionally intense two days. This paper is one outcome of that conference; written just as societal dynamics were turning toward the populism and authoritarianism we have since seen develop more fully.

For two consecutive years, the Erikson Institute's Fall Conference had studied the transmission of trauma, the clinical relevance of which was becoming increasingly clear. Papers from these conferences were published under the title *Lost in Transmission: Studies of Trauma across Generations* (Fromm, 2012). They joined a literature that began with Selma Fraiberg's classic paper "Ghosts in the Nursery" (1975) and expanded enormously as the suffering of second-generation Holocaust survivors became known and treated. These studies have taught us that what human beings cannot contain of their experience – what has been traumatically overwhelming, unbearable, unthinkable – falls out of social discourse, but onto and into the next generation, as an affective sensitivity, a strange symptom, a chaotic urgency, in the words of one of our presenters, Gerhard Wilke, "an encapsulated presence", and sometimes an unconscious mission.

The challenge of empathy

This new conference was radically different from the earlier two in the subjects of its focus. As Wilke pointed out in the conference brochure, "psychoanalytic understanding of the working through of such traumatic material is largely based on work done with survivors, émigrés, refugees and their children. What we know less well are the transgenerational phenomena of children of perpetrators" – a generation not guilty by deed but so often caught up in feeling ashamed, guilty, responsible and horrified by association. In this conference we hoped to learn about the configuration and dynamics of this particular traumatic history.

In a clinical case conference some time ago, a young male patient told the staff that the hospital "is haunted by the forces of the dead. They are here as much as there are helping people here." To the degree that a person is unconsciously preoccupied with what may well be a haunting family history – who even at times may represent this hauntedness to and for his family – to that degree, the person's subjectivity is "lost in transmission", sometimes with tragic consequences: the German patient whose grandfather worked in the V-2 program at the beginning of World War II and who, years later, hurled himself from his dormitory balcony, thereby becoming a human missile. The Austrian patient whose suicide attempts always involved the products of his grandfather's pharmaceutical company, itself implicated in a horrific Holocaust history.

The task of the "Legacy of Perpetrator Trauma" conference was to explore this phenomenon through the stories of post-war German and Austrian generations. We hoped to help clinicians and scholars revisit and understand more deeply the psychological aftermath of the Third Reich through a consideration of the inner conflicts of those who may carry this psychic burden, on behalf of their families, their society and, in fact, for the rest of us. What might we learn about individual, family and group dynamics associated with the offspring of perpetrators, and what are the implications of this learning for society?

The tradition of the Erikson Institute is to hold interdisciplinary *working conferences*, by which we mean that learning occurs through active dialogue among presenters and members; and that the process dimension of the conversation sometimes illuminates what we are talking about. In this conference, that process dimension was inescapable. We were dealing with an extremely serious subject and highly charged material. Members' joining this conference represented an act of courage

Thoughts on the legacy of perpetrator trauma **137**

because it inevitably meant encountering genuinely disturbing feelings, and inevitably challenged us to think more deeply, more discerningly and, as Heinz Kohut suggested, more empathically about those feelings.

Freud spoke about every family's "archaic heritage" (1939, p. 38), and one task of transmission turns out to be the generational struggle to resist the dissociation of that heritage, to recognize, in Davoine's and Gaudilliere's phrase, the "cut-out" unconscious (2004, p. 61) – cut out, that is, from the official narrative, whether that narrative is the family's or the society's – and to bring its full, tragic story into social discourse. How the unconscious gets "cut out" – and an astonishing 1930s dream journal kept by Charlotte Beradt (1968), to which I will return later, may open a window onto that process – leads to one set of questions. How it gets re-inscribed – the profound task of telling the story – is where the conference began.

The danger of love

The first theme to emerge in the conference was a simple but powerful one: How to love when the object of that love is implicated in horrific crimes. Alexandra Senfft, a freelance journalist, whose personal story, *Silence Hurts: A German Family History*, was published in 2007, put it in hypothetical form: "What if my grandfather had taken me onto his lap and I had begun to love him?" (This and other quotes come from the presentations and discussions at the conference.) Other similar, not at all hypothetical, statements spoke to the visceral experience of trying to contain the good and the bad at the same time, of vomiting out at the moment of taking in, of genuine love and horror at the feeling of loving.

It was as though it fell to the next generation to at least attempt to integrate what they experienced with their parents and what they also knew about them, an integration that the parents themselves seemed not to make at all. Rather the perpetrator generation, the generation of "knowing and not knowing", seemed essentially to be living out what Melanie Klein (1946) called the paranoid-schizoid position, the place where at all costs good and bad must be kept separate. The maturational effort toward the depressive position, that is, the task of holding the good and bad in the same space toward some sort of integration, fell to the next generation. It was a profoundly difficult emotional assignment.

Part of the integrative task that fell to the children of perpetrators included feeling the guilt and shame of their parents' actions, which they themselves had warded off. Their children's responses took more than one form. We heard examples of essentially manic efforts at reparation, not necessarily directed to the victims of Nazis, but to other suffering people in far-off countries. Not only were these efforts frenetic and obsessive, manic reparation defensively kept at bay the very feelings of guilt motivating it. We noted as well friction between this generation and their children when the latter did not want to continue the reparation project but rather hoped to go on with their "own lives". This was extraordinarily difficult, given their parents' excruciating pain and the daunting task of individuating from the chaos of such immense family disaster.

Another form this effort to process parental perpetration took, in the second and third generations, was identification with the victims, sometimes very literally and to a quasi-psychotic degree. Vamik Volkan in his recent book *A Nazi Legacy* (2015) tells the story of a man who in his sleep leaves his bed to frantically open windows night after night. Though this man's troubles were many and complex, this particular stubborn and mysterious symptom was eventually understood in relation to his Nazi grandfather, who murdered Jews by gassing them inside a school bus. His victims – like his grandson years later – frantically tried to open windows.

Alexandra Senfft brought two questions to her presentation: her mother's question, "Why did they kill my father?" and her own, "Why did my mother die?" In the story, Ms. Senfft's mother loved her own father and was devastated when he was hung for war crimes when she was 14. Over time, as she learned about his Nazi career and his role in deporting 65,000 Jews, she became increasingly depressed and alcoholic. In a family context where her own mother refused to believe, or to speak about, what had happened and who admitted no guilt or shame at all, Ms. Senfft's mother spiraled into madness.

Or perhaps into a mad sanity. In her alcoholic state, she would panic about being closed in and scream for help. Davoine and Gaudilliere (2004) are convinced that the psychotic patient is madly conducting a research into the rupture between her family and the social fabric, a rupture brought about through trauma and betrayal. Beyond her screaming about the suffocating silence of her family, was Ms. Senfft's mother also living out her fragmented imagining of what her father's victims might have experienced? And was that part of her tragic death, self-inflicted while drunk, in scalding water?

One more thing Ms. Senfft's mother did while drunk, much more in the direction of an active transmission: She talked to her oldest child and as Ms. Senfft said, "I let her". Frightened of "becoming" her, Ms. Senfft needed to know why her mother died, one year after her grandmother did, and boxes of letters left to her became a way into that terrible story. Ms. Senfft took up the task of inscription of a cut-out history, the task of "how to give my mother a voice".

But she then encountered the same terror her mother felt, the terrifying dilemma of exploding the silence or sinking into it. In a sense, by taking the risk of learning and then speaking the truth of her family history, she found herself in another transmission role: destroying the family myth, she *became the perpetrator*, the one who inflicts on her family, *for the first time*, the horrific images and feelings that have been so strenuously split off and kept at bay. The psychoanalyst Donald Winnicott once articulated a remarkable intuition: "The patient needs to 'remember' . . . but it is not possible to remember something that has not yet happened, and this thing of the past has not happened yet because the patient was not there for it to happen to" (1974, p. 105). It's as though Ms. Senfft's family had dissociated themselves so thoroughly from their own lives that, in a very powerful sense, they were at risk of experiencing *in the future, at her hands* the trauma of what they had already done.

Ms. Senfft experienced enormous and sustained family resistance to her writing her book. She was criticized, demeaned and shunned. "Drive carefully" after one

Thoughts on the legacy of perpetrator trauma **139**

such family meeting had a menacing ring to it. Ultimately she lost her family when her book came out, though, crucially, not her whole family: her father supported her throughout the project. As she said, "I don't know what I would have done if he had turned against me." And, in a sense, her mother was there too, as the "open wound" of her family that "nobody treated". Until her daughter did by writing her story.

The word "therapist" has an ancient Greek root in the word "therapon", the second-in-combat, the one who *attends to the burial ritual of the warrior*. In a sense, this is the role that Ms. Senfft served for her mother. In his enigmatic statement that the symbol is "the murder of the thing" (1977, p. 104), the psychoanalyst Jacques Lacan evokes the varying levels at which inscription – and the witnessing embedded in it – destroys something. He also refers to its role in a person's fundamentally separating from the traumatic context: the way that inscription on a tombstone allows leaving the dead – and the trauma leading to the death – because now one knows where to truly find them.

A delegated life

Another presenter, Gerhard Wilke, a sociologist and organizational consultant (Wilke, Binney, & Williams, 2005), referred to present-day Germany as a "post-traumatic society". Today's understanding of PTSD includes three major elements: overwhelming exposure to horror, manifested in the symptom triad of flashbacks, dissociation and hyper-arousal; the experience of sudden unbearable loss; and what has come to be called "moral injury" (Shay, 2014; Litz, 2014). The latter refers to a deep sense of betrayal of "what's right", committed by someone in legitimate authority or by oneself, in a high-stakes situation. This often involves witnessing or participating in something that fundamentally violates one's most basic sense of moral order. All three elements occur simultaneously and with extraordinary intensity in perpetrator families.

Wilke captures one aspect of the second and third generations' sense of themselves in the statement that "We live a delegated life". From his point of view, his generation is always representing, and indeed working out, something for someone else, one reason why the longing for "one's own life" is both urgent and naïve. Wilke attempted to get a personal grasp on this phenomenon by leaving Germany for London, from which vantage point two things happened. First, he was constantly seen as a Nazi, which he actually found useful; in the safer, more playful context of London, he could dare to face the Nazi in himself. But his former countrymen did not have the luxury of this perspective, so the second thing that happened was Wilke's dedicating himself to helping them achieve it, as best he and they could. He did this through consulting to their work lives and helping them see the playing out of war trauma in their daily relation to authority, to ordinary assertiveness, to their need for order and so on.

Following Wilke's presentation, we set aside a considerable amount of time for conference discussion. The first half of that time was to be a space for volunteer members to express freely what they had experienced in the conference, to which Wilke consulted; the second half was to be a more reflective and integrative conversation for everyone, to which both he and I consulted. But the initial effort was simply to bring out whatever members were carrying emotionally. This was not an easy task, even if it promised some degree of relief, learning and even intimacy. As I had from the very beginning of the conference, I told myself once again to try to "hold the whole thing", meaning that I was keenly aware of how critical it was for the staff to contain this process, to manage boundaries and to be present as sensible authority.

In the first discussion, members were very attentive to the presence of two Holocaust survivors in their midst. Nevertheless – or perhaps because of this – the unfolding conversation was extraordinary in its emotional scope and detail. Stories about members' families came out, many associated with wartime experiences. References to the conference material included very personal reactions, sometimes of feeling things from both sides. Anxiety ebbed and flowed, and, at one point, in the midst of the unstructured opening up of experiences, one of the Holocaust survivors spoke with feeling about "needing a framework" for what was happening. Not long thereafter, a second Holocaust survivor began to speak at some length and rather theoretically about trauma. Interesting as his comments were, the effect was to interrupt the expression of what members were carrying and how it linked to their personal experiences.

Wilke consulted to what might be the group's need, via this member's discourse, to protect itself from the intensity of feeling that had been emerging. Nevertheless, members deferred to the Holocaust survivor, who continued what felt like a lecture, which limited the opportunity for other members to speak about their experiences. Eventually, a German member and Wilke again intervened with the speaker but in ways some felt to be too confrontational. And suddenly, just as this part of the discussion was coming to a close, we were back to the old roles of German perpetrator and Jewish victim. Sadly, a framework of sorts had fallen into place, and the flow of conversation – and, to a degree, of history – had stopped.

In the broader reflective discussion that followed, the group tried to process what had happened. Feelings were still running high and tended toward polarized positions. The group did its best to reflect on the first discussion and at least allowed members' different perspectives to be articulated. The hypothesis I found myself with, and offered to the group, was that, as this powerful conference was coming to its end – and therefore as we were all about *to be silenced permanently* – there was something unbearable about, in Kohut's terms, "empathic observation". No one wanted to end up on the wrong moral side of history, nor to be stuck with unbearable identifications. The old roles – and the sense of being back to square one – disappointing as they were, were nevertheless reassuring. We knew where, in a projective sense, to leave the good and the bad. Though it was hard to know what members did with my intervention and indeed how they actually understood what had happened, it seemed to me that the potential learning from and about the group's process was invaluable.

The destruction of dream life

"What haunts are not the dead, but the gaps left within us by the secrets of others." This quote from the Hungarian psychoanalyst Nicholas Abraham begins a recent book – part legal treatise, part Holocaust history, part family study – by Phillipe Sand (2016). As we have seen, one generation's secrets become the next generation's gaps, and also their hauntedness. But a remarkable dream journal from the 1930s suggests the ways that, in the context of terror and destructive group processes, the earlier generation attempted to keep secrets from itself, leading to profound, collective dissociation and the licensing of horrific destructiveness. A natural experiment in what Gordon Lawrence (1991) called "social dreaming", the journal illuminates the steady assault on a person's inner life and the way that massive social trauma and malignant authoritarianism turn an essential privacy into dangerous secrecy, even from the self.

As I have argued elsewhere,

> Adaptation requires that we "see" the Other on whom we depend so fully throughout development, and psychic change relies to some extent on our seeing the Other whose conflicts speak to and through us. In certain contexts, . . . envisioning the Other may move beyond the familial environment to larger social realities. . . . (E)ach dreamer is potentially a "seer" of his or her "people" and of the relationship to that Other. This has been described (Lawrence, 1991) as "social dreaming". In my own terms, I consider it an aspect of unconscious citizenship.
>
> *(Fromm, 2000, p. 289)*

But what if the Other is all-powerful and ruthlessly dangerous? And what if that Other sees that you see it?

This is the framework from which I would like to reflect on the earlier question about how the unconscious may become "cut out" and on the remarkable journal mentioned above. Throughout the 1930s, the journalist Charlotte Beradt kept a notebook, published in 1968 with the title *The Third Reich of Dreams*, in which she recorded the dreams of ordinary, "non-political" German citizens, just after National Socialism came into power. Here is one of those dreams:

> It was about nine in the evening. My consultations were over, and I was stretching out on the couch to relax with a book, when suddenly the walls of my room and then my apartment disappeared. I looked around and discovered to my horror that as far as the eye could see no apartment had walls anymore. Then I heard a loudspeaker boom, "According to the decree of the 17th of this month on the Abolition of Walls . . ."
>
> *(Beradt, 1968, p. 21)*

This is the dream of a middle-aged doctor, who that day, in response to the block warden's apparently casual, half-joking observation that he had no flag outside his apartment, thought to himself "Not on my four walls" (p. 22). The consequence in his dream is that his walls and all others are abolished. The physical boundary between private and public life no longer exists, just as, during the day, the boundary between private thought ("Not on my four walls") and public communication (no flag) did not exist either. Stunned by this experience, the doctor wrote his dream down, only to be accused of doing so in the next night's dream.

Beradt thus documents the penetration of the totalitarian Other into private life, including the private life of dreaming. She thereby raises for us questions about the effect of such serious boundary disturbance, and presumably both sleep and dream deprivation, on a terrorized group. From a different context, the psychoanalyst Christopher Bollas (1989), considering the problem of sexual abuse, argues that the invading Other "electrifies the dream process" itself (p. 175), rendering it too charged with anxiety to be at all useful in the processing of wishes and the development of symbolic functioning. The epigram to Bruno Bettelheim's Afterword to Beradt's book is: "Sleep no more. Macbeth doth murder sleep" (Beradt, 1968, p. 149).

Here is another dream on this theme:

> I dreamt I was talking in my sleep and to be on the safe side was speaking Russian (which I don't know, and anyway I never talk in my sleep). I was speaking so that I would not even understand myself and so no one else could understand me.
>
> *(p. 52)*

The dreamer dreams in a language that not only those around her but she herself cannot understand. As I wrote elsewhere: "If dreaming represents an effort, albeit ambivalent, to process important inner and outer life events, what does it mean to dream in order not to understand yourself?" (Fromm, 2000, p. 292).

What I believe we see here is "a desperate effort not only at safety but at anything that would feel like a boundary; the dreamer's demand that she have a private life is paid for by her keeping that private life from herself" (Fromm, 2000, p. 292). Beradt is remarkably attuned to the profound absurdity in these dreams, which she also sees in the dreams of many young Germans in which they express shame and horror at having the wrong color hair or the wrong kind of nose. Beradt is astonished by the utter silliness and arbitrariness of these physical ideals, bought into, however, with a teenager's deadly seriousness and enforced with brutality, either by the State or one's peers.

A third dream on the theme of the public and the private:

> In place of the street signs which had been abolished, posters had been set up on every corner, proclaiming in white letters on a black background the twenty words people were not allowed to say. The first was "Lord", the last was "I".
>
> *(p. 23)*

Thoughts on the legacy of perpetrator trauma **143**

In this dream of an educated young woman, reference points, represented by street signs, are abolished. Given the words that have been censured, the more fundamental reference points of "Lord", representing a higher power or a moral order, and of "I", that is, personal subjectivity, are forbidden as well. The disoriented dreamer is left in a terrorized dyadic relationship with the unseen authority behind the posters. So, this woman's comments, to some degree like the previous dreamer, that "To be on the safe side, I must have dreamt this dream in English" (p. 23).

Jacques Lacan returned Freud's foundational description of the trajectory of clinical psychoanalysis – "Where Id was, there Ego shall be" (1933, p. 80) – to its original German: "Where It was, there I must come to be" (1977). This last dream suggests that the totalitarian process perversely reverses this trajectory: Where I was, only It will be, It referring to the dominant-submissive pairing between the State and its subjects. There is no Third (Muller, 1996), through which to ground the pair in a larger symbolic and moral order. As Beradt puts it, these dreams were "dictated . . . by a dictatorship." She suggests that this "(d)ream imagery might thus help to describe the structure of a reality that was just on the verge of becoming a nightmare" (p. 9).

Beradt adds that:

> The dreams we are concerned with were not produced by conflicts arising in their authors' private realm, and certainly not by some past conflict that had left a psychological wound. Instead they arose from conflicts into which these people had been driven by a public realm in which half-truths, vague notions, and a combination of fact, rumor, and conjecture had produced a general feeling of uncertainty and unrest. These dreams may deal with disturbed human relations, but it was the environment that had disturbed them.
>
> *(p. 15)*

She records many dreams in which this social dimension of fear, uncertainty and miscommunication plays out with predictable results. In many dreams, she observes a "chorus" who intone statements like "There's not a thing one can do" (p. 72) or whose silence accuses the dreamer of a costly and misguided refusal to join.

Indeed, so many dreams include, to the dreamer's shock, "silent and expressionless faces" (p. 25), no human response at all when the dreamer expects and desperately needs one. In a sense, these dreams foreshadow the child development research of many years later having to do with the "still-face experiment" (Tronick, 2007), in which the mother is instructed to break the communicative rhythm of looks, smiles and sounds with her infant, and instead present a "still face" for a short time. After efforts to re-engage mother – to restore what Erikson would call "basic trust" in this intimate social process – the infant invariably withdraws into what looks like hopelessness and reflexive shame.

If one essential function of the dream-work is overcoming trauma-induced helplessness, Beradt shows us dreams in which the collapse analogous to that in

144 M. Gerard Fromm

the still-face experiment occurs, and terrorized helplessness is recurrently justified. In one dream, the dreamer is "no longer able to speak except in chorus with my group" (p. 87) and another person dreams "I was saying, 'I don't *have* to always say *no* anymore'" (p. 119). About this last quasi-delusional contortion seemingly in the direction of freedom, Beradt comments: "Amid all the 'musts' of life under totalitarian rule, this almost touching magic formula, 'don't have to,' demonstrates once again what effort it costs to be against the state when freedom is a burden and bondage comes as a relief" (p. 119).

Beradt calls this group process the "imperceptible and undramatic . . . transition from suggestion to autosuggestion" (p. 119), as insidious as it is terrifying. Erikson (1959) writes that "Where the human being despairs of an essential wholeness, he re-structures himself and the world by taking refuge in totalism" (p. 133). By totalism, he means "a Gestalt in which an absolute boundary is emphasized. Nothing that belongs inside must be left outside; nothing that must be outside should be tolerated inside" (p. 133). Beradt's book documents this despair of an essential wholeness and the subsequent disastrous splitting and re-structuring. As I noted elsewhere,

> Relentlessly, we see the ethno-syntonic (Erikson, 1954) but ego-dystonic conflict resolved in favor of membership rather than identity or conscience. The totalitarian outcome is the self-alienated subject rather than the citizen, and the destruction of dream life – one space for self-other confrontation – is at the heart of the totalitarian method.
>
> *(Fromm, 2000, p. 293)*

In the name of the father

The concluding chapter of Kohut's *A German Generation* is titled "The Authority of Historical Experience", with the word "authority" connoting, to my mind, not only the power historical experience unconsciously exercises over people (Frie, 2017) but also the set of rights or claims one generation makes on the other. One could argue that the transmission of trauma from one generation to the next reflects this complex authority issue. To some degree, the experience of the next generation has been "authored" by the unspoken, indeed unspeakable, traumas in their parents' histories, and some of these children – Ms. Senfft's mother perhaps – are lost in this transmission.

Others, like Ms. Senfft herself, may have been especially, if unconsciously, "authorized" to carry her parent's trauma into the future. "She talked to me, and I let her." This may take the form of a symptom, of an "unthought known", in Christopher Bollas' apt phrase (1987) or of an urgent question: for example, "Why did my mother die?" One way or the other, such transgenerational experience "must come into being as emotional understanding if the (person) is ultimately to take authority for his or her own life as distinct from that of the traumatized parent" (Fromm, 2012, p. 113). Ms. Senfft's story suggests that the authority of one

Thoughts on the legacy of perpetrator trauma **145**

generation's historical experience – and its raw, unconscious power over the next – can be mitigated by that next generation's finding the authority – and, to be sure, the courage – to become its author, and to somehow inscribe this "archaic heritage" (Freud, 1939, p. 38) into the larger human discourse.

Ms. Senfft needed her father to find this authority, and fathers are a major part of the story Kohut tells in *A German Generation*. He argues that the defeated, humiliated and lost fathers of World War I – from the PTSD perspective, a set of profound losses, horrific shocks and moral injuries – set the experiential stage for the next generation's driven merger with collective peer relationships, which in turn made them vulnerable to, indeed hungry for, the return of a powerful, idealized father. Beradt reports a dream in which the phrase "In the Name of . . ." is proclaimed over the radio repeatedly, but its last word is "Fuhrer" (1968, p. 40). In this dream, Hitler supplants all fathers, including the Heavenly One.

In the Preface to *Young Man Luther* (1958), Erikson – the son of a German Jewish woman and a Danish Gentile father whom, to his great pain, he never knew – concludes with

> a memory . . . utterly covered by the rubble of the cities and by the bleached bones of men of my kind in Europe. In my youth . . . I stayed one night with a friend in a small village by the upper Rhine. His father was a Protestant Pastor; and in the morning, as the family sat down to breakfast, the old man said the Lord's Prayer in Luther's German. Never having "knowingly" heard it, I had the experience, as seldom before or after, of a wholeness captured in a few simple words . . .
>
> *(1958, p. 10)*

Once again, the longing for wholeness and its being found, however temporarily, through a father.

Thomas Kohut concludes his introductory chapter with a memory too:

> My own interest in history can be traced back to fishing trips with my father in rural Wisconsin when I was very little. I do not recall us ever catching anything, but I vividly remember listening with rapt attention as my father told me stories of the Persian and Peloponnesian wars as we sat in a little rowboat in the hot sun on a lake . . .
>
> *(2012, p. 18)*

Barely fifteen years after his escape from Vienna, Heinz Kohut and his son together, alone on a boat, safely separate from other people, warmed by the sun, waiting for nature to offer something special from its depths, telling and listening to stories of long ago and far away wars. From which comes a life's vocation, a story of too close a war, and our gratitude that some transmissions are more profoundly generative than others.

References

Beradt, C. (1968). *The third reich of dreams*. Chicago: Quadrangle Books.

Bollas, C. (1987). *The shadow of the object: Psychoanalysis of the unthought known*. London: Free Association Books.

Bollas, C. (1989). The trauma of incest. In *Forces of Destiny: Psychoanalysis and human idiom* (pp. 171–180). London: Free Association Books.

Carney, M. (2007). *The end of the Neubacher project.* A documentary film written and directed by Marcus J. Carney.

Davoine, F., & Gaudilliere, J-M. (2004). *History beyond trauma*. New York: Other Press.

Erikson, E. (1954). The dream specimen of psychoanalysis. In R. P. Knight & C. R. Friedman (Eds.), *Psychoanalytic psychiatry and psychology: Austen Riggs center* (Vol. 1, pp. 131–170). New York: International Universities Press.

Erikson, E. (1958). *Young man Luther*. New York: W. W. Norton & Company.

Erikson, E. (1959). The problem of ego identity. In G. S. Klein (Ed.), *Psychological issues* (pp. 101–171). New York: International Universities Press.

Fraiberg, S., Adelson, E., & Shapiro, V. (1975). Ghosts in the nursery. *Journal of the American Academy of Child Psychiatry, 14*, 387–421.

Freud, S. (1933). *The dissection of the psychical personality*. Lecture XXXI. New Introductory Lectures on Psycho-Analysis. S.E. 22. London: Hogarth Press.

Freud, S. (1939). *Moses and monotheism. S.E. 23*. London: Hogarth Press.

Frie, R. (Ed.). (2017). *History flows through us*. London: Routledge.

Fromm, M. G. (2000). The other in dreams. *Journal of Applied Psychoanalytic Studies, 2*, 287–298.

Fromm, M. G. (2012). *Lost in transmission: Studies of trauma across generations*. London: Karnac.

Klein, M. (1946). Notes on some schizoid mechanisms. *International Journal of Psycho-Analysis, 27*, 99–110.

Kohut, H. (1969–70). On leadership. In P. Ornstein (Ed.), *The search for the self: Selected writings of Heinz Kohut* (Vol. 3, pp. 103–128). New York: International Universities Press, 1991.

Kohut, T. (2012). *A German generation*. New Haven: Yale University Press.

Lacan, J. (1977). *Ecrits*. New York: W. W. Norton & Company.

Lawrence, W. G. (1991). Won from the void and formless infinite: Experiences of social dreaming. *Free Associations, 2*, 259–294.

Litz, B. (2014). Clinical heuristics and strategies for service members and veterans with war-related PTSD. *Psychoanalytic Psychology, 31*(2), 192–205.

Muller, J. (1996). *Beyond the psychoanalytic dyad*. New York and London: Routledge.

Sand, P. (2016). *East West street: On the origins of "genocide" and "crimes against humanity."* New York: Knopf.

Senfft, A. (2007). *Silence hurts: A German family story*. Berlin: Claassen Verlag.

Shay, J. (2014). Moral injury. *Psychoanalytic Psychology, 31*(2), 182–191.

Tronick, E. (2007). *The neurobehavioral and social-emotional development of infants and children*. New York: W. W. Norton & Company.

Volkan, V. D. (2015). *A Nazi legacy*. London: Karnac.

Wilke, G., Binney, G., & Williams, C. (2005). *Living leadership*. Harlow: Pearson Education Limited.

Winnicott, D. W. (1974). Fear of breakdown. *International Review of Psycho-Analysis, 1*, 103–107.

12

SOCIAL MEMORY OF THE HOLOCAUST IN POLAND

Katarzyna Prot-Klinger and Krzysztof Szwajca

Introduction

What has Europe, as a patient, repressed from its consciousness, and what could it remember and work on while lying on the couch? For us, as therapists from Poland, what lives on in our country's social memory is important. This is what we hear from our patients, manifested in collective memory in group therapy, during large group sessions or in the course of a Social Dreaming Matrix.

Based on these therapeutic experiences, we believe that the most important, unresolved problem residing in our patients' subconscious minds is the Holocaust heritage being ignored. Work by cultural researchers shows that what we see in our offices not only concerns individual patients, but also features in Polish society (Kowalska-Leder, Dobrosielski, Kurz, & Szpakowska, 2017, Niziołek, 2013). In his recently published book, literary historian Tomasz Żukowski states:

> A characteristic feature of Polish culture is guilt in connection with the Holocaust. This surfaces from time to time, but it is not acknowledged or considered. The slightest suggestion about complicity [of Poles] in the Holocaust evokes immediate resistance before it can even reach consciousness.
>
> *(2018, p. 7)*

According to the author, cultural messages in the form of stories and films build a subtle narrative that protects Poles' self-perception as rescuers of Jews, as "Righteous Among the Nations" – contrary to historical facts, which demonstrate the active participation of Polish citizens in murders of Jews.

We single out Poland because the Holocaust took place mainly in Poland. The research of historians, to which we refer in the first part of the chapter, clearly shows that the term "bystander" – an indifferent witness – is not appropriate to a situation in which, after the liquidation of the ghettos in Poland,[1] there was a hunt for other Jews who then died at the hands of or as a result of denunciation by Poles. In addition, Poles benefited materially from the Holocaust by occupying houses and social spaces previously occupied by Jews.

Poland is also set apart as a country in which, since 2000, a public debate about the Holocaust has been taking place. The suppressed subject of the Holocaust in Poland has re-emerged in studies by historians and in new cultural messages, but also in a strengthening of calls for the defense of the "good name" of Poles. Political scientist Piotr Forecki describes this using a term borrowed from sociology – "backlash" (2018). This is a defensive group mechanism involving displacement and the distortion of reality. In practice, these are actions of individuals and state institutions attacking historical research that are a threat to specific formulas of historical memory and national identity.

To us, this process seems interesting and important in the face of growing national-fascist movements (not only in Poland). The basic question for Poland, and indeed for the whole of Europe, is how we could explain the crisis of liberal democracy and the collapse of the European project.

One possible explanation is "the return of the repressed" – the repetition or reconstruction of the unresolved trauma/guilt, in "new clothes". This can be confirmed by an event which took place in Wrocław in 2015. During a demonstration against immigrants, organized by the National Radical Camp, participants burned an effigy of a Jew. In this way, the refugee became identical with the orthodox Jew, a stranger among the Polish nation, arousing extremely aggressive feelings and a desire to annihilate.

In the first part of the chapter, we attempt to present the social process taking place in Poland, together with an example of a collaborative attempt at a group-work process by psychotherapists of the Polish-Israeli Mental Health Society. In the second part, we present material from a workshop conducted at a psychotherapeutic conference in Kraków in 2017, regarding the social memory suppression of the Holocaust.

Polish collective memory and the memory of the Holocaust

We live in an important moment. The last witnesses of the Holocaust are dying. We will not learn from them anymore. We are already almost satisfied with the social concepts of the past given to us by pop culture, school education, the official practice of commemoration and museums. And yet there were hundreds of thousands of witnesses in this country. The extermination of European Jews took place mainly in Poland and, above all, Jewish-Polish citizens died in front of their neighbors. For years, in historiography as in the collective consciousness, the predominant description of Jewish deaths lay somewhere distant and hidden – in extermination camps and behind restrictive walls, strictly isolated in big city ghettos. Yet, before the war, Jews constituted about 10% of the country's population. They lived, and then they were killed, mostly in hundreds of small towns scattered all over occupied Poland (Engelking & Grabowski, 2018). It was here, much more than anywhere else, that witnessing the Holocaust was a real mass experience.

Jewish fate and Jewish deaths have not become an important component of the Polish experience of the Second World War (Szurek, 2006), and so it continues today. Polish memories of those times contain surprisingly few and rather marginal references to the Holocaust (Szacka, 2006; Kwiatkowski, 2008). Today's collective memory is populated with other stories; something else, with its own symbolic and meaningful experiences, interests us. There is no Holocaust in this. The Holocaust is not experienced as an integral part of our own past, despite the great progress of historical knowledge (Szacka, 2010).

After 1989 the level of professional, historical debate about the Holocaust heightened, with tremendous progress in Holocaust research, especially in the area of the attitudes and actions of Poles. No difficult issue has been omitted – not the blackmail and exposing of those in hiding, not the threat posed to the hidden and their rescuer neighbors, not the exploitative trade with starving ghettos, not the informing to the occupation authorities, not the theft and takeover of "post-Jewish" property and business, not the attitude of people making money from hiding Jews, and finally, not the direct involvement of Poles in murder. Polish discourse is considered the most advanced amongst all post-communist Central and Eastern Europe countries. The discourse is accompanied by an explosion of initiatives, debates, associations, educational programs, festivals, books and artistic performances devoted to Jewish heritage and the Holocaust. Despite the generated tensions, it has continued and deepened. In addition, the demythologizing discourse that began in the 1980s in the low-circulation Catholic press or publishing houses (issued outside the political censorship of the opposition press) is spreading ever more and becoming a social fact through its presence in popular media. The dispute over the publication of *Neighbors* by Jan T. Gross (2001) turned into a national debate about the role of Poles in the Holocaust. Gross describes a pogrom in a provincial town where the mass murder of Jews was carried out by their Polish neighbors – the massacre was not mandated by the occupiers but occurred during the chaos just after the German army entered. This debate was reported in the biggest media outlets, and involved politicians, publicists and journalists, even reaching people who had previously shown no interest in the subject. There was no one in Poland who had not heard about this town: Jedwabne.

There is great interest among historians, as well as among culture-forming elites, in the problems of the Holocaust, and greater availability of reliable knowledge about it, and yet . . . none of this changes "what everybody knows", and even strengthens convictions that persist in the social consciousness that Poles were only heroes during the Second World War (Krzemiński, 2015). This contrast surprises us.

The prevailing vision of history remains a heartfelt tale of a heroic Polish nation, which suffered the most at the hands of the Germans (Poles, according to opinion polls, constitute the largest group of victims of the Second World War) (Szacka, 2010), but nevertheless behaved heroically, fighting on all fronts and above all across the country in mass guerrilla units, whose members jointly and with all their might helped their Jewish brothers in distress (TNS Polska, 2015). Thus the nature of Jewish "misery" is unclear.

The lack of stories about executions of Jews, and the lack of memory of Jewish deaths in towns where they often accounted for more than a third of the population – towns in which they starved and then died in front of their neighbors – cannot be considered a natural process of memory eliminating the irrelevant. We must recognize that this forgetting was active, a form of post-traumatic defense. The absence of the Jewish Holocaust in the Polish collective memory is a social amnesia, an active forgetfulness. This lack can be called "oblivion" and understood as a gap in the collective memory about an event of vital importance, which has been actively forgotten. This distinguishes "oblivion" from the natural process of forgetting.

The Holocaust cannot be told "well"

Agnes Heller stated, with the Holocaust in mind, that one cannot genuinely remember things that are unbearable and meaningless and not die from it (Heller, 2001). There are, therefore, such sufferings about which we must be inauthentic, which we ritualize and adapt to, or actively forget. The problem of the inadequacy of language, the sense of "weaning" language from events, suspicion about language when words skirt tragic events but are unable to reach them, are frequent conclusions accompanying the attempt to describe the Holocaust.

Everywhere, not only in Poland, we were faced with an immediate and feverish post-war attempt to "tell everything", an attempt that was dramatically unsuccessful and suppressed within a few years. The fundamentally important testimony of the Holocaust, *If This Is a Man* (Levi, 1947), despite a run of barely a few thousand copies, remained in Italian bookstores for several years. There were no readers. Stories told have been suspended in a void, because there is no "empathic listener" (Laub, 1992). This was true not only on the "Old Continent", with its perhaps impure conscience, but also in the "New World", to which Polish-Jewish Holocaust survivors immigrated. Their truth was too different from the socially dominant narratives to be heard. In Israel they found themselves in confrontation with the Israeli founding myth and were perceived as "meekly going to slaughter" rather than being received by society with their stories (Dasberg, 1987). The reception was similar in the richer United States. The world failed to understand the accounts of witnesses, too frightening and disturbing for comfort, in a way that could resound, more or less until the 1980s.

Specific polish Holocaust "oblivion"

Conducted by the Germans with unusual consistency and brutality, the process of the annihilation of Jewish communities took place in Poland in front of hundreds of thousands of Polish witnesses. Its cruelty exceeded everything experienced hitherto by Polish society. The Polish witnessing of the Holocaust was a terrible, complex, intense and massive experience. It involved listening to the call for help of those sentenced to death and very different reactions – aiding in escape or hiding, exposing the hidden, participating in robbery and even murder. It involved terrible mass deaths seen from up close. It was horror, fear, helplessness, compassion, disgust, guilt and being wronged (the victim who made us vulnerable to accompany their misfortune also harms us), voyeuristic excitement, defensive rationalizations (they had to be guilty because people get what they deserve), but above all reluctant passivity, refusal of compassion and empathy. This was partially intentional, connected with ideology, growing pre-war anti-Semitism, the greed of those who were waiting for the division of "post-Jewish" spoils. But with witnesses to such a terrifying trauma, the refusal to empathize is a reflexive, defensive salvation against trauma. The witnesses of the mass crimes saw only a small part of the crime, and only for a moment. They felt a terrifying distance – terrifying in essence also to themselves, because witnessing crimes humiliates. One cannot do anything that would be "right", which would be adequate or sufficient. Witnesses arouse revulsion rather than compassion. They behaved as we would never like to behave. Therefore, the witnesses do not tell. They have nothing to tell, because their experience is unthinkable, their narrative is unauthorized (because they were not victims), they cannot reproduce the psychic defenses that made them the way they were then. Traumatic experience, which cannot be dealt with, can only be supplanted, pushed out of consciousness, forgotten.

Individuals and communities were simultaneously witnesses, perpetrators, beneficiaries, but also victims of crimes. The mass victims of the war were also ethnic Poles and other communities inhabiting the then-multinational Poland. The German occupation of Poland and Eastern Europe was ruthless, cruel and exterminating.

In addition, in Poland, which as a state had not existed for more than a hundred years (between 1795 and 1918), the myths had a special meaning. "Polishness" was in fact not embedded in institutions, monuments, offices and law, but rather in symbols and unofficial, mythical stories which tugged afresh at heartstrings. That mythology embedded in the romantic tradition was most vital in constructing Polish identity. There have been questions about how that tradition shaped Polish memory and collective life (Józefik & Szwajca, 2011). The basic element of the romantic myth is the ennoblement of suffering and sacrifice. The experiences of the Second World War have become part of this mythical tradition. The Polish collective memory was filled with successive disasters. And since the Poles always played the role of victims, others could be perpetrators, or at most co-victims; they could not suffer more. The competition for martyrdom had to have an influence on the Polish memory of the Holocaust.

The Polish-Israeli Mental Health Association

The decision to found a bi-national association was made in Savion (Tel Aviv) on April 19th 2000, by 30 Israeli and Polish mental health professionals. Annual

152 Katarzyna Prot-Klinger and Krzysztof Szwajca

meetings, held alternatively in Israel and in Poland, formed the basis of the Association's activity. The titles of these meetings show the process of working through trauma:

> *The Past in the Present: coming to terms with memories – our own and those of our patients* (Jerusalem 2000); *Guilt and responsibility* (Haifa 2003); *Guilt – Responsibility – Forgiveness* (Kraków 2004); *Painful memories* (Nazareth 2008); *Shoah – between the Past and the Present* (Warsaw 2016).

The foundation of the Association and its various activities are described in detail in an article by Jacek Bomba (2013). In the context of this paper, we find relevance in the reflection on the group process between Poles and Israelis. During the aforementioned conferences, meetings of small groups were held outside the framework of the lectures. The Israelis talked emotionally about their experience of Poland and their own Polish heritage, about the construction of their own identity and the importance of the Holocaust and anti-Semitism for this process. The Polish participants were not prepared for the seminar to take on such a personal character. The speeches of individuals, although during the meeting co-creating a polemical dialogue, are in fact the "internal" voices that were presented in every participant: a voice demanding "objective truth", a voice seeking justification and purification, and a voice defending against anything that would violate the myth of a noble Pole (de Barbaro, Józefik, & Szwajca, 2004). Difficulties of the group process were further analyzed later (de Barbaro, Józefik, Drożdżowicz, & Orwid, 2007; de Barbaro, Józefik, Drożdżowicz, & Szwajca, 2011) concluding that the deconstruction of myths important in building Polish identity, although necessary, faces mounting problems.

What certainly happened was the suspension or disbanding of the Association's "small groups". The 2009 Symposium commemorating Professor Maria Orwid, the Holocaust survivor living in Poland and one of the Polish-Israeli Mental Health Association's co-founders, who had passed away suddenly six months earlier, was the last one with the small groups. The question of what caused the suppression of the trauma process arises. Jacek Bomba (2013) speaks of a transgenerational transmission of trauma, an unconscious process that can lead to destruction. Of note, the dialogue within the Association halted after the death of Maria Orwid – a survivor of the Holocaust in Poland who always emphasized that she owed her life to Poles. In view of this testimony, it was difficult to find a place for the anger of the "second generation", children of the survivors, primarily from Israel, who often did not have their own connection to the Righteous (Poles) and for whom, in the memories of their parents, the Poles cooperated in the Holocaust. One of the hypotheses may be that this anger led, over the years, to the dissolution of "small groups". Work in small groups has been replaced by activities of the "third generation" meetings between Polish and Israeli students. Perhaps this is another element of the intergenerational message – we delegate to children the task of working through traumas in a manner that we have been unable to do ourselves.

Social memory of the Holocaust in Poland **153**

Case study

In September 2017, an annual conference of the psychotherapeutic community in Poland was held in Kraków under the title *Obcy. Inny. Taki Sam.* [Aliens. Others. The Same.] As members of the Polish-Israeli Mental Health Association, we proposed a workshop focused on the memory of the Holocaust. The aim of the workshop was, through individual experience, to confront the relationship to the "others" in Polish society. We decided that the memory/oblivion of the Holocaust was an important aspect of the attitude towards "others". We hypothesized that processes related to the history of the Holocaust in Poland and the participation of Polish society in it influence the current attitude towards others – minorities, immigrants and refugees. In invitations to the workshop we stated that it would consist of an experimental part and a large group reflecting on experience.

In the first part of the workshop, the participants read texts chosen by us about the Holocaust. These texts comprised narratives of victims, perpetrators and observers, along with contemporary commentary about the memory of the Holocaust. The extracts were short, so as to be delivered in the course of discussion. For example:

> We went there on bicycles, and before that we went to the forge and tipped sticks with iron to make them better for killing. After an hour, two carts arrived from the Bzura estate . . . We drove the Jews out of the cellar and told them to get to the cart. We took them to the edge of the forest, where a trench was dug. There, we ordered all the Jews to strip to their shirts and underwear. We led them to the edge of the trenches and killed them with the sticks. Tkacz killed four Jewish women. Before a fifth was killed she was raped violently. I took a wooden stick from Tkacz and personally killed a Jewish woman, beating her about the head with it thrice, and she fell into the trench. After the murder, I received the slippers and dress of the Jewish woman.
>
> *Murderer from Bzury (Domanowska, 2012).*

Relatively young people – grandchildren of victims, perpetrators and witnesses – attended the workshop, about 20 to 30 people. Grandchildren of witnesses came with anxiety that perhaps their grandparents were perpetrators to some degree. In the first part of the workshop, the names of the towns where the Holocaust was carried out by

Poles – Jedwabne, Gniewczyna and Markowa – came up. In the second part, psychotherapists identified their family origins, pointing to the locations on the map – not far from Jedwabne, near Markowa. The second part of the workshop was short, lasting only 45 minutes. But the dynamics were clearly visible, from the first "professional" statements, in which participants tried to maintain their roles as psychotherapists, talking about interest in the transgenerational message and their work with patients, to the accounts of two people from Jewish families who made very personal statements that ascribed guilt or indifference to the Polish reality. The most important topic was Holocaust oblivion, the approach to which varied from anxiety and the search for "guilty parties" to shared mourning.

At the beginning, one of the participants noticed the difference regarding the attitude towards the Holocaust from contact with the international environment:

> It was striking to me how much the memory of the Holocaust is alive in psychotherapy, and how much I feel that for us it is not. That is why it was important for me to come here, because now I will know to which e-mail address to send an inquiry, or with whom I can start a discussion, because I am interested in such a discussion. I did not know that anyone is really interested. I do not remember that, during supervision, I ever spoke about the Holocaust, even if I knew from the basic genogram that such a story was in the family. The truth is also that I did nothing about it while being aware of it.

Interestingly, people for whom, "for unknown reasons", the topic of the Holocaust became important, began to look for Jewish "roots" in their families, as if the fact that this tragedy happened in Poland, in their home places, was not sufficient a reason to sympathize with the victims. We understand this as a contrast to their family environment, where this tragedy remained unspoken:

> A large part of my adult life has been connected to the fact that I am looking for Jewish traces, a Polish-Jewish identity, which is important to me. And I do not know if this is an attempt to connect somehow . . . or whether I was in an anti-Semitic climate where the homes that were once Jewish had been taken over are inhabited by Poles . . . I do not actually know anyone who would speak openly about their origins, or about the fact that they

returned. I have a need to check, research and hunt for traces. I would like to know why.

(A person from near Kielce)

There is concern about neighbors, and maybe one's own family:

I lived in Podlasie. In April 1941, all inhabitants were murdered. Nothing was said about it directly. Something about the fact that someone got rich, that there was some gold . . . There is nobody to talk to. There was no way to approach it. I could not read the story of Anna Bikont, because it was a story about my home, my area and the places I know. I lived there for 15 years, I met people and maybe I knew these people . . .

The story, reminiscent of a dream, of one of the participants, was a breakthrough moment:

I was in Kazimierz and I took pictures of my daughter. And she started to spin, to dance, I took her pictures, and these photos were so beautiful, I felt sad, I did not know why. And then I thought that this sadness was because it could be me, it could be her. I'm talking about the Holocaust.

Then there is an exchange between participants (so far separate testimonies):

- "There are traces. The traces are terrifying. I was talking about this sewing machine, an old Singer, not working. It's my imagination that it came to me from a Jewish property. It is not that there are no traces . . ."
- "I don't mean in the sense that there are no such things, but that they have lost their identity."
- "The fact that we are talking means that they are not lost. This world exists somewhere, despite the fact that someone wanted to obliterate it. The traces are there."

The workshop ended with a reflection on taking responsibility:

I am Polish, I do not have Jewish roots, but I also investigated very intensely at a certain moment why it moves me so intensely, and I think it is because I am Polish.

> And on identifying oneself in the transgenerational transmission of trauma:
>
> We say that so many years have passed since the war, but from a different perspective these years are two generations.
>
> As organizers, we tried to create a safe place, an experience that in psychotherapy is referred to as a "holding" or "containing" environment.

Interpretation of the workshop experience

Alessandra Cavalli writes about the "deadly" transmission, which is the result of the inability to understand and find representation for the experiences that have been placed in the body and psyche of the next generation. She writes: "events become experiences when they become meaningful, have a name, become known". If there is no environment that is able to contain them, they become non-representation. The goal of transgenerational trauma therapy is to give language to the "unrepresented" (Cavalli, 2012).

It is important to distinguish between loss and absence. "When an absence approaches loss, it can become a subject of mourning", writes LaCapra (1999). In the comments of the workshop participants, first absence was disclosed – "I understood that in my town half the inhabitants were Jews" and then a sense of loss. To start a process of bereavement in a society, loss must be named. Therefore, it is important who died, where and how. It is important to find the burial places. This will fill a void. This emptiness is described in the individual context as a "hole" in the psyche of a child whose parent was exposed to trauma. Different researchers working with the "second generation" notice and try to conceptualize this emptiness. Laub speaks of the "empty circle" – "the absence of representation, the rupture of the self, the erasure of the memory and the accompanying sense of void that are the core legacy of massive psychic trauma" (1998, p. 507). Gampel believes that unsymbolized losses become psychic holes. These internal voids are filled with emptiness that contains "some radioactive remnants that cannot be transformed into memory" (Gampel & Mazor, 2004, p. 547). In that silence, parents transmit "the wounds but not the memories" (Gampel, 1998). Green created the concept of *psychosis blanche* – a blank or white state, absent anxiety or mourning (1972). Green linked this state to an emotionally absent mother – a "dead mother". Dori Laub extends the Green construct. In her opinion, psychosis blanche can cause other traumatic losses of the good internal object at any age (Laub, 2012). Gerson writes of "a dead third" – the legacy of the trauma and loss without someone to empathically witness these experiences. This is connected with a lack of societal concern for their well-being while the inhumane victimizations are being perpetrated (Gerson, 2009). All these descriptions of emptiness and absences seem to "fit" the statements

Social memory of the Holocaust in Poland **157**

of the workshop participants. However, the participants were not, in most cases, the children of survivors. So who were they? Considering the presence of Jews in the towns they come from, it is highly probable that their grandparents witnessed the Holocaust. We assume that most often this witnessing was "indifferent", or in many cases there was a satisfaction with the disappearance of half of the inhabitants of the town, after which one might take over their property (Grabowski & Libionka, 2014). This is not to say that their disappearances were not a traumatic event. This complexity of feelings – horror of crime, but also satisfaction with the benefits obtained, seems to block the narrative completely. Trauma can lead to dissociation within the self, and to the experience described by Sullivan as *not-me* (1953). Faimberg believes that the child inhabits an unacceptable part of the parent, an unconscious *not-me* experience. This identification the author defines as "alienating identification", and believes that, in this type of identification, three generations are always involved. Interestingly, the discovery of this process was due to a patient whose father emigrated from Poland while the entire family who remained was killed in the Holocaust. According to Faimberg, the son became a container for the reality, which the father did not accept, of losing a family (2005). Feinberg, introducing the concept of "telescoping generation",[2] states that three generations always take part in transgenerational transmission. Similarly, Apprey believes that three generations are needed to define a human subject, and states that a mother as auxiliary ego to her child must simultaneously work through the psychical connection to her own mother (Apprey, 2017).

This meeting showed that there is perhaps a chance to change the transgenerational message, in which we are doomed to remain in the position of a descendant of the victim, perpetrator or observer, in a world where one cannot say "sewing machine" without feeling guilty. Work experience shows a readiness to deal with the guilt of "grandparents". It seems that the "second generation" – victims, witnesses and perpetrators, protect their "parents" from pain, guilt and shame, while the third has more courage to be identified with the generation of their ancestors, and thus to start the process of facing loss. Jill Salberg suggests containing disturbing feelings and events (2017). This does not mean ending mourning, but that we are close to being in the sphere of "closure".

Freud clearly showed the differences between mourning and melancholy (depression). The task of mourning is to withdraw the libidinal energy from the object (Freud, 1917). Above all, one must recognize the de facto lack of an object. In melancholy, the person who has been lost is idealized, without awareness of feelings of anger and rage that destroy the ego. Freud writes that in the case of mourning, the world has become impoverished and deserted – in the case of melancholy, it is "I" itself that is impoverished and deserted (1917). The benefit of melancholy is that it maintains the illusion that the object has not been lost. Identification can occur even with a damaged or dead object. In his work on mourning and melancholy from 1917, Freud saw the possibility of working through mourning by transferring libidinal energy to other objects. Freud's thought about the processes occurring in melancholy have been developed by Jewish psychoanalysts from Hungary,

Nicolas Abraham and Maria Torok, working in France (Abraham & Torok, 1994). They understand the characteristic of melancholy incorporating a lost object as a literal absorption and placement within the "psychic crypt". Such "phantoms" are transmitted transgenerationally, without the knowledge of a descendant, and are sometimes referred to in colloquial language as "skeletons in the closet". The task of mourning, according to Abraham and Torok, consists of moving the libido from the lost object by the creation of a metaphor. Then, incorporation changes into introjection – the ability to assimilate, to give meaning, which leads to the development of the individual and the enlargement of the ego. Referring to Freud's theory and Abraham and Torok's concept, Jacques Derrida (a personal friend of Torok) writes about the need for a constant mourning process, which he describes as *demi-deuil* (semi-mourning) (Derrida, 1995a). This assumes the impossibility of complete mourning over the lost object, but of remaining in the "in between" position oscillating between incorporation and introjection (Derrida, 1995b). In a conversation, the French psychoanalyst Elisabeth Roudinesco says:

> Mourning must be impossible. Successful mourning is unsuccessful mourning. In a successful mourning, I incorporate the deceased, assimilate him, agree with death and, consequently, disagree with death and the otherness of the deceased. So I am unfaithful. Wherever introjection succeeds in mourning, mourning cancels out the other. I take the other upon myself, and consequently negate or limit its infinite dissimilarity.
>
> *(Derrida & Roudinesco, 2016)*

Judith Butler underlines the difficulties of mourning in situations when there is no public recognition or discourse which allows naming and grieving of the identification and loss (2004). Butler refers to the difficulties of grieving in relation to gender. This might also be extended to other identifications. This means that, if the loss is connected with secrecy, such as the participation of Polish society in the Holocaust, for example, the process of mourning cannot take place. Without this space for reflection, paranoia about the outside world grows and a strictly defensive stance does not allow new information to be accepted. The grandchildren of the witnesses face the transgenerational trauma of the witness, but also suffer the loss of the national myth about the nobility of Poles during the war.

Summary

The question of the need for space for mourning, which the workshop clearly showed to be transferred to the social arena, remains. Poland stands guilty of eager participation in the Holocaust, in the "mob", on the "social margin", thus protecting the rest of society (Tokarska-Bakir, 2014). This is in line with the thesis expressed in Leder's book (2014) that "bad things" were done by "others".

Withdrawing this projection from external objects causes depressive feelings – guilt and a sense of responsibility for crimes – and subsequent manic defenses such as megalomania and omnipotence. Social functioning regresses from a depressive position, in which there exists the ability to recognize both one's aggression and the possibility of experiencing a sense of guilt and mourning, to a schizoid-paranoid position with its mechanisms of denial, cleaving and projection. The ability to function in reality and make reparation is replaced by a relation with a partial object, in which there is no place for care and empathy (Segal, 1987). A manic relationship with the object encompasses triumph, contempt and a sense of control. There is no remorse, and there are no regrets, because the subject feels that they have everything and are not dependent on internal or external objects. This can be seen in the aggressive reactions of a part of Polish society following reports on the killing of Jews by Poles during and after the war.

Recent developments in Poland – above all the amendments to the Act on the Institute of National Remembrance, according to which it would be an offence to "attribute responsibility to the Polish State or the Polish people for the Nazi crimes committed by the Third Reich" – show that there is a tendency to deny and encourage manic defenses. This occurred on the 50th anniversary of the events of March 1968, when anti-Semitism unleashed by the authorities led to another wave of Jewish emigration from Poland. On the other hand, books demythologizing the history of the Second World War and thoroughly, honestly analyzing the Holocaust have been published.

While in contact with those suffering from trauma, psychoanalysts developed theories of witnessing. Witnessing is the creation of a space where there can be a "live" or "moral third" (as opposed to a "dead third") and recognition (Benjamin, 2009; Feldman & Laub, 1992). Central to the literature on witnessing is the privileging of words, to "hold" vs. to "interpret" (Gentile, 2017). In the individual treatment of the traumatic transgenerational message, it is therefore important to tell a story that has never existed before. "It is only when survivors remember with someone, when a narrative is created in the presence of a passionate listener that the connection between an 'I' and a 'you' is remade" (Auerhahn, Laub, & Peskin, 1993, p. 436). In transferring this to the social arena, it is important to tell stories in the presence of the "passionate listener". It is essential to refer to specific facts. As in therapy for the children of Holocaust survivors, it is important to reconstruct specific facts from the lives of their parents. According to Grubrich-Simitis, such reconstruction allows them to resume the process of metaphorization (1984). The workshop experience, along with the processes taking place in the social arena, shows that more space is being created for these witnesses.

Notes

1 The so-called "third phase of the Holocaust".
2 "Telescoping generations" in biology means that a mother, her daughter and her granddaughters are housed in the same body. It can occur in parthenogenetic species and is characterized by a viviparous female having a daughter growing inside her that is also pregnant with a daughter cell.

160 Katarzyna Prot-Klinger and Krzysztof Szwajca

References

Abraham, N., & Torok, M. (1994). New perspectives in metapsychology; Cryptic mourning and secret love. In N. Abraham & M. Torok (Eds.), *The shell and the Kernel, Nicholas Rand* (pp. 99–176). Chicago and London: The University of Chicago.

Apprey, M. (2017). Transgenerational haunting and healing. In S. Grand & J. Salberg (Ed.), *Trans-generational trauma and the other: Dialogues across history and difference* (pp. 16–37). London and New York: Routledge.

Auerhahn, N. C., Laub, D., & Peskin, H. (1993). Psychotherapy with Holocaust survivors. *Psychotherapy: Theory, Research, Practice, Training, 30*(3), 434–442.

Benjamin, J. (2009). A relational psychoanalysis perspective on the necessity of acknowledging failure in order to restore the facilitating and containing features of the intersubjective relationship (the shared third). *International Journal of Psychoanalysis, 90,* 441–450.

Bomba, J. (2013). Psychodynamic groups as used to work through collective trauma memory. *Archives of Psychiatry and Psychotherapy, 3,* 41–48.

Butler, J. (2004). *Precarious life: The powers of mourning and violence.* London: Verso.

Cavalli, A. (2012). Transgenerational transmission of indigestible facts: From trauma, deadly ghosts and mental voids to meaning-making interpretations. *Journal of Analytical Psychology, 57*(5), 597–614.

Dasberg, H. (1987). Psychological distress of Holocaust survivors and offspring in Israel, forty years later: A review. *Israel Journal of Psychiatry and Related Sciences, 24,* 243–256.

de Barbaro, B., Józefik, B., Drożdżowicz, L., & Orwid, M. (2007). Polsko-Izraelskie Towarzystwo Zdrowia Psychicznego: Dynamika i dylematy grupy polskiej. [Polish-Israeli mental health association: Dynamics and dilemmas of the Polish group]. *Psychiatria Polska* (Supl. 3), 32.

de Barbaro, B., Józefik, B., Drożdżowicz, L., & Szwajca, K. (2011). In the face of anti-semitism: Thoughts of Polish psychotherapists. *Archives of Psychiatry and Psychotherapy, 13*(1), 55–60.

de Barbaro, B., Józefik, B., & Szwajca, K. (2004). Problem żydowski? Refleksje nad procesem grupowym krakowskich psychoterapeutów [A Jewish problem? Some reflections on the group process of psychotherapists in Kraków]. *Psychoterapia, 3,* 73–79.

Derrida, J. (1995a). Ja or the fauxbond II. In E. Weber (Ed.), *Points: Interviews, 1974–1994* (p. 48). Stanford, CA: Stanford University.

Derrida, J. (1995b). The subject. In E. Weber (Ed.), *Points: Interviews, 1974–1994* (p. 321). Stanford, CA: Stanford University.

Derrida, J., & Roudinesco, E. (2016). *Z czego jutro . . . Dialog [For what tomorrow . . . dialog].* Warsaw: Wydawnictwo Naukowe Scholar.

Domanowska, A. (2012, March 6). Mord Żydówek w Bzurach. IPN po 71 latach wszczyna śledztwo. [Murder of Jewish women in Bzury. After 71 years, the institute of national remembrance initiates an investigation]. *Gazeta Wyborcza.* Retrieved June 25, 2018, from http://wyborcza.pl/1,76842,11289917,Mord_Zydowek_w_Bzurach__IPN_po_71_latach_wszczyna.html

Engelking, B., & Grabowski, J. (Eds.). (2018). *Dalej jest noc. Losy Żydów w wybranych powiatach okupowanej Polski [Night goes on: The fate of Jews in selected counties of occupied Poland].* Warsaw: Stowarzyszenie Centrum Badań nad Zagładą Żydów.

Faimberg, H. (2005). *The telescoping of generations: Listening to the Narcissistic links between Generations* (pp. 4–18). London and New York: Routledge.

Feldman, S., & Laub, D. (1992). *Testimony: Crises of witnessing in literature, psychoanalysis and history.* New York: Routledge.

Forecki, P. (2018). *Po Jedwabnem Anatomia pamięci funkcjonalnej [After Jedwabne anatomy of functional memory].* Warsaw: Instytut Badań Literackich PAN.

Freud, S. (1917). *Mourning and melancholia*. SE 14, 243–258.

Gampel, Y. (1998). Reflections on countertransference in psychoanalytic work with child survivors of the Shoah. *Journal of American Academy of Psychoanalysis, 26*(3), 343.

Gampel, Y., & Mazor, A. (2004). Intimacy and family links of adults who were children during the Shoah: Multi faced mutations of the traumatic encapsulations. *Free Associations, 11*, 546–568.

Gentile, K. (2017). Cresting conditions for emergence. In: J. Salberg & S. Grand (Eds.), *Wounds of history: Repair and resilience in the trans-generational transmission of trauma* (pp. 169–188). London and New York: Routledge.

Gerson, S. (2009). When the third is dead: Memory, mourning and witnessing in the aftermath of Holocaust. *The International Journal of Psychoanalysis, 90*, 1341–1357.

Grabowski, J., & Libionka, D. (Eds.) (2014). *Klucze i kasa. O mieniu żydowskim w Polsce pod okupacją niemiecką i we wczesnych latach powojennych 1939–1945 [Keys & cash: The fate of Jewish property in occupied Poland, 1939–1945]*. Warszawa: Centrum Badań nad Zagładą Żydów.

Green, A. (1972). *On private madness*. London: Rebus.

Gross, J. T. (2001). *Neighbors: The destruction of the Jewish community in Jedwabne*. Poland: Princeton University Press.

Grubich-Simitis, I. (1984). From concretism to metaphor: Thoughts on some theoretical and technical aspects of the psychoanalytical work with the children of Holocaust survivors. *Psychoananlytic Study of the Child, 39*, 301–319.

Heller, A. (2001). Pamięć i zapominanie. O sensie i braku sensu [Memory and forgetfulness: About sense and lack of sense]. *Przegląd Polityczny, 52–53*, 25.

Józefik, B., & Szwajca, K. (2011). Polish myths and their deconstruction in the context of Polish-Jewish relations. *Archives of Psychiatry and Psychotherapy, 12*, 35–41.

Kowalska-Leder, J., Dobrosielski, P., Kurz, I., & Szpakowska, M. (Eds.). (2017). *Ślady Holokaustu w imaginarium kultury polskiej [Traces of the Holocaust in the imaginarium of Polish culture]*. Warsaw: Instytut Kultury Polskiej Wydział Polonistyki UW, Wydawnictwo Krytyki Politycznej.

Krzemiński, I. (Ed.). (2015). *Żydzi – problem prawdziwego Polaka [Jews – the problem of a real pole]*. Warsaw: Uniwersytet Warszawski.

Kwiatkowski, P. T. (2008). *Pamięć zbiorowa społeczeństwa polskiego w okresie transformacji [The collective memory of Polish society during the period of transformation]* (Vol. 2, pp. 220–311). Warszawa: Wydawn. Nauk. Scholar.

LaCapra, D. (1999). Trauma, absence, loss. *Critical Inquiry, 25*(4), 696–727.

Laub, D. (1992). Bearing witness or the vicissitudes of listening. In S. Felman & D. Laub (Eds.), *Testimony: Crises of witnessing in literature, psychoanalysis, and history*. New York: Taylor & Francis.

Laub, D. (1998). The empty circle: Children of survivors and the limits of reconstruction. *Journal of the American Psychoanalytic Association, 46*, 507–529.

Laub, D. (2012). Traumatic shutdown of narrative and symbolization. In M. Gerard Fromm (Ed.), *Lost in transmission: Studies of trauma across generations* (pp. 31–53). London: Karnac.

Leder, A. (2014). *Prześniona rewolucja. Ćwiczenia z logiki historycznej [A dreamed revolution: Exercises in historical logic]*. Warsaw: Krytyka Polityczna.

Levi, P. (1947). *Se questo è un uomo [If this is a man]*. Turin: De Silva.

Niziołek, G. (2013). *Polski teatr Zagłady [Polish theater of the Holocaust]*. Warszawa: Wydawnictwo Krytyki Politycznej.

Salberg, J. (2017). The texture of traumatic attachment: Presence and ghostly absence in transgenerational transmission. In J. Salberg & S. Grand (Eds.), *Wounds of history: Repair and resilience in the trans-generational transmission of trauma* (pp. 75–99). London: Routledge.

Segal, H. (1987). Silence is the real crime. *International Review of Psycho-Analysis, 14*(1), 3–12.

Sullivan, H. S. (1953). *The interpersonal theory of psychiatry.* New York: W.W. Norton & Company.

Szacka, B. (2006). *Czas przeszły, pamięć, mit [Past time, memory, myth].* Warszawa: Wydawnictwo Naukowe. Scholar.

Szacka, B. (2010). II wojna światowa w pamięci rodzinnej [World war II in family memory]. In P. T. Kwiatkowski, L. M. Nijakowski, B. Szacka, & A. Szpociński (Eds.), *Między codziennością a wielką historią. Druga wojna światowa w pamięci zbiorowej społeczeństwa polskiego [Between everyday life and great history: The Second World War in the collective memory of Polish society]* (pp. 82–83). Gdańsk-Warszawa: Wydawnictwo Naukowe. Scholar.

Szurek, J. C. (2006). Między historią a pamięcią: polski świadek Zagłady [Between history and memory: Polish witness of the Holocaust]. In B. Engelking, J. Leociak, D. Libionka, & A. Ziębińska-Witek (Eds.), Zagłada Żydów. *Pamięć narodowa a pisanie historii w Polsce i we Francji. Wybrane materiały z kolokwium polsko--francuskiego [Holocaust: National memory and writing history in Poland and France. Selected materials from the Polish French colloquium].* Lublin: Wydawnictwo Uniwersytetu Marii Curie-Skłodowskiej.

Tokarska-Bakir, J. (2014). Rozum w Polsce wysiada. *Wiadomości.onet.pl [Reasoning in Poland ceases to function].* Retrieved July 13, 2015, from http://wiadomosci.onet.pl/prasa/joanna-tokarska-bakir-rozum-w-polsce-wysiada/

TNS Polska. (2015). *II wojna światowa w pamięci Polaków – w 75 lat od wybuchu [World War II in the memory of Poles – in 75 years from the outbreak].* Retrieved 2019, from www.tnsglobal.pl/wp-content/blogs.dir/9/files/2014/09/K.059_II-wojna_swiatowa_w_pamieci_Polakow_O08a-14.pdf

Żukowski, T. (2018). *Wielki retusz. Jak zapomnieliśmy, że Polacy zabijali Żydów [Great retouching: As we forgot that the Poles were killing Jews]* (p. 7). Warsaw: Wielka Litera.

13

NEGOTIATION BETWEEN THREE AMBIVALENTLY CONNECTED NATIONS

Finding common ground through metaphors in multinational large group sessions

Marie-Luise Alder and Stephan Alder

Trialog Conference

In the spring of 2013, Stephan Alder (one of the authors) met with colleagues in Krasnodar (Russia) during a supervision session of the Router Program of the International Association of Analytical Psychology. In the course of the seminars and supervision sessions, they realised that their common traumatic history, in particular with regard to World War II, was very much a part of their discussions. It became obvious to them while working together that they were grandchildren of former enemies who most probably fought against each other in World War II. Together they developed the idea of organising a conference that focuses on this issue. Since then, an organising team[2] formed in Berlin (Germany). To date, two psycho-historical Trialog Conferences were held in Potsdam (Germany), in 2015 and 2017. We invited Ukrainian, Russian and German colleagues to a four-day exchange on individual, family-related and psycho-historical issues. Most of the participants were psychological and medical psychotherapists, who all are the children and grandchildren of victims and perpetrators, soldiers and civilians in various roles, positions and faiths. We established a framework of small and large group analytic work.

Social background and the aim of the conference

In 2014, while we were busy planning the first Trialog Conference for the next year, a war broke out between Russia and Ukraine, which continues to this day. At first we doubted whether a conference would still be possible in these circumstances. Some Russian and Ukrainian colleagues cancelled their participation because they refused to talk to the enemy. Nevertheless, we decided to continue the project. Those who were open to an encounter felt that this confrontation was more important than ever in the light of current events. So we aimed to understand and reflect the diverse past and present, personal and collective experiences and projections. The aim is to reduce prejudices and increase mutual trust through talking (Alder, 2018). Furthermore, due to our common history (from World War I and the revolution of 1917–1918 to World War II and up to the end of the Cold War in 1989) we will not only realise what separates us but also what connects us. The choice of the title "Trialog" is motivated by the idea of the necessity of triangulation (Abelin, 1980; Thomä & Kächele, 1987). We aim to involve citizens from three countries in a dialogue because a dialogue between two parties often requires a third position in order for new insights to develop. During the conference, different participants alternately assume the triangulating, perspective-giving position. We are convinced that this facilitates communication and deepens the dialogue.

We would like to learn from each other, not teach each other. The participants working as psychotherapists, supervisors or organisational consultants can act as multipliers in their working fields where they can share the experience they have gained.

Conference structure

The group work was organised in such a way that each participant was part of a small group moderated by two group leaders and one interpreter. In the small groups (no more than ten) participants and two group leaders sat in a circle facing each other. The large group consisted of several circles with the outer circle being the largest and the inner circle the smallest. All seats faced the centre and everyone could choose their seat, including the large group leaders. Outside of the group's circle in each small group, two silent observers took notes, and all the six to nine observers in the large group. They recorded everything they heard and saw but were asked to avoid active participation.

The small groups met up to three times a day. Additionally, once a day all the participants and group leaders met in the large group. The same counts for the Social Dreaming session (following Lawrence, 2005), which was only held once. Every group session (be it a small or large group or the social dreaming) was supported by interpreters for the three languages (Russian, Ukrainian and German). What was said was immediately translated. Each group had two group leaders. Each leading couple consisted of one German and one Ukrainian or Russian group analyst. All German group leaders were formally trained group analysts and the Ukrainians and Russians were experienced psychoanalysts. The group leaders made sure the interaction was safe, trusting and open.

The small and large group leaders are referred to as staff. Staff and interpreters met as a group with supervision each night during the conference, in order to share their thoughts on their experiences in the process and regarding the subject at hand. The observers' group met independently outside these supervised sessions (see Alder & Buchholz, 2017 for previous work).

These different group models delineate the parameters for the participants. This framework, while providing safety and support, also allowed for space for the development of reflection. The three group models served to organise psycho-historical knowledge. For the participants, they represented open spaces in which both the unconscious and the conscious was verbalised. The general rule for contributions was the rule of "Free-Floating Discussion" (Foulkes, 1964; Schlapobersky, 2016) related to the psychoanalytic idea of Free Association (Freud, 1959 [1925]). However, the focus is meant to be on sharing thoughts and biographical imprints relating to the overall conference subject of a shared historical background.

Group analytic theory

The group work we followed in the Trialog Conferences draws on the tradition of Group Analysis (Foulkes, 1964; Burrow, 1926; Hopper, 2003). Group Analysis is guided by the assumption that there is an unconscious that connects group members. This connection is conceptualised in the metaphor of a *matrix*. According to S. H. Foulkes (1964, p. 292), "the matrix is the hypothetical web of communication and relationship in a given group. It is the common shared ground which ultimately determines the meaning and significance of all events and upon which all communications, verbal and non-verbal, rest." More recent works on the matrix concept and its application in the field of group analysis are mentioned for instance in Schlapobersky (2016). While the matrix describes the general conditions governing encounters of people in groups, American psychoanalyst Vamik Volkan's (2000, 2004, 2015) concept of a *large group identity* draws on social and cultural attributions. Just as there are different aspects of a personal identity (Straub, 2016; Volkan, 2004) that arise through temporal (diachronic) and interactive/communicative (synchronic) difference (Assmann, 2006; Straub, 2016, p. 162), there are also forms of group identity. According to Volkan's concept of large group identity, group identity needs to be distinguished from the individual core identity. The former is intimately interwoven with the latter (Volkan, 2004, p. 33). Nevertheless, large group identity, which is a cultural and a social identity, is communicated to us from the earliest stages of individual development. Large group identity circumscribes the affiliation to large groups of people who usually do not know each other individually, but are connected by certain characteristics, for instance shared convictions, a shared faith and a common language. This might be paraphrased as a "feeling of inner sameness" (Volkan, 2015, p. 111) and is expressed in a "we form: [. . .] we are Lithuanian Jews, we are Slavs, we are Germans, we are Sunni Muslims, we are Communists" (Volkan, 2015, p. 111). This identity, he says, gives pleasure on the one hand, but on the other hand it is also a source of prejudice against other groups and their members. It can serve to legitimate the murder and repression of other large groups, or to find a cooperative attitude towards the others.

Cultural complex

In parallel to the large group concept, Thomas Singer and Samuel L. Kimbles (2008) developed the concept of the *cultural complex*, referring to C.G. Jung's (1934)

166 Marie-Luise Alder and Stephan Alder

complex theory. Complexes as a whole are mainly emotion-based, repetitive, autonomous and stable patterns acting in the minds of individual people (Jung, 1934; Kast, 1994; Roesler, 2010). In the context of social events, a shared language, religion, social conflict and traumata (for instance shared experiences of wars, displacement, imprisonment or flight), typical experiences, events evoking fear or shame or great successes that are a matter of pride to a whole group of people (like victory in war or a win in a World Cup) combine into a structure or shape. It is this shape, a partly conscious but often unconscious configuration, that Singer and Kimbles (2008) call a cultural complex. Both concepts emphasise the strong emotional reaction of people as individuals and group members and focus on cultural memory (Assmann, 2006).

Activating cultural memory and making it useful for a group is what group analytic encounters focus on. Besides the Trialog Conference, there are several other projects that bring people from different nations, beliefs and generations together in order to confront, understand and, consequently, overcome prejudice, hate, idealisation or other kinds of inauspicious dispositions (Friedman, 2017; Levin, 2017; Erlich, Erlich-Ginor, & Beland, 2009). Just like at Trialog Conference, these group analytic encounters always have staff and participants. The group work of the Nazareth Conference mostly focuses on Germans who have lived through the Nazi era, and on descendants of Germans and Jews who are either survivors of the Shoah or the descendants of survivors (Erlich et al., 2009).

Silent note takers at Trialog Conference

We would now like to take a closer look at the large group protocols from the Trialog Conferences. As described above, silent note takers accompanied the group session and were instructed to avoid active participation in groups. During the group sessions, they were allowed to take notes and record their observations according to a focus they determined themselves. In this manner, more than 500 pages of material were generated. In their large group protocols, which the following remarks are based on, the observers attempted to write down as much as possible of the conversational turns. Nevertheless, these minutes should not be misconstrued as verbatim protocols, but understood as a shorthand recording of what was said, without any claim to being a full word-for-word transcript. The goal was to quickly record the sequential development of subjects, words and scraps of conversation. The excerpts quoted below have all been translated from the original German to English for this publication. To our knowledge, this is a rare example of actual minutes of a large group interaction, if not the only one. This allows us not just to reconstruct interactions from minutes taken from memory or from re-narrations, but actually to retrace an interaction in a large group. The value of studying psychotherapeutic processes with the help of detailed transcripts has already been demonstrated elsewhere (Peräkylä, Antaki, Vehviläinen, & Leudar, 2008; Buchholz, Spiekermann, & Kächele, 2015). In the following, we will present some fragments of these protocols in order to keep the analytic process transparent and allow readers to understand it. Readers can follow the unfolding conversation. Even though the transcripts are limited in our case because of the stenographic style, they clearly show the associative manner of talking in the large group.

Common ground activity and the use of conversational objects

When people talk to each other, they relate to the smallest common knowledge and continuously increase this knowledge. This common ground (Tomasello, 1999) includes knowledge of the knowledge of the other: the other knows what you know yourself, and you know that the other knows that you know (Clark, 2006). In group processes like Trialog in particular, with individual participants from different cultures, establishing common ground is essential. Without an awareness of the significance of common ground, it is impossible either to resolve conflicts or to achieve reconciliation.

In conversation we create conversational objects. This means we turn something (e.g. a thought, a feeling, a perceivable object) into words that henceforth can be talked about. Think of initiating small talk. We often start with a reference to the weather or a picture on the wall, things we as interactants can easily access. This directs our joint attention and ensures the first step onto common ground. For example, a feeling can be turned into a conversational object through metaphor (Buchholz, 2016), which then can be talked about. The experience of a relationship can thus be captured in an image. Buchholz (2016) describes this process as part of the common ground activity in one-on-one psychoanalytic conversations, attributing the highest level of the common ground activity to this creative achievement of developing metaphors. He describes the first level as the transformation of an object that the participants of the interaction can see or hear into a conversational object; the second level is the integration of conversational objects into the course of the dialogue; on the third level, conversational objects are related to each other (e.g. A relates to B like A to C); on the fourth and highest level, metaphorical objects for this relation are created. This provides an opportunity to talk about something "as if", which enables change.

These common ground activities and the search for a conversational object were observed both in the first large group in 2015 and in 2017. To the best of our knowledge, this is the first description of such a process in groups.

Common ground activity facilitates personal exchange

In 2015, at the first Trialog Conference, sixty-two people participated in the large group sessions. What we can observe is how an external object from the shared perceivable world develops into a conversational object and encourages self-disclosure. The following fragment is taken from a protocol of the large group during its meeting on the second day of the conference. Everyone had already met in one of the small group sessions, so this large group was the second session they attended.

Outside, it was a sunny spring day in May. After a short silence, the free-floating discussion started. One participant, person A in the protocol, began to speak. He referred to a bird that could be heard, thus creating a conversational object (first level of common ground activity) that was then used in the further course of the conversation. Person A interprets the birdsong that is heard outside as the bird's fundamental wish to connect with another. The large group hears this as a comment on itself, and other participants start to integrate the bird in the course of the conversation and refer it to themselves.

1)   *Excerpt from a large group protocol (Nedtwig, 2017) of Trialog 2015:*

> *[While referring to the sound of a bird from outside]*
> *Person A starts by saying: "Birds who still sing now must be losers since they still haven't found a wife."*
> *Person B: "Birds seem to be closer to art in depression."*
> *Person C: "It might just be a typical Berlin 'single bird.'"*
> *Person D tells about his feeling of loneliness in his small group because [there] he is the only Ukrainian.*
> *[Person E], a Russian woman, gives him a look of understanding and declares that she too feels lonely.*

The bird is related to the group because one participant reckons it was better in the art of expressing its depression than the group itself (third level of common ground activity). The metaphorical image of a lonely bird expressing its solitude enables the large group members to express their need of belonging and relating.

In the process of the large group, the bird serves to build a conversational object from a sensory experience that, while it is located outside the group, can be heard by everyone. This provides a starting point in which joint attention (Tomasello, 1999) is built on something that everyone can have access to by listening. The joint attention allows the group to negotiate how the image of a singing bird may be interpreted and made useful. Through the idea of singing as an expression of loneliness, the subject is made available and is used by a group member. Again, he is talking about his loneliness in a small group, yet outside the actual group. The process develops and gradually approaches the here and now until one group member can express her loneliness in this particular large group.

This lands us in the participants' direct experience of relationships in the large group. From the lonely singing bird, other images of singing came to the surface of conversation. The lonely singing bodes ill and is continued in the imagery of the myth of the Sirens. This opened the large group to a very painful and transgenerational experience. First someone mentioned Odysseus plugging his crew's ears as protection from the Sirens. Another one mentioned Orpheus who escaped them with even louder singing. The underlying question could have been: How is it possible to escape the loneliness and seductive danger in a large group? Suddenly the image of the Sirens was transformed when one participant told of his childhood experiences, which still influence him today: "'When the sirens sound, I cannot work', and then [he] draws a parallel to the air raid alarm sirens in World War II. The ambiguity of the 'sirens', which has already made itself felt, is expressly described here" (Dreyer, 2017, p. 207). The Sirens not only became a symbol of utter destructive seduction, like the singing bird with its mating call, but also of the life-saving signal before air raids.

The images of the Sirens and the bird's loneliness were utilised as a conversational object. These became metaphors which functioned to provide access to shared experiences, to find common images and to associatively connect these to personal stories and feelings.

Metaphors in a large group and their meaning for the group

From Trialog 2017, with forty-two participants from the three countries, we would like to show the extent of the large group's struggle to establish common ground and include destructive large group attributions. Trialog 2017 differs from Trialog 2015 in that most of the members already knew each other from the first conference, and they already knew what to expect from the setting. Due to the limitation of space, we can only give an account of the first minutes of the large group session, and will then return to the protocols in order to understand the development of a powerful metaphor.

Immediately after the opening of the conference, we started with the first large group session. In the early stages of this session, the question was how the group, and also individual members, would be able to contact each other and the large group leaders. Everyone knew there was one female Ukrainian and one male German group leader.

The experience of relationship was in a way added on in the same large group session, which was later developed into the following scenario: should amorous relationships develop among the participants, this would be a union between people of different nations, two of which actually were at war – a hot issue for the Russian and Ukrainian participants. As soon as they got involved, the German participants would be unable to avoid aligning themselves to one or the other side. This issue was skilfully negotiated in the following narratives in an attempt to establish common ground: first, a female participant tells of an encounter with a Norwegian man on the airplane on her way from Russia to Germany, and her astonished reaction to his question about marriage between Russians and Ukrainians: "[T]hat was like asking about gay marriage, in its significance. As though it wasn't legal" (see excerpt 2 below, turn 30). The moral question of who is allowed to do "it" with whom is negotiated. With the dung heap (*Misthaufen*) metaphor (in excerpt 2, turn 37) we come to a highlight of symbolic creation. The group members tried to approach the issue of pairing, and taboo constellations between Russians and Ukrainians, between same sexes and between Jews and Russians.

Let us now take a look at the stenographic protocol with the sequence about the Norwegian and the first appearance of the dung heap metaphor. The protocol's written style reflects the participants' associative speech. Once more we can observe how a theme evolved in a large group process and how an ambiguous metaphor was proposed. The note taker did not specify who said what, new turns in the conversation are therefore indicated by numbers in the sequences. Each freshly numbered turn is equivalent to a turn-taking.

2)   *Excerpt from the first large group session of Trialog 2017*

30   A female participant tells of her encounter with a Norwegian man. He asked how marriage between Russians and Ukrainians is viewed in Russia. She comments: "But that was like asking about gay marriage, in its significance. As though it wasn't legal."

31   Another woman reports that her neighbour couldn't deal with the fact that she was Jewish and Russian at the same time. It seems he couldn't understand how a Russian man could have married a Jewish woman. For her, the question was more plausible the other way round.

32   "Let's see where else the subject of love will take us."

33   "But you might also say that Russians and Ukrainians used to be married and are now in the process of separating. What becomes of love?"

34   "It seems it was one-sided love."

35   "Some also confuse love and possession."

36   "Marriages of convenience."

37   A German woman says: "Marry across the dung heap (*Misthaufen*) and you'll know what you'll get." (German proverb: *Heirate über'n Mist, dann weißt du was du kriegst!*)

Speaker 32 opts for the subject of love and comments on the process: "Let's see where else the subject of love will take us." This comment neither touches upon the anti-Semitism nor on the sensitive issue of transnational relationships. It can be classified as an attempt to reveal a common ground in these two preceding turns, and thus allow it to be used by the participants. It is an attempt to relate the participants to each other – the third level of common ground activity. The following turns in the conversation are also descriptive, trying to filter a common ground from an observer's position: People from different countries talk about love without borders. The current war between Russia and Ukraine is finally verbalised in the image of a divorced couple (turn 33). The confusion of love and possession (turn 35), too, is ambiguous and involves normative ideas of love and its justified claims. Ultimately, the German proverb "Marry across the dung heap and you'll know what you'll get" is derived from the marriage of convenience. While the Germans did not seem to play any role in the discussion on fantasies of pairing, what their side contributed was the offer of the dung heap as an initiator of relationships. This had a triangulating effect.

Finding common ground in large group sessions **171**

From the proverb, the participants seized on the metaphor of the dung heap and went on to discuss it. This meant they metaphorically grasped the experience of a relationship, going on to negotiate its possible meanings – the fourth level of common ground activity. The dung heap was considered and discussed as an ambivalent metaphor, and with it the ambivalence of Good (fertile manure) and Bad (poisoning) (see next excerpt 3). De Masi (2010) distinguishes between love and hatred, which are similar in their object relatedness, while self-satisfied destruction poisons and destroys all that connects. What we would like to draw attention to briefly is that the members of the large group negotiated both the connecting forces (love), the limiting forces (hate) and the poisonous destructive forces. This enabled them to reveal the complexity, which implied a detoxifying capacity. This is apparent in the logged utterances (39 to 48) in the next excerpt:

3)   *Continued excerpt from the first large group session of Trialog 2017*

   39   "The Wild East."
   40   "But this was meant more in a symbolic manner, wasn't it?"
   41   "Talking about borders seems to be risky."
   42   "As long as we talk without coming to blows, that's ok."
   43   "Marriage of love is something new, after all. It all used to be about the exchange of goods. Marrying across borders meant expanding one's territory."
   44   "Dung heap – what does that mean? You throw everything together and in the end, you have to untangle it all again."
   45   "Actually, every farm has its own dung heap. A large farm has a large dung heap."
   46   "You have to marry so you aren't left with your own heap [*Haufen*, heap or turd, translator's note]."
   47   "Farmers poison the groundwater with liquid manure."
   48   "Now it's starting to get ugly."

The dung heap is a rural metaphor that all three nations were able to embrace as a common and shared cultural background. This may be understood as an example of shaping a cultural complex (Singer & Kimbles, 2008), which in this case does not separate but connect. The differentiation of the metaphorical meaning occurs by way of the double meaning of dung heap (*Misthaufen*) and turd (*Scheißhaufen*) and continues to the poisoning of groundwater.

From a group analytic perspective, this is a process of developing and consolidating group cohesion, the experience of togetherness among group members. Thus, the concept of a common ground in its dynamics can be understood as one aspect of the realisation of the group matrix through the participants' group activity. The relationship and the relatedness[3] of the large group leaders amongst themselves might also be considered to reflect the dynamics of this process. The female large group leader was Ukrainian, the male large group leader German. Both connected

Closing remarks

Today, there is a war in Ukraine, a country neighbouring the European Union; people lived side by side there for more than a hundred years. People married across ethnic divides, something that is becoming impossible for many today. Families are divided by the current war, couples are destroyed because one of them feels they owe allegiance to the Russian nation, the other to the Ukrainian. Behind this societal conflict, the painful past between Germans and people(s) from the former Soviet Union, including Russians and Ukrainians, was alive. However, these days Germany is the best compromise for such a meeting to be realised. We are grateful and delighted to find that, in spite of a history informed by war, the Russian and Ukrainian participants trusted the German hosts enough to accept the invitation to Germany. All participants were open to meet each other against the backdrop of history.

The struggle for recognition of differences and reconciliation pervaded the conference as a whole. This struggle became manifest in the search for a common language, a common ground through common metaphors. Step by step, the members of the large group developed the capacity for love, hate and detoxication. This is a process that may be regarded as a proxy for a variety of social conflicts in societies.

The compilation of the large group protocol sequences showed that:

a) Conversational objects are found and translated to become the group's topic.
b) Common ground activities are an essential component of the differentiation of a given group's matrix, which initially was only a hypothetical assumption.
c) We were able to show with group processes, too, how the creation of metaphors reflects *and* promotes creative cooperation.
d) Metaphors serve as vehicles to facilitate a process of negotiating and understanding.
e) Group leaders may find it useful to identify the details of common ground activity and harness its potential for the group.

As a political statement, we believe that it is worthwhile to talk to each other in a good enough and safe enough setting. Group analysts can thus enable an encounter between nations or communities or organisations. This kind of group work generates a capacity to reduce prejudices, anxiety and egocentric convictions. It is helpful to understand that human beings are strongly influenced by their large group identities, with their cultural complexes forming a part of their individual psyches. The real encounter with the other is necessary to learn this. We support a culture of a balanced ego, group and other centred view, keeping the dignity of the individual central.

Acknowledgements

We would like to thank all participants of these conferences in their different functions and roles, in particular all those who gave their time and expertise as group leaders, as participating observers, as supervisors or who provided financial support. Many thanks to the observers, in particular Florian Dreyer, Michael M. Dittmann, Camellia Hancheva, Juliana Nedtwig, Tatjana Jacob-Bekfani, Olga Janzen and Christopher Mahlstedt.

Notes

1 Translated from the German by Brita Pohl.
2 This includes not only the two authors, but also the active members of the organisation team of the conference and their supporters – for names and details, please, see www.trialog-conference.org/en/.
3 In Group Analysis some aspects of the knowledge by W. R. Bion are used (Bion, 1961; Lopez-Corvo, 2003). In group-related work (Tavistock model) the concept of relatedness and relationship is used. Relationship is a way of relating to an "other" which derives not from relationship in reality but from a totality of feelings, associations, fantasies and attributions that the other evokes. Relatedness has a real impact on what happens in and between groups. This is comparable with the matrix concept.

References

Abelin, E. (1980). Triangulation, the role of the father and the origins of core gender identity during the rapprochement subphase. In R. Lax, S. Bach, & J. Burland (Eds.), *Rapprochement: The critical subphase of separation-individuation* (pp. 151–169). New York: Jason Aronson.

Alder, M-L., & Buchholz, M. B. (Eds.). (2017). *Trialog: Beobachtungen einer Konferenz zur ukrainisch, russisch, deutschen Begegnung von Psychotherapeuten* (pp. 202–215). Retrieved from http://hdl.handle.net/20.500.11780/3771

Alder, S. (2018). *The trialogue conference, 2015 and 2017: A psycho-historical focus for group analytic work.* Retrieved December 5, 2018, from www.internationaldialogueinitiative.com/volkan-scholar-dr-stephan-alder-reports-on-trialogue-conference/

Assmann, J. (2006). *Thomas Mann und Ägypten: Mythos und Monotheismus in den Josephsromanen.* München: C.H. Beck.

Bion, W. R. (1961). *Experiences in groups.* London: Social Science Paperbacks.

Buchholz, M. B. (2016). Conversational errors and common ground activities in psychotherapy – insights from conversation analysis. *International Journal of Psychological Studies, 8*(3), 134–153.

Buchholz, M. B., Spiekermann, J., & Kächele, H. (2015). Rhythm and Blues - Amalie's 152nd session: From psychoanalysis to conversation and metaphor analysis – and back again. *The International Journal of Psychoanalysis, 96*(3), 877–910.

Burrow, T. (1926). Die Gruppenmethode in der Psychoanalyse. *Imago, 12*, 211–222.

Clark, H. H. (2006). Social actions, social commitments. In N. J. Enfield & S. C. Levinson (Eds.), *Roots of human sociality* (pp. 126–150). Oxford: Berg.

De Masi, F. (2010). *Die sadomasochistische Perversion. Jahrbuch der Psychoanalyse, Beiheft 23.* Stuttgart-Bad Cannstatt: frommann-holzboog.

Dreyer, F. (2017). Resonanz im Trialog. In M-L. Alder & M. B. Buchholz (Eds.), *Trialog: Beobachtungen einer Konferenz zur ukrainisch, russisch, deutschen Begegnung von Psychotherapeuten* (pp. 202–215). Retrieved from http://hdl.handle.net/20.500.11780/3771

Erlich, H. S., Erlich-Ginor, M., & Beland, H. (2009). *Gestillt mit Tränen – Vergiftet mit Milch: Die Nazareth-Gruppenkonferenzen Deutsche und Israelis – die Vergangenheit ist gegenwärtig*. Gießen: Psychosozial.

Foulkes, S. H. (1964). *Therapeutic group analysis*. London: George Allen & Unwin [reprinted London: Karnac, 1984].

Freud, S. (1959 [1925]). An autobiographical study. In J. Strachey (Ed.), *The standard edition of the complete psychological works of Sigmund Freud, Volume XX (1925–1926)*. London: Hogarth Press and Institute of Psycho-Analysis.

Friedman, R. (2017). Enemies' love story: Reconciliation in the presents of foes. In G. Ofer (Ed.), *A bridge over troubled water: Conflicts and reconciliation in groups and society* (pp. 173–186). London: Karnac.

Hopper, E. (2003). *Traumatic experience in the unconscious life of groups: The fourth basic assumption: Incohesion: Aggregation/massification or (ba) I:A/M*. London: Jessica Kingsley.

Jung, C. G. (1934). *Allgemeines zur Komplextheorie (Collected Works, Vol. 8)*. §194–219. Olten: Walter-Verlag.

Kast, V. (1994). *Dynamik der Symbole: Grundlagen der Jungschen Psychotherapie*. Trimbach: Walter.

Lawrence, W. G. (2005). *Introduction to social dreaming: Transforming thinking*. London: Routledge.

Levin, U. (2017). Us and them: An object relations approach to understanding the dynamics of inter group conflicts. In G. Ofer (Ed.), *A bridge over troubled water: Conflicts and reconciliation in groups and society* (pp. 155–172). London: Karnac.

Lopez-Corvo, R. E. (2003). *The dictionary of the work of W. R. Bion*. London: Karnac.

Nedtwig, J. (2017). Was ist eine Stimmung in einer Gruppe? In M-L. Alder & M. B. Buchholz (Eds.), *Trialog: Beobachtungen einer Konferenz zur ukrainisch, russisch, deutschen Begegnung von Psychotherapeuten* (pp. 216–228). Retrieved from http://hdl.handle.net/20.500.11780/3771

Peräkylä, A., Antaki, C., Vehviläinen, S., & Leudar, I. (Eds.). (2008). *Conversation analysis and psychotherapy*. Cambridge: Cambridge University Press.

Roesler, C. (2010). *Analytische Psychologie heute: Der aktuelle Stand der Forschung zur Psychologie C. G. Jungs*. Freiburg: Karger.

Schlapobersky, J. R. (2016). *From the couch to the circle: Group-analytic psychotherapy in practice*. London: Routledge.

Singer, T., & Kimbles, S. L. (Eds.). (2008). *The cultural complex: Contemporary Jungian perspectives on psyche and society*. London: Routledge.

Straub, J. (2016). *Religiöser Glaube und säkulare Lebensformen im Dialog: Personale Identität und Kontingenz in pluralistischen Gesellschaften*. Gießen: Psychosozial.

Thomä, H., & Kächele, H. (1987). *Psychoanalytic practice: Principles*. Heidelberg: Springer.

Tomasello, M. (1999). *Origins of human communication*. Cambridge, MA: MIT Press.

Volkan, V. (2000). *Das Versagen der Diplomatie. Zur Psychoanalyse nationaler, ethnischer und religiöser Konflikte*. Gießen: Psychosozial.

Volkan, V. (2004). *Blind trust: Large groups and their leaders in times of crisis and terror*. Charlottesville: Pitchstone.

Volkan, V. (2015). Großgruppenidentität, schweres Trauma und seine gesellschaftlichen und politischen Konsequenzen. In S. Walz-Pawlita, B. Unruh, & B. Janta (Eds.), *Identitäten: Eine Publikation der DGPT* (pp. 111–130). Gießen: Psychosozial.

14

THE BALKANS ON THE REFLECTIVE-CITIZENS COUCH UNRAVELING SOCIAL-PSYCHIC-RETREATS

Marina Mojović

> "*The Balkans is Europe's myth,*
> *It has been the screen onto which the Europeans*
> *projected their dreams, and that has been their doom.*"
>
> —*Žižek (2018)*

Serbian Reflective-Citizens (RC) is a new psycho-social methodology combining in a certain way approaches from the psychoanalytic family aimed for all interested citizens to reflect on their communities, exploring the social unconscious (SU) in its various manifestations. Complex psycho-social phenomena, such as "social-psychic-retreats" (SPR), are often encountered, their unraveling initiated with deeper individual and collective understanding, which includes relationships of local/regional with other European or global processes. More about RC and SPR follows after a short vignette. Further illustrations are offered from social-historical themes, a Nobel Prize-winning novel and Kusturica's film "Underground", returning then for elaborations of the vignette from that RC event.

Serbian and Ex-Yugoslav Reflective-Citizens

A recent RC workshop, held in a village close to the historic Višegrad on the river Drina near the Bosnian/Serbian border, started with a Social Dreaming session.

> An old farmer began: "*I dreamt many times about my bull Thunder, but yesterday's nightmare really scared me. My grandfather, my father, my son and I are all engaged in traditional bull-fighting. This competition, who's bull is the strongest, was absent only during WWII and the last war. In this nightmare, Thunder suddenly dug his hooves — stared into the depths of my soul, turned around to the crowd, people moved, but he*

gazed just at one beautiful girl. Chased by Thunder, she ran away through the woods, threw herself into the green depths of the Drina – Thunder stopped at the bank, his nostrils flaring and hooves buried – I woke up sweating!" Associations to the dream came fast: "The bull was lost, possessed by archaic powers, urging help from his master . . . I know about Thunder from our village, with his flattened horns, trained not to kill, but. . .!". Another image was of abused women throwing themselves into the historic Drina "better drowned than raped!"; an older woman was reminded of Serbian children who were taken away along the Drina by the "Ottoman Bull" – leaving their mothers forever frozen in grief on the river-bank. "As if time is frozen, too . . . Then in these new wars, it was our sons who did horrendously shameful things. So much hate and evil! We are cursed!" she moaned. A younger man linked this to his recurrent dreams about falling-exams, and "wanting only to get out of this mud." A participant from another town asked: "Wasn't it in Greek myth that Princess Europa was kidnapped by Zeus disguised as a white bull, then swimming together to Crete?" Another woman's voice replies: "Oh, yes, and the statue of Europa riding the Bull placed there in Brussels at the central EU building!"; "But wasn't it actually the rape of Europa? Bizarre for the EU?! " A retired guest-worker from France joins: "My recent bizarre dream emerges now: Višegrad was floating to Paris. My family stood on its old-bridge looking at Parisian bridges, ashamed and proud at the same time." A further association: "It is like the ending scene of Kusturica's film 'Underground', part of the miserable land floating down the Danube with ghostly people, as if alive." Sarcastically, a car mechanic lamented: "Living in Austria, I often felt seen as dirty, wild 'Balkanian', even barbaric rapist." A student adds: "I read about fears of 'Balkanisation' of Europe!"; "And for centuries we have played this game well!"; "Yes, no surprise, even Kusturica abused this image of the Balkans in his films, as if we are reduced to obscene, dirty killers." A student of linguistics brought her dream: "I was a teacher in a school with a ghostly atmosphere, children only had nicknames, no family names, single mothers, various nationalities – wasn't sure what kind of school it was – I didn't know and, at same time, I somehow knew that they had all been conceived by rape."

This vignette is a glimpse into the initiation of an RC event. Embraced with carefully created settings and RC methodology as a whole, people are invited to share dreams, associations to dreams, to be then followed by other psycho-social sub-sessions. Events are open, free of charge for any interested citizen as a voluntary activity. The network of events has been developing over 15 years continuously in Serbia in different locations. New branches are growing throughout the region (Bosnia and Herzegovina, Montenegro, Slovenia, Croatia) – named Ex-Yugoslav Reflective-Citizens. Enrichment continues also in cooperation for RC events in other European regions like in Turin, Malmo, London and Moscow or RC-inspired events in Warsaw (Zajenkowska, 2016).

These citizens' groups grow in grassroots style, from the trust in the capacity of raw human exchanges of learning through experience, true culture of dialogue and citizens' responsibility. Cradled by psychoanalytic and group-analytic traditions,

The Balkans on social-psychic-retreats **177**

RC aspire to provide space for free sharing of thoughts, feelings, fantasies, dreams, drawings and hypotheses, opening up the minds to the chaotic and uncontrollable unconscious of communities within "safe-enough" dialogue situations – thus keeping the psychoanalytic flame of liberal and cosmopolitan ideals burning. Similar to other psychoanalytic areas, there is always a struggle to balance two opposite paradigms: the totalitarian and the liberal, overtly and covertly being parts of the world we live in (Mojović, 2018b, 2018c). RC involves some elements of grassroots movements regarding encouraging citizens to take responsibility for their communities and self-organizing, but without aiming to become a political movement (Mojović, 2018d).

RC events always reveal many layers of personal, community, regional, European and global dynamics in their complexity of human interactions. Therefore, appreciation of complexity is strongly present in its core values. RC is not aiming to arrive jointly to any sort of homogeneous conclusion. Such human needs are, of course, often encountered, acknowledged and contained as much as possible. On the contrary, among its basic principles is the tendency to have participants from as many as possible different professional, age, gender, class, ethnic, religious and ideological/political areas. Thus, RC is primarily a space for freedom of diversity, for learning to listen and to be heard, for allowing difficult feelings like despair, hate, fear, guilt or shame to be expressed, defenses from them eventually seen/understood, as well as a place to learn to allow positive feelings like hope, love, etc. Opening up new perspectives, learning about others and one-self in relation to others, includes also the convener-participants, without any assumed privileges to own the "Truth". Essential is the challenge for all participants to open their minds for the diversity of discourses/paradigms and curiosity for their interactions, while keeping (or repairing) core human values.

RC roots, developments and applications are many – elaborated in "Serbian Reflective-Citizens Flourishing in the Leaking Containers", a response to Foulkes Lecture 2016, and elsewhere (Mojović, 2015, 2016, 2017, 2018b, 2018c, 2018d). Bauman (2005) claim that "people balance on the tightrope between freedom and stability" are related to certain phenomena rooted in the Balkans' SU and revealed through RC. Linked to people's existence on the faultlines of civilizations (Huntington, 1993), where the need for survival is constantly forcing perilous balancing between historical powers, the Balkans often "falls off that tightrope". Due to recurring regional social traumas with long-lasting consequences, for understanding the Balkans foundation matrices in their dimensions of homogeneity/diversity or stability/freedom, significant are specific social defenses, which I conceptualized as "social-psychic-retreats" (Mojović, 2011, 2015, 2017, 2018b).

Social-psychic-retreats in foundation matrices

"Social-psychic-retreats" are complex and obscure psycho-social phenomena, which originate in peoples' experiences of despair during extreme and cumulative social traumas. I have conceptualized them developing the psychoanalytic concept of "psychic retreats" (Steiner, 1993) through my group-analytic and psycho-social work. According to Steiner (1993, p. 2) psychic retreats (PR), as spaces of withdrawal from human contact which is experienced as threatening, are internal "pathological organisations" involving closely knit systems of defenses. Formed initially out of desperation, these sabotaging, self-protecting and self-organizing internal sub-systems provide alternative shelters for human relationships and for reality in general. In their very essence lies a paradox: they both protect and imprison the vital parts of the self.

As equivalence phenomena of internal PR, SPR are formations of social systems co-created by recursive externalisation and internalisation processes between personal psyche and society, which simultaneously occur in both directions. SU vastly operates through these figurations, which involve highly-structured systems of social defenses and create alternative shelters to social mainstreams. They indirectly influence a lot the dynamics of social discourses and power relations. They are being discussed in both their positive forms – as survival maneuvers – and negative, as obstacles to development. The latter underlie much of the social pathology aggravating with time and trans-generational transmission, becoming vicious psycho-social spirals causing unforeseen troubles. For example, in this region, extreme fear of losing freedom has often lead to isolation, unwise or even self-destructive decisions like protests in Belgrade 1941 against Hitler: "Better war than pact! Better grave than slave!" resulting immediately in extreme casualties during total bombing – one of the four within a single century. In Tito's time, slogans turned into the anti-communist: "Better dead than red!"

It is important to consider positive/negative aspect of SPR in relation to liberal/totalitarian aspects of the macro/micro-systems. Usually a version opposite to the mainstream of the macro-system is taking place in the particular micro-system of SPR: More positive SPR serve to protect from the threatening/totalitarian/terrorizing environment (life in ghettos, or underground homes). Negative SPR characteristically develop totalitarian patterns with loss of faith into good relations (like mafia, or partisan guerilla initially protecting people, but turning into persecuting regimes). So, depending on the features of the immediate macro-system environment, whether more liberal or more totalitarian, the opposite version of power relations is lodged in the alternative space, walled off in the micro-system of SPR (Mojović, 2011, 2018b).

Thus, SPR are a sort of "illusionary containers" (Armstrong, 2005) or "as-if-transitional" spaces (Steiner, 1993; Mojović, 2011, 2018b), but in contrast to these phenomena, in the Serbian and Balkans foundation matrices there exist also true transitional spaces (Winnicott, 1971; Bridger, 2001), bridging different paradigms as creative psycho-social holding environments (like in Serbian community traditions of supportive fellowship, "koinonia").

My learning on the subject came through various roles (professional and citizen's), yet the group-analytic field was the major source. In the laboratory of the group-analytic matrices, the personal PR of a few members might meet with each other. The "coming-into-being" of SPR (group version) often becomes visible in

The Balkans on social-psychic-retreats **179**

the dynamics of their construction/deconstruction. However, for my further learning, RC was the most meaningful resource – in analogy to small groups, within these events, the SPR of various communities become more transparent by mirroring each other.

Upon questioning whether a society without at least some trauma experience exists at all, SPR might be regarded as quite universal phenomena – certainly in the Balkans and Europe in general. Although we are now carefully and cooperatively learning about regional similarities/differences, still the bulk of my competence on these phenomena comes from Serbia (most examples in the chapter). Complex intertwining within the wider global social matrices remains to be further explored.

Living in the socio-cultural borderland

Throughout the centuries Serbs and other South Slavs, as small European peoples, were destined to persist between the largest world empires and their great clashes, exactly where the historical storms of antagonizing power forces with their divergent cultures, ideologies and religions repetitively met – either for their major fights, sometimes in struggles to extinction, or for their political negotiations to embrace peace. So, probably these nations must have been predestined for the position of suffering, and for an existence which is difficult to understand by either the conflicting powers or their orbiting countries. It has certainly impacted much of their relating to others, for example chronic frustration of their needs to be really seen and understood, as well as to belong. When disillusionment from their unrealistic expectations from neighbors and allies was unbearable, then the dissociation from those needs was pushing them into SPR. Serbs developed a strong (whether overestimated or not) urge to defend the independence and identity of their homeland with historically valued readiness to sacrifice themselves for such ideals – a disposition imprinted into much of their social defenses, but which resulted also in major losses during wars: in WWI only, a third of the overall population (58% of male population) perished – a percentage far ahead of any other nation – with then-Prime Minister Pašić saying: "We lost everything, but kept our honor."

Being small between the large countries, at the same time – as an additional complexity of their "small-big" position (Stojanović, 1997) – the Serbs happened to be the largest among the South Slavs. Thus, often leaders of the unification of the "brotherly nations", they were seen as either supporting their "siblings" in reaching freedom from the surrounding empires or as patronizing them with hegemonic inclinations, suppressing their identity and independence. All those historical turbulences are happening in the mountainous Balkan Peninsula – the whole region being a crossroads between continents and cultures – but Serbs were "building the house in the middle of the road", living exactly around the division line between the Eastern and the Western World – historically often along the river Drina.

Suffering the horror of extreme social traumas would have been totally unbearable, leading to extinction, if the "childhood" had not been relatively serene. The peaceful prehistoric cultures of the "Old Europe", Lepenski Vir and Vinča

180 Marina Mojović

civilisations (Vinča's center was 10km from Belgrade, its writing system predating the Sumerian) and the "old Slavic proneness to democratic way of life" (Kobylinski, 2005; Herder, 1952, 1965) can be traced in the foundation matrix. In the early Serbian kingdoms the land was experienced as "good enough mother" and the way of adopting Christianity and changes went through soft transition spaces with pagan and ancient cultures. It was not until the 10th century that extreme social trauma occurred. Traces of shared memories from those early centuries with internalized ideals, accumulated faith, love and beauty, like a long period of primal idealization, may be found manifested in the SU, for example, in the Serbian folk poetry or beautiful frescoes (UNESCO Heritage).

Changes of the social-psychic-retreats regarding historical turning points

Thus, dispositions for co-creation of positive SPR and of warm/soft transitional spaces including tendency to somewhat infantile features, *enfant-de-nature*, like unrealistic expectations/naivety in relationships, was probably due to lack of immunity to extremely violent situations. In better circumstances, Serbs might have had opportunities for gradual growing up, but their journey towards nation's maturity was traumatically interrupted in the 14th century with the Ottoman invasion – to be continued in completely changed circumstances. Strong defense mechanisms had to come into use for surviving the dramatic encounter with most cruel abuse of the population, customs and religion in the infamous Ottoman style of public torture by tearing out the fingernails, decapitating, burning of Orthodox saints' relics, publicly raping women and impaling people, constructing towers out of Serbian skulls along the roads . . . Among the most painful was the abuse of core identity by violently taking Serbian children, converting them to Islam and making them Janissaries – high-class infantry units of the Turkish army. A lot of poetry describes pains of the mother-child separations or reunion in fantasy (as in Andrić's story, later in this chapter). This new, cruel reality impacted the shaping of "false-self defensive organizations", while the nation's "trueself" turned mainly to live in various "underground spaces".

Thus, only after the death of Emperor Dušan and the Battle of Kosovo in 1389 against the Ottomans, the historical turning point (*caesura*), dramatic developmental changes ensued, creating a need for additional social defenses, particularly the rise of negative SPR. I suggest that during the centuries of the Ottoman rule, SPR (both positive and negative) increased and that in the later history of the Uprisings in 1804 and the later wars, SPR played a significant role – helpful for survival, but more mature nation's development was sabotaged.

Additional malignancy of these mechanisms occurred after 1918 with the confusion of identity linked to unification into Yugoslavia, especially with the unexpected turn of the country to communism during WWII (1943 Churchill-Tito Agreement). The resulting confusion was the outbreak of a terrible civil war. The consequences of the U-turn to communism tearing the social fabric of prewar civil societies were mass persecution of intellectuals and emigration of the elite – causing further darkening of SPR, adding more perverse layers. SPR turned their ugly head up in their full monstrousness later in the Yugoslav civil wars in the nineties.

Complexity of the border position: swinging between wisdom and confusion

Having to struggle with such difficulties of their historical position, the Serbs and their leaders aspired, on one side, to understand complexity, to wisely find ways to develop facilitating skills and transitional spaces for their identity within all the cultural differences around, to learn to cope with the constrains of the divergent paradigms being so close to each other. On the other side, they were often confused and lost in the overwhelmingly complicated projective/introjective inter-cultural processes – rise of the incohesion: aggregation/massification – (ba) I:A/M (Hopper, 2003) with falling into a range of traps – "psycho-social black holes" (Mojović, 2018a), such as:

1   Grandiose messianic tendencies (for example, in medieval times, the idea of defending Judeo-Christian Europe from the Ottomans; the "small-big" identity in self-destructive opposing empires: Austro-Hungarian, Ottoman, the Third Reich, the big "No!" to Stalin; after both world wars, to be the unifiers of Yugoslavia, certainly in collusion with the interest of the large world powers; or during the Cold War, when Tito seduced Yugoslav citizens into playing the peacemaker role between the East and the West Blocks, to be among the founders of the Non-Aligned Movement for the sovereignty of two-thirds of the UN member states in their struggle against imperialism).
2   Victimhood – ranging from inevitable true tragedies, innumerous mixed forms, to all those fueled masochistically or by the grandiosity mentioned above.
3   Scapegoat roles (e.g. when during the Yugoslav wars in the nineties Serbs were seen as the only perpetrators); manifested also in the fact that in the 20th century Serbia was bombed four times.
4   Enacting monstrous behaviors of atrocities in the civil wars of the nineties. Centuries-long mass emigration.

Extreme traumatic experiences with various psycho-social distortions were never worked through enough, but internalized as bad, often perverse objects within the sabotaging sub-systems of the SU – obstacles to mature coping with reality. Instead of the more acceptable defensive organizations, from which the self can emerge more easily into transitional spaces, negative SPR increased. The border position is now the opposite of the opportunity for relational understanding of different paradigms – it is the fertile ground for the repetitive, perverse circles of simultaneous acceptance and disavowal of truth and addiction to falsity, increasing the viciousness. For illustration of efforts to turn vicious circles towards a positive direction, here follows an excerpt from a famous story.

The Bridge on the Drina

As mentioned, the Drina was exactly the division line of the Great Roman Empire between its Eastern/Greek and its Western/Latin parts in the 4th century, which later created one of the major religious-cultural schisms, known as the Great East-West Schism, dividing the Christian Church into the Eastern Orthodox and the Roman Catholic (Fine, 1991). An additional significant schism happened later in the same region with the Turkish occupation and forced conversion to Islam. The major theme of the novel *The Bridge on the Drina* by the Serbian Nobel Prize winner Andrić, is the people living along the banks of Drina sharing the specific paradigm of both dividing and bridging the opposite worlds with the richness of diversity, but enormously suffering as well. The basic story is historically grounded: at the beginning of the novel, Andrić focuses on a Serbian boy taken from his mother for "blood tribute" as part of the levy of Christian people to the Sultan; it describes how mothers follow their children wailing. The boy becomes a Muslim convert, Mehmed. Around the age of 60, he becomes Grand Vizier Mehmed-Pasha Sokollu. Yet that moment of separation haunts him and he decides to commission the building of a bridge at the point on the river where he was separated from his mother. It should have the power "to bridge the steep banks and the evil water between them . . . and thus link safely and forever Bosnia and the East, the place of his origin and the places of his life" (Andrić, p. 42).

The pain in Pasha's chest

"Always the same black pain which cut into his chest with special well-known childhood pang which was clearly distinguishable from all the ills and pains that life later brought to him" (Andrić, 2011, p. 41). The pain, from which he couldn't ever find relief, was obviously holding many layers of imprisoned/encrypted traumata: personal/family/leadership and social-cultural. Being so cruelly separated from his mother/motherland, he needed a strong denial of the trauma experience for the survival of his body and soul. If not to be killed by such a horror, he had to push the contents into the very depths of his unconscious. We may imagine that it was also a way to keep the primal good objects safe in the internal home and the internal motherland of his personal PR, on a secure distance from other parts of his life. Still, the pain from his chest reminded him of having lost contact with vital parts of his self, crying for reunion. So, his two selves belonged to two countries, which were enemies for centuries and had to be kept at a distance. Building the bridge over the Drina was an appeal for a reunion of his two personal and social selves, and of his family as well. His brother Makarije Sokolović was at the time the Serbian Patriarch, the leader of the Serbian Orthodox Church, so they literally and historically represented the two sides of the Serbian people which, since the Ottoman invasion onwards, experienced painful difficulties in reuniting or in "bridging the unbridgeable".

The amount of pain and annihilation anxieties was so big that the creation of true bridging areas (transitional) could only occur with strong engagement.

Directly linked to this is an interesting contemporary example of a large cultural centre, Andrić-Town, built at the memorial Višegrad (by the film director Kusturica), intended for sharing, in the presence of "the other", people's memories, dreams, art, debates . . . in an appeal for reconciliation.

The film "Underground" by Kusturica is an illustration of phantasmal life in malignant SPR since WWII; in a story about two communist comrades, one climbing up the party ladder by betraying and manipulating, the other, a disabled war veteran, living in a bizarre shelter for decades, believing the war is still going on. The film ends with a surreal wedding scene, in which the living and the dead are reunited on a piece of land floating down the Danube, lost in confusion and despair.

Transitional spaces and social-psychic-retreats in the foundation matrix

During the six decades of the totalitarian communist rule, the external transitional spaces reduced so much that they were almost non-existent. They were sucked into multi-layered SPR ranging from relatively healthy defensive to malignant versions or dispersed in fragmentation within (ba) I:A/M. Free talk was not possible at all, neither at work nor in public places or families, as children, who all had to be "Tito's pioneers", could be exposed to dangers, too. Not only members of the Party and its orbiting organizations, such as Tito's Communist Youth, but also the spies of the regime, were spread all around in the social matrix. It was almost impossible to know which neighbor, "friend" or even family member could be involved into such roles. The field of neighborhood and relatives, traditionally being important transitional spaces (*koinonia*), became poisoned by inauthentic communication, scapegoating, suspiciousness and other paranoid anxieties.

Žižek, a social philosopher, has pointed out that "just at the point when the West is narcissistically admiring the incarnation of its Ego-Ideal of democracy in a more passionate form than it usually has in the routine politics of the West" (1990, p. 52), Yugoslavia as the East-West non-Allied transitional space was just about to explode/disintegrate. Yet Žižek himself uses jokes in a way typical for Yugoslav intellectuals – interchangeably creating matrix of cynicism about any truthful world, and only at moments finding cracks in such a world as random slips (Rustin, 2001); playing with paradox to discover space in which truth remains at least briefly possible for the true selves, but always being ready to sarcastically turn it all into a secure attitude of contempt, or "just joking". These phenomena originated to some degree from the internalization of Tito's manipulative skills. Unlike other communist leaders, Tito virtuously played with "as-if freedom" for citizens like his "self-management socialism" and open country borders. Emigration as refuge from endurable reality, both external and "inner emigration" (Arendt, 1994), were often the only solutions for true creative selves. In such ambiguity and blurring of borders between the true transitional and the as-if transitional spaces, between real freedom and as-if freedom, between truth and as-if truth, special mental and social mobility had to be learnt and yet you were never sure in which space you were. Internal images of *hajduks*

184 Marina Mojović

(traditional guerillas/outlaws), with both positive and negative potential, are part of this heritage.

Reflective-Citizens unraveling social-psychic-retreats

Returning now to the RC event vignette at the beginning: after closing the Social Dreaming Matrix with its "infinity", participants are asked to sit in circle and to freely share what comes to mind from their various citizens' roles (neighbor, parent/child, student, work roles, sports, soldier, political, traveler. . .). Contrary to previous rather impersonal matrix, here, in a face-to-face setting, participants slowly begin to co-create "psycho-social dialogue". Later, they continue the dialogue in small leaderless groups, only to return later to the whole-RC event group. From the richness of the contents, I will select few related to our subject:

1   The theme of the aggressive power of the bulls, holding both human destructiveness and passion – tamed through sports, but turned wild in wars – was unraveled through memories and concerns for the future. Many traditional rituals, although helpful, keep lives locked in circular repetitiveness (positive SPR).
2   The meaning of the bulls since ancient times in the Mediterranean and Minoan civilization were explored in relation to Slavic archetypes of bears and wolves.
3   The Balkans, seen as Europe's uncivilized area, is kept excluded from the EU – condemned to *damnation memoriae*. How did it happen that the land of some of the most ancient civilizations, as is eleven-millennia-old Lepenski Vir, the first city of Europe, and the Vinča civilisations, turned to the most horrendous human destructiveness?
4   The significance of the region's history with Turkish cruelties is still present in societal/family/personal stories. The stare of the bull was seen as an infantile/archaic intrusive appeal for decisions at social crossroads, although leaders were often incompetent or confused. Barbaric snatching of the beautiful youth (Serbian beauty) influencing victim-rapist relational perversity became obstacles for true contact with the *anima* (personal or collective) like in the "Beauty and the Beast" dynamics (perverse SPR).
5   People are stuck in "black-and-white", swinging between the victim's position of accusing only the "others" for bullying their families/communities or only one-selves, falling then into endless self-destructive lamenting. Real responsibility of taking ownership of perpetrator aspects slowly emerges; horror of rape and massacres is still difficult to look at, and to believe that happened massively on all warring sides, including within families; the Srebrenica/Bratunac theme activated a clash between denial in deadly silence, sighs from the tombs facing the evil.
6   One leaderless group identified themselves as Disney's bull "Ferdinand", wanting only positive vision in contrast to "the mud of the earlier generations", and visited other groups curious to understand their place in the event's

The Balkans on social-psychic-retreats **185**

system – their SPR shifted between further withdrawal from reality and opening to transitional spaces with jokes as mini-recoveries.

7   Difficulties in owning the complexity of one's identity, but rather split into clichés of "Europeanised intellectuals" and nationalists' "primitive bloody warriors" as the "two Serbias" (voiding more mature responsibility), were brought by previous participants.

My colleague Dr. Jelica Satarić, the co-creator of the RC program, often emphasizes that "RC is the society working on itself". In terms of the tightrope metaphor, in every RC event we experience swinging between denying and owning split-off psycho-social aspects. Still, in that up-and-down flow we testify moving towards RC learning the "art of listening" and "art of dialogue" – indeed, transforming hate into a culture of dialogue. These might be just "drops in the ocean" of social destructiveness. Yet, like some "beams of darkness" (Bion, 1973) enabling sighs and tears from the crypts to emerge – they remain meaningful.

Ending thoughts – Reflective-Citizens "bridging the unbridgeable"

The Balkans' position as a screen onto which Europe projects its dreams, in Žižek's terms, "Europe's mirror image" (Bjelić, 2011) or "Europe's shadow" holding chaos and destructiveness, is in our times, perhaps, at the new historical crossroads: Will this relationship repeat its pattern of misunderstanding and lead into new Europe/ World catastrophe? Or will it advance towards more mature levels of relatedness with taking back historically projected identity aspects of one's side onto the other – extending maturity and complexity capacities – questions often emerging through our RC lenses?

Europe was often doomed to smash its self-idealization, and if, even after being politically and historically in various ways involved in the Balkans' recurrent social traumas, it is not willing to thoroughly reconsider the dynamics of rejection/ acceptance of its "Balkans orphan/outlaw", then the vicious spirals might indeed continue. Europe's keeping the blind eye for the co-responsibilities for many Balkans tragedies might be linked to a need to protect the images of innocence and superiority, refusing some serious shifts in self-perception – perhaps, staying insulated in defensive "complacency" (Lousada, 2018). Is Europe forever doomed to crashing its (and ours) teeth onto the "Mountainous Balkans"? Or might "beams of darkness" in the cracks and blackholes of the Balkans' matrices illuminate some jewelry and wisdom kept safe for a long time in "inner migration"? Will some "RC guerilla" gain enough complexity skills with navigating through imaginaries with half-dead/half-alive people in their "flouting ghostly lands", or through the tricky discourses with slippery post-communist jokes, equip us for coping with our Post-Truth World? The "art of recycling true human treasure" was developed in the Social Dreaming of the Belgrade EFPP Conference 2018. Are the dreams of

186 Marina Mojović

"bridging the unbridgeable worlds" just in minds of artists, social dreamers and in Reflective-Citizens' fairytales?

In the myth Princess Europa dreamt about two women-continents fighting for her, Asia as her origin, and another without a name. Was it the "nameless dread" (Bion, 1962) of the intercourse(s) to come? Gazing at this *namelessness*, I think about speechlessness and un-bearableness of our Evil deeds: Jews excised from Europe; colonialism, racism and neo-liberalism annihilating whole communities, their identities and their histories; manufactured civil wars with children warriors; migrants drowning in the Mediterranean while dreaming about Europe; human trafficking ... Responsibilities keep shifting – ghosts keep haunting (Frosh, 2013; Mojović, 2015).

As citizens of Europe, we all might have parts of our personal/family/community/social matrices being conceived in "rape", that we want to disown. Perhaps, like those nameless children in the ghostly school dream (RC vignette), we need to continue learning how to embrace our painful destinies and of our fellow people – dissolve hate in warmth and dialogue within networks of *koinonia* (DeMare, Piper, & Thompson, 1991) as are Reflective-Citizens.

References

Andrić, I. (2011). *The bridge on the Drina*. Beograd: Dereta.

Arendt, H. (1994). *Eichman in Jerusalem: A report on the Banality of evil*. Harmondswoth: Penguin.

Armstrong, D. (2005). *Organization in the mind*. London: Karnac.

Bauman, Z. (2005). *Liquid life*. Cambridge: Polity Press.

Bion, W. (1962). *Learning from experience*. London: Karnac.

Bion, W. (1973). *Brasilian lectures*. London: Karnac.

Bjelić, D. (2011). *Normalizing the Balkans: Geopolitics of psychoanalysis and psychiatry*. London and New York: Routledge.

Bridger, H. (2001). Foreword. In G. Amado & A. Ambrose (Eds.), *The transitional approach to change*. London: Karnac.

DeMare, P., Piper, R., & Thompson, S. (1991). *Koinonia: From hate, through dialogue, to culture in the large group*. London: Karnac.

Fine, J. (1991). *The early medieval Balkans*. Ann Arbor, MI: University of Michigan Press.

Frosh, S. (2013). *Hauntings: Psychoanalysis and ghostly transmissions*. Hampshire: Palgrave Macmillan.

Herder, J. G. (1952). *Die Geschichte der Europaishen Volker*. Berlin: Aufbau.

Herder, J. G. (1965). *Ideen zur Philosophie der Geschichte der Menschheit. 2 Bände, Band 2, Herausgegeben von Heinz Stolpe*. Berlin und Weimar: Aufbau.

Hopper, E. (2003). *Traumatic experience in the unconscious life of groups*. London and Philadelphia: Jessica Kingsley.

Huntington, S. (1993). *Clash of civilisations?* New York: Simon & Schuster.

Kobylinski, K. (2005). The slavs. In F. Paul (Ed.), *The New Cambridge medieval history* (pp. 524–547). Cambridge: Cambridge University Press.

Lousada, J. (2018). *The challenge of social traumata – the inner worlds of outer realities*. Keynote at EFPP Conference in Belgrade, 2018.

Mojović, M. (2011). Manifestations of psychic retreats in social systems. In E. Hopper & H. Weinberg (Eds.), *Social unconscious in persons, groups and societies* (pp. 209–234). London: Karnac.

Mojović, M. (2015). Disrupted matrices: Challenges and changes. *Group Analysis, 48*(4), 540–557.

Mojović, M. (2016). Serbian reflective-citizens flourishing in the leaking containers. Group *Analysis, 50*(5), 370–384.

Mojović, M.(2017). "Untouchable infant gangs" in group and social matrices as obstacles to reconciliation. In G. Ofer (Ed.), *A bridge over troubled water: Conflicts and reconciliation in groups and society* (pp. 119–139). London: Karnac.

Mojović, M. (2018a). *Social traumata "Black Holes" in matrices.* Presentation at EFPP-Conference, Belgrade.

Mojović, M. (2018b). Totalitarian and post-totalitarian matrices: Reflective-citizens facing social-psychic-retreats. In B. Huppertz (Ed.), *Approaches to psychic trauma: Theory and practice.* Washington, DC: Lexington Books.

Mojović, M. (2018c). *Serbian reflective citizens coping with social trauma black holes.* Presentation at International Interdisciplinary Conference, Prague, Oct. 2018.

Mojović, M. (2018d). *Serbian reflective-citizens & Otpor Power with(out)money.* Workshop at OPUS Conference. London.

Rustin, M. (2001). *Reason and unreason: Psychoanalysis.* New York: Science and Politics.

Steiner, J. (1993). *Psychic retreats: Pathological organizations in psychotic, neurotic and borderline patients.* London: Routledge.

Stojanović, S. (1997). *The fall of Yugoslavia: Why communism failed.* Amherst, NY: Prometheus Books.

Winnicott, D. W. (1971). *Playing and reality.* London: Tavistock.

Zajenkowska, A. (2016). *Polska na kozetce: siła obywatelskiej refleksyjności.* Sopot: Smak Słowa.

Žižek, S. (1984). *Birokratijaiuživanje.* Beograd: SIC.

Žižek, S. (1990). East Europe's Republics of Gilead. *New Left Review, 183*(1), 50–52.

Žižek, S. (2018, February). *Lürzer's Archive.* Interview.

15

EUROPE ON THE COUCH IN SOCIAL DREAMING MATRICES

Gila Ofer

Introduction

This paper was written following my experiences as host to Social Dreaming Matrices (SDM) at international conferences in Europe and in various eastern and western European countries. The Social Dreaming Matrix is a method of working with dreams and associations to the dreams shared by a gathering of people, coming together for this purpose.

Throughout history, people met to share their dreams and learn how to use them to guide and inform their lives. We dream about important initiatory experiences from birth to death, to make sense of our waking lives. Freud called this "the royal road to the unconscious" (Freud, 1900) and offered his view of dreams as an experience of wish fulfillment. Later neo-Kleinian and object relations theorists looked at dreams as expressions of transference experiences in psychoanalytic relations (Segal, 1991). Self-psychologists regarded dreams as a map for solving problems and organizing mental life (Fosshage, 1997). Relational psychoanalysts looked at dreams as bringing forth dissociated affective stories of the dreamer (Bromberg, 2008). Ogden defines dreaming as "internal communication in which a dream presentation is generated by one aspect of self and understood by another aspect of self" (Ogden, 1990, p. 233). He argues that a dream is "internal communication involving a primary process [. . .] that must be perceived, understood, and experienced by another aspect of self" (ibid., p. 234). Dream data must undergo some form of psychological transformation in order for dreaming to occur.

The Social Dreaming Matrix emphasizes the social aspect of dreams and the social process of dreaming. There is a different kind of relationship between the dream and dreamer to that explored in psychoanalysis: a relationship not so much between different aspects or experiences of the self, rather it is between 'the Self' and 'the Other', where the dreamer gives voice to the dream that is in the person but not just of the person, and can understand the Other's voice through meeting others' dreams. A dialectical process occurs through the meeting of the participants' dreams and the social working hypotheses given by the conductor (host) of the SDM.

The key evidence that led to the formulation of the Social Dreaming Matrix as invented by Gordon Laurence was gathered through a reading of Charlottte Beradt's *Third Reich of Dreams* (Beradt & Bettelheim, 1968). Charlotte Beradt collected reports of dreams of Jewish citizens in Germany during the Third Reich. She asked a network of doctors to elicit dreams from their patients in the course of diagnosing them. In this way she was able to piece together their dreams which they themselves could not give voice to. What emerges is a horrific story. People dreamt of the fate that was to befall them. While in daily life they thought they could resist, their dreams told them otherwise. This was a clear example that dreaming and dreams can voice concerns of a social nature. The dreams dreamt were far beyond personal concerns, and referred to what was happening to them in the culture of the society.

The Social Dreaming Matrix can be as much a part of contemporary life as it always was in some societies. In it, participants are invited to share their earlier dreams while everyone is encouraged to provide associations for these dreams, let them float throughout the room seeking resonance, and witness how dreams create images which reveal something about social processes. The idea is not to claim ownership of the dream, but to let it make its own way, meeting other dreams and associations of the other participants (Lawrence, 1998). 'Matrix' is a place out of which something grows but it also refers to the network of 'all individual mental processes' (Foulkes, 1965, p. 26; Foulkes & Anthony, 1957). In a Social Dreaming Matrix, the focus is on the dream and not on the dreamer.

There is a sense of the most primordial of communication including feelings and nonverbal cues. Dreams in the matrix inevitably initiate conversations with one dream leading to another, creating associations, enabling participants to bring dreams from the infinite, recognizing them as a source of creativity and meaning available for their daily lives.

Dreaming and dreams are the currency of the matrix and not the relationships among participants. In this aspect, SDM is different from Friedman's model of dream-telling (Friedman, 2008). Issues of transference and countertransference are not meant to be part of the SDM. The reasoning is that if transference issues of the matrix are addressed directly in the 'here and now', the dreaming would be robbed of this material. In actuality, once transference issues are voiced in a dream any participant can pinpoint them. It is not the transference to the takers of the matrix that is important but rather to authority figures in the mind that are given substance in the dreams. ('Takers' or 'Hosts' are chosen as the name for the conveners of the matrix, in preference to 'consultants'.)

Social dreaming helps us understand processes that take place in the context of a certain organization or even in society at large. As each dream has a personal as well as a social aspect, the individual dreams for him/herself, as well as for a group, an organization, or a society. (While Bion (1967, 1970) spoke of thoughts looking for a thinker, Lawrence (1998) mentioned dreams looking for a dreamer.)

Our post-Freudian culture makes it difficult for people to consider dreams in terms of social commonalities rather than latent wishes and intimate thoughts. This is why, at first, many find it hard to adjust to this manner of working with dreams. One must forget what one knows, or thinks one knows, about dreams, must leave behind the theoretical framework and traditional ways of working with dreams, and enter open-mindedly into a different kind of play – play in the Winnicottian sense of the word (Winnicott, 1971). For this to happen the individual must be able to see the multifaceted nature of him/herself and the other.

Dreams can reflect personal and social aspects at the same time (Ofer, 2014, 2017; Lipmann, 1988). As the dreams, rather than dreamers, are the focus, each dream returns to its dreamer through someone else's dream. One must learn how to surrender control and allow oneself to be surprised by new discoveries. The metaphor of a 'casual tourist' in the dreaming space is quite appropriate here (Lawrence & Biran, 2009). In essence, social dreaming actually liberates people from the need to delve into their personal biographies with respect to attempting to understand their dreams, thus enabling them to travel along various paths to the unconscious meanings of their dreams.

Another explanation of what happens in the SDM is understanding the two properties of human thinking which Elias (2007) refers to as 'involvement' and 'detachment'. Involvement consists of relating contents of knowledge to the 'we' perspective and preference for immediate concerns. It focuses on the group to which the thinker belongs, whereas detachment is a property of knowledge which is oriented towards the object of thinking (the 'it'), group focus being removed for the sake of a more distanced view. In the 21st century we live in a global matrix and we can hardly talk about a local foundation matrix or species-based social unconscious. Yet, we can think of regional foundation matrices – the European foundation matrix, where there is interpenetration of cultures leading to a trans-societal foundation matrix, which can be seen in the SDM.

The Social Dreaming Matrix is usually followed by Social Dialogue and Reflection in which the focus is on thinking about the dreams and what they reveal about the shared context: social, political, organizational, and human. The Social Dreaming Matrix facilitates an encounter between the personal matrix and the group matrix; the internal group touches the dreaming group. Memories, feelings, thoughts, anxieties, unconscious phantasies, and personal traumas all come together in the matrix, through a trans-personal process. The 'unconscious' becomes conscious and a set of unconscious meanings is constructed through the mutual communication of sharing of dreams and associations, thereby alleviating loneliness and enabling both social and inner work.

SDM as containment for trauma

While its chief purpose is not therapeutic, the Social Dreaming Matrix is, nevertheless, therapeutically valuable. The richness of its perspectives, the act of listening to other people's dreams, the abundance of associations – all help the individual

Europe in Social Dreaming Matrices **191**

relinquish control and reach a different level of depth. This was clearly seen in an SDM taken at a Group Analytic Society International (GASi) conference in Lisbon in 2014 where most, if not all the participants were European.

SDM in traumatic situations in Europe

Operation 'Protective Edge', a 2014 military operation in the Gaza Strip, began on July 8th and ended in a ceasefire on August 26th. The operation entailed heavy shelling of the Gaza Strip by the Israeli air force, armored corps, and artillery corps, while Israel was bombarded with hundreds of rockets launched from Gaza and faced infiltration of armed terrorists by sea or through tunnels. The shelling of considerable areas in Gaza caused much destruction of property and the killing of innocent civilians. In Israel, the feeling was both one of fear, seeing rockets landing all over the country, and also one of guilt. The overall feeling at the time was that the entire world was against Israel. Some in Israel thought this operation was wrong and excessively brutal; others felt persecuted. All of us, however, felt isolated. On July 28th, a GASi conference was scheduled to begin in Lisbon. Some twenty-five Israelis flew over from Israel to attend, myself included, and five more Israelis came from the United States. On July 23rd, most international airlines had stopped flying to and from Israel. The days leading up to the conference were very tense for the Israelis who were ready to attend yet did not know whether they would be able to leave the country or not. Until the final hours before leaving the country, I had no idea whether I would be able to make it to the conference on time. I was late for my first session. For four days, I conducted a Social Dreaming Matrix together with Joanna Skowrowska from Poland. About forty people attended, all from different countries in Europe, as well as three other Israelis. (Apart from a handful of people who asked to join this particular matrix, most people were assigned to this activity by the conference organizers.)

I had no doubt that this was a traumatic situation, at least for the Israelis present. It certainly was for me; I didn't know how people from other countries felt. One indication of awareness in the room of the traumatic situation was the overwhelming number of dreams. Almost every day, the 75 minutes of matrix included about seventeen dreams. There were also many associations, though these did not prevent more dreams from surfacing. There were also several people who were totally unable to dream.

On a personal level, trauma is defined as a state which overwhelms one's mental coping capacities, thus giving rise to extreme feelings of helplessness and despair. Traumatic situations cause very difficult material to surface. We also know that in traumatic situations, people succumb to feelings of extreme loneliness, feeling that no one can understand them; they thus remain isolated and alone with whatever is overwhelming them, or enter a dissociated state, in which their emotions are detached from their present experience.

In his book, *Tongued with Fire: Groups in Experience*, W. Gordon Lawrence (2000) describes the 20th century as a century of man-made catastrophes in which

192 Gila Ofer

humanity caused the deaths of hundreds of millions of people. He therefore offers the following general working premise: "a future cannot be brought into being until we experience and consciously call to mind the meaning and significance of tragedy, both as a private problem, and as a public issue at this point in history" (p. 209). One can conclude that, by conducting a Social Dreaming Matrix, our expectation is that the sharing of dreams will bring about a feeling that those present understand the meaning of shared tragedy, even though they come from different backgrounds and different situations (Ofer, 2016). The expectation is that the individual attending the matrix will not feel that the trauma is uniquely their own. Social Dreaming can potentially allow trauma to bring the strong and the weak together in the same space, to evoke powerful feelings and break the barriers of isolation and loneliness. Following are several dreams illustrating some of the main themes that emerged in the Lisbon matrix:

1   **No Home to Go Back To** – the first shared dream:

I'm riding on the slow 561 bus from Tel Aviv to Kfar-Saba (another Israeli town), *where I used to live as a teenager. The bus gets emptier and emptier and goes further and further away; suddenly there's no driver, there isn't even a road. It's not going to my home. I realize that it's not going to get me home. I don't feel anything.*
Another dream:
I drove into the city. A friend let me borrow her car. I used the key but couldn't start it. I didn't know where the apartment I was going to was located. Suddenly, I have no memory and no key.
The associations that came up during the first day in relation to this theme:

 - I remember riding the bus on my way out of Serbia, not knowing if I'll ever make it home.
 - There is this flight to Mars, which is basically a one-way ticket, and still there are thousands of people signing up (this association was accompanied by a lot of crying).

2   **Am I the Killer or the One Being Killed?** – Here are some of the dreams that emerged connected to this theme:

 - *I'm swimming in the ocean and there's this vague figure there. I'm afraid that he's going to kill me and suddenly I merge into him.*
 - *I'm sort of running away – running and shooting.*
 - *I was catching masks (or maybe Mosques) and drowning them in water.*
 - *I was a murderer, it felt unbearable. How am I going to deal with this? How am I going to hide this? But I can't hide it.*

3   **No Way of Knowing What's There – Behind Curtains, Behind Walls, Inside People – an Unclear Future:**

 - *I go into this house that I've never been in before. There's this long corridor with no doors and billowing white curtains. I ask myself – what's hiding there? Is my*

Europe in Social Dreaming Matrices **193**

husband behind one of those curtains? I didn't make a sound. I had to be quiet. I was on the street and I walked into a skyscraper. I took the elevator that was empty. The walls had thick curtains with strong light coming through. I realized the building had no walls.

4 **Serious or Terminal Illness**:

- *I'm in a dark place and I have liver cancer. It's stage four cancer.*
- *I met this woman I know. Her son is sick and is going to die. Does he know? He's a teenager.*

These few examples illustrate the extent to which the dreams in the matrix expressed despair, fear, anxiety, the feeling that there is no way back, that you can't trust anyone, as well as feelings of guilt and seeing yourself as a murderer. This mixture of emotions – fear, despair, and guilt – is characteristic of traumatic situations. However, I would also like to demonstrate how this chain of dreams and associations by participants from all over Europe facilitated a process of understanding and provided meaning. I return to the first dream:

I'm riding on the slow 561 bus from Tel Aviv to Kfar-Saba, where I used to live as a teenager. The bus gets emptier and emptier and goes further and further away and suddenly there's no driver, there's no road. It's not going to my home. I realize that it's not going to get me home. I don't feel anything.

It was followed by this dream:

It was a scary dream. I was so afraid that I woke up. I met this woman I know in a group of people. She told me that her teenage son was sick. He was going to die. I asked her if he knew that he was dying.

And then this dream:

It's 1961, because that's when I was in South Africa. I was riding on a bus full of Australians. They kept laughing the whole way and I felt something else entirely. I was alone and depressed.

The final dream:

I had this green shawl that I put on and it occurred to me that I didn't want to wear an Arab color.

With this brief presentation of three dreams and one association, we can see how every dream explains the previous one. The theme of fear is present from the very beginning, but the first dreamer seems to be detached from his emotions. The next dream highlights the theme of fear that was there from the start and makes

194 Gila Ofer

dissociation impossible. The dream about the bus that was full of Australians carries with it the sense of alienation and loneliness which was present from the start of the matrix. Then, the theme of the ongoing war floods the matrix.

Each dream sheds light on another aspect and clarifies the emotions that are present in the matrix. Thus, the traumatic state is understood and given meaning. Personal, national, and general social trauma merged. At the end of that session, the final dream was:

> *I dreamed that I came here, to the conference, and this was my home.*

Overall, you could say that people were willing and ready to share these difficult emotions, to understand and to be understood. The dream that captures this most poignantly is the following:

> *I'm on a plane which is plummeting to the ground. I run and fall into the arms of someone I don't know, but I'm looking for comfort and relief.*

Indeed, the matrix was not restricted to the context of the 'protective edge' war; rather, it went on to a different, more general context, in which we could see how this war, the plane crash in the Ukraine, the Balkan wars, and the effects of the Second World War affected everyone.

At the end of the week, when we had a panel devoted to reflection on what had happened during the social dreaming sessions, people said that when they surrendered to the matrix, they were also able to engage in profound internal work, alone. For example, one participant said that despite not having had any dreams during the week and having been unable to offer dreams she had had in the past, she was constantly crying, confronting different parts of herself, and engaging in internal work, alongside the work done in the matrix.

The three preconditions for a constructive Social Dreaming Matrix were met: the presence of a shared context; shared emotional prevalence; and ambivalence, vagueness, and unconscious aspects of those participating.

SDM in different countries in Europe

When SDM is conducted in a specific country, dilemmas, conflicts, and solutions are more particularly related to that country. The specific cultural historical economic infrastructure has a stronger impact on the matrix. For example, I hosted a Social Dreaming Matrix in Estonia at a conference concerning treatment of difficult patients. The participants were generally Estonians and Russians. (Note: Baltic Estonia was occupied by Soviet Russia. Stalin intended to settle it with hundreds of thousands of Russians who were sent there. For many years, the only official language was Russian.) When Estonia gained its independence, about fifteen years ago, this Russian population found itself trapped . . . abandoned by 'Mother Russia'. The official language was changed to Estonian and these people became even

Europe in Social Dreaming Matrices **195**

more restricted. It is important to note that Estonians are a peaceful people and their struggle for independence was conducted through song, rather than armed revolt.

Here are some of the dreams brought into the matrix on the first day:

Dream One: *There's a party with many people dancing but set in the middle ages. All the people dancing taught us a well-known dance: everyone should have a magic wand, made of wood. The magic is that inside the wand there is a magnetic wire. We are supposed to gather together, holding our wands to create a culture of skirts. The wands change color so that they are black on the inside and red on the outside.*

Dream Two: *A dream about Cinderella. The scenery is beautiful, much more so than any ordinary landscape. The wind is very strong. At the center of the field there is a female figure. It is difficult to be there, but I'm hoping that things will turn out for the best. Suddenly, a boy appears, holding a magic wand. The woman says: We're going to have a new government.*

Dream Three: *I am looking for a nicer home.*

Dream Four: *I am looking for a house with my late mother, a house for everyone. She always said we were living in the wrong house.*

Dream Five: *This dream also seems to take place in the middle ages, in a fortress. There's a kitchen with a kind of altar. Four or five people are preparing a meal: diced chicken, peas, and potato casserole. There's plenty to eat. Suddenly there's a dead body on the floor. We are afraid. We saw hunters come in and take the body, they said it was a mistake.*

Dream Six: *I was working at a morgue, starting to peel the layers off a body. It wasn't at all scary. It was interesting.*

It is apparent that the dreams share quite a few common elements: the magic wand, the other-worldly atmosphere, something extra-temporal, losing one's way, women with skirts or Cinderella. I raised the idea that Estonia has a feminine culture in which men may act as saviors but may also be very dangerous and corrupt and one never knows whether to wait for them or not.

The suggested working assumption (interpretation in the matrix) related to the fact that there is a lot of food of a very particular kind (dreams). The peeling is also that of different layers of the unconscious. Beyond this, the common element is the feeling that something bad is happening in the country; the house is unsafe. People are afraid that what happened in Russia will happen in Estonia as well (fear of loss of democracy). The women want power and receive it through a process whereby they must learn not to wait for a male partner, to count less on men but more on their relations with the group, and themselves as society.

The impact of the particular context in this matrix was expressed by a search for the way history is revealed to us, embodied through appearance of older wise grandparents in the dreams; the cultural context of the country (the dancing, the feminine culture); the current political situation (fear of being swallowed by bigger countries in dreams like "a truck towing a small car and ruining it").

196 Gila Ofer

Another example of a matrix in a specific country was one held in Belgrade for local citizens. The impact of the former Yugoslavian country and ongoing wars was heavily present in the dreams, the associations, and the reflections. However, history of traumatic wars with the Turks was also part of the foundation matrix. Dreams repeatedly expressed no help from the outside, not enough food, being left alone ... loss of hope expressed in the dreams through abortions and ectopic pregnancies, falling trees killing people. In addition, there were repeated dreams of changing identities, changing gender identities, changing money, dangerous injections, that all pointed to identity crisis and fear of the future repeating the past. The dreams relating to this issue expressed ambivalence regarding having children as there was a dangerous person hiding in the house, the decision to sell the baby for money, and the armed threatening policemen on the streets.

In another SDM conducted in one of the Balkan countries, many of the dreams were about the beautiful place with demons, or a beautiful landscape in the country that becomes a place of evil.

Commonalities and differences in themes across Europe

While conducting SDM across Europe, some common themes could be found in most of the countries. Issues regarding confusion of identity, searching for safety and for meaning were common to participants in both Western (e.g. Greece, Denmark, Spain) and Eastern European countries. However, the ambivalence, guilt feelings, responsibility, and fear in connection with the refugees entering Europe were not reflected in the matrices in countries like Ukraine, Poland, Estonia, Serbia, and Russia.

Here are some of the topics as manifested in the dreams in different countries:

1   *Searching for the right way and turning to the old people to find it.*

- *I had a dream about the last supper – the dreamer lost his way but was able to enter the picture of the last supper and talk with the characters.*
- *I was walking in the lower level of a building. Suddenly the whole building turned upside down, but I was not scared because an older man showed me the way out.*

2   *Globalization vs. group identity.*

We are living in a world where group identities are getting stronger to protect people from incohesion and fear of annihilation. A common theme in SDM worldwide is the conflict between globalization (wish for merging with others) vs. apathy toward the others. This issue was stronger in Western countries than in Eastern countries. Here are some dreams from different countries which pointed to this issue:

- *My family (Greek) wants to go to London but finally we stay in Yoanina (the local town).*
- *Repeated dreams about failed marriages.*

Europe in Social Dreaming Matrices **197**

- *A couple where the woman is headless.*
- *Looking for a bridge to connect to the other side.*
- *My friend's family was supposed to be united but was still apart. The husband was sleeping on a sofa, but the wife was in a different country with the children.*
- *My family went on a trip to another country. The father had his back to his family and could not speak the language of the locals. The mother and the children wanted to talk with them.*

3   *Ambivalence regarding the problem of refugees – between responsibility and guilt.*

- Waves of immigrant refugees in the last five years have had an impact in shaping identity and testing tolerance of locals; this is reflected in almost all the matrices across Europe. In one of the Scandinavian countries there were dreams about *layers of people falling off cliffs into a ditch* followed by another dream of *frozen faces, neutral faces opposite suffering people.* The working hypotheses was that this could look like a computer game with no feelings attached to what is going on or to mass graves of refugees nowadays, or during the Holocaust with guilt feelings around neutrality. In another country a typical dream was: *I was walking between many people. I saw a man and I did not know if he was a terrorist or not. He knew I recognized him. He was contaminated by radioactivity and everybody said don't touch him. But I could not avoid it. Other people did not realize that I myself was already contaminated.*

The reflection illustrated that whether we want to or not, we are all affected (contaminated) by the problem of refugees, we either help them or feel guilty, and we must deal with it.

4   *Having to take care of children but failing to do so.* Common to all SDM is the theme of uncertainty and concerns regarding the future, mainly regarding children and the worries of the difficulty of taking care of them. Some examples:

- *In a building, there is chaos. A man had a small child but forgot to look after him. I wanted to do it. I followed the child, but he ran away and fell. I was afraid.*
- *I was with a colleague, looking at some children. They needed some help.*
- *I was working taking care of an infant with skin problems. The child drowned in the bathtub. I was scared; how can this not be my fault? I knew it was me, but I did not want to accept it.* (This dream was related by a woman who also works with refugees and could also be connected to ambivalence regarding the refugees in Europe.)

Conclusion

Working, hypothesizing, or interpreting dreams take place in an area of play. The Social Dreaming Matrix teaches us the degree to which the dream is an extended invitation to observe, study, and play, rather than restricting ourselves to

198 Gila Ofer

interpretation and the search for a definite, precise meaning. It has the potential of manifesting the hidden knowledge that is present in systems – the 'unthought known' (Bollas, 1987), revealing issues that are in some way known, but have previously not been able to be thought about. The dream has the potential of conveying a vision, as Martin Luther King said in his "I have a dream" speech on August 28th, 1963. In SDMs across Europe, we could participate in gatherings that reflected shared anxieties, fears, conflicts, fights, burdensome differences, and guilt, as well as wishing for cooperation, bridging, and responsibilities toward others who are less privileged.

References

Beradt, C., & Bettelheim, B. (1968). *The third Reich of dreams: The nightmares of a nation, 1933–1939*. Chicago: Quadrangle Books.

Bion, W. R. (1967). *Second thoughts*. London: Karnac.

Bion, W. R. (1970). *Attention and interpretation*. London: Karnac.

Bollas, C. (1987). *The shadow of the object: Psychoanalysis of the unthought known*. London: Free Association Books.

Bromberg, P. (2008). Bringing in the dreamer: Some reflections on surprise, dissociation, and the analytic process. *Contemporary Psychoanalysis, 36*, 685–705.

Elias, N. (2007). *Involvement and detachment*. Dublin: University College Dublin Press.

Fosshage, J. L. (1997). The organizing functions of dream mentations. *Contemporary Psycho analysis, 33*, 429–458.

Foulkes, S. H. (1965). Psychodynamic processes in the light of psychoanalysis and group analysis. In S. H. Foulkes (Ed.), *Therapeutic group analysis* (pp. 108–119). London: Karnac, 1984.

Foulkes, S. H., & Anthony, E. J. (1957). *Group psychotherapy: The psycho-analytic approach*. Harmondsworth: Penguin; reprinted 1984 London: Karnac.

Freud, Z. (1900). *Interpretation of dreams*. SE, ch. 2, 107.

Friedman, R. (2008). Dream telling as a request for containment: Three uses of dreams in group therapy. *International Journal of Group Psychotherapy, 58*(5), 327–344.

Lawrence, W. G. (Ed.). (1998). *Social dreaming at work*. London: Karnac.

Lawrence, W. G. (2000). *Tongued with fire: Groups in experience*. London: Karnac.

Lawrence, W. G., & Biran, H. (2009). The complementarity of social dreaming and therapeutic dreaming. In C. Neri, M. Pines, & R. Friedman (Eds.), *Dreams in group psychotherapy: Theory and technique* (1st ed., pp. 46–67). London: Jessica Kingsley.

Lipmann, P. (1988). On the private and social nature of dreams. *Contemporary Psychoanalysis, 34*, 195–221.

Ofer, G. (2014). The personal, the relational, the group and the social in a globalized world – a perspective through working with dreams. *Group Analysis, 47*(4).

Ofer, G. (2016). *Social dream matrix in traumatic situations*. Lecture given on a conference to the memory of Gordon Lawrence in Tel-Aviv.

Ofer, G. (2017). Personal, group and social dimensions of dreams. In R. Friedman & Y. Doron (Eds.), *Group analysis in the land of milk and honey*. London: Karnac.

Ogden, T. H. (1990). *The matrix of the mind*. London: Jason Aronson Inc.

Segal, H. (1991). The function of dreams. In S. Flanders (Ed.), *The dream discourse today*. London: Karnac.

Winnicott, D. W. (1971). *Playing and reality*. New York: Basic Books.

INDEX

Note: Numbers in bold indicate a table. Numbers in italics indicate a figure.

20 Minutes 86
1968 generation 11

Abraham, Nicolas 141, 158
absence 156
affect 35, 38–41
Afghanistan 32, 47, 65, 100, 108
Afghans 35
Africa 16–17, 106; North 65, 67; South 193
African Americans 94
After the Internet (AI) 69
Aggregation/Massification 2
aggression 53, 69–71, 127, 159; and anger 48; and sex 52
Ahmadinejad, Mahmoud 127
Ahmed, S. 41
Alder, Stephan 163
Al-Samaloty, N. 77
Alternative für Deutschland 36, 100
Amenhotep IV 128
amnesia: historical 15; social 150
Amnesty International 12, 28
Andrić, I. 180, 182
Andrić-Town 183
anima 184
Animus 128, 131
anti-democracy 71
anti-globalism 114
anti-growth 24, 25
anti-migration 5, 32, 33, 34, 36; party 36
anti-pain 24

anti-Semitism 46–47, 65, 151, 170; Christian 57–58; in East Germany 12; in Poland 70, 152, 154, 159; in the United States 60
anti-thought 24
anxiety 24, 59, 62, 172, 193; and aggression 71; about Brexit 120; depressive 23; displacement 32; and the Holocaust 140, 153, 154; internal 83; and the Other 80, 82, 142; persecutory 27, 60; about refugees 32, 115; unconscious 63–64
Arab countries 57, **73**, 74
Arab 193; in Poland 71–83, **73**
Arafat, Yasir 107
Argentina 12
Armenians 15
Asia 91, 106, 186
assimilation 71, 74, 76, 79, 130
asylum seekers 34, 91, 95, 100
atomic bomb 21
atrocity 11, 13, 60, 61, 181
Auschwitz 88, 93
Austen Riggs Center 135
austericide 25
austerity 32, 102, 104, 115
Austria 9, 12, 114, 136, 176
Austro-Hungarian Empire 181
authoritarianism 135

Bachmann, Ingeborg 14
"backlash" 148

200 Index

Bain, A. 129
Balkanisation 176
Balkans 85, 88, 175, 185, 196; social
    unconscious 177; transitional spaces 178;
    as "uncivilized" 184
Balkan wars 91, 101, 108, 194
Balkan Peninsula 179
Baltic states 13, 88, 194
Basic Assumption Oneness 129
Bauman, Zygmunt 69, 177
Baumeister, R. F. 2
Before the Internet (BI) 69
Belfast 45
Belgrade 178, 180, 185, 196
Beradt, Charlotte 137, 141–145, 189
Berlin 15–16, 48, 64, 86, 163; West 89
Berlinale Film Festival 15
Berlin Wall 9, 21
Berlusconi, Silvio 126
Bettelheim, Bruno 142
Bikont, Anna 155
Bion, Wilfred 28, 115, 189
blood libel 57
body, bodies 38, 41, 156, 182, 195
Bollas, Christopher 142, 144
Bomba, Jacek 152
border(s) 10, 12, 16; Bosnia/Serbian 175;
    closed 45, 85; Croatia/Hungary 87;
    and the dispossessed 41; European 14,
    113; and the Internet 28; love without
    170–171; mental 15; national 35; of
    North Ireland/Eire 116, 119; opening 46,
    70, 81; of Poland 82; position 181–183;
    shutting 15; of the United Kingdom 115;
    world without 22
borderland (socio-cultural) 179–180
borderspace 39–40
Bosnia 14, 65, 175, 176, 182
bourgeoisie 20
Bratunac 184
Breivik, Anders Behring 106
Brentano, Heinrich von 17
Brexiteers 118
Brexit referendum 47, 50, 104; and the
    European Union 129–131; and national
    identity 114–116; post- 117, 118–122;
    pre- 112–114; and social processes
    116–118
Bridge on the Drina, The (Andrić) 182
Britain 118, 133; economy of 122; *see also*
    Brexit; United Kingdom
Brit(ish): On Race, Identity and Belonging
    (Hirsch) 119
Brundtland, Gro Harlem 99, 105

Brunetta, Renato 126
Brunning, Halina 113
Brussels 115, 118, 119, 120, 176
Budapest 14
Bulgaria 26, 65
Bundestag 16
Bundeszentrale fuer Politische Bildung 88
Butler, Judith 39, 158

'Calais Jungle' 115
Cameron, David 113, 118, 124–125, 127,
    130
Carney, Marcus 135
catastrophic change 21, 27, 28, 30
Catholic Church 68, 74
Catholicism 45, 63, 70, 149; Roman 182
Cato the Younger 128
Cavalli, Alessandra 156
Center for Political Beauty 15
child 12, 47, 60, 71, 130; adoption of
    76; anti-Semitic 46; in danger 131;
    development 143; dreams of 197; father's
    duties toward 77; of former enemies 163;
    guilty feelings of 93, 95, 136, 137; and
    the Holocaust 61, 152, 153, 156, 157,
    158, 159; in Madagascar 101; in Norway
    104; refugee 29, 85, 91; of refugees 136;
    role 184; Serbian 176, 180; of single
    parents 126; "in-trash" 186; and war 95,
    186; of Zeus 128
child abuse 24
childbirth 130
childhood 53, 62, 78, 89, 168–169, 179
Chile 91
China 15
Chirac, Jacques 94
Christian, Christianity 35, 60, 180; anti-
    Semitism 57; church 72, 73, **73, 74**, 182;
    European 65, 106, 130, 181; in Norway
    106; unconscious anxiety toward 63–64
Churchill-Tito Agreement 180
Churchill, Winston 8
Clinton, William J. ("Bill") 107
closure 157
Cold War 12, 15, 17, 21, 164, 181
Colombia 108
colonialism 11, 16, 17, 104, 115, 186;
    neo- 17; post- 13
colonization 26, 94
common ground activity 165, 167–169,
    172
communism 12, 13, 180
complacency 185
complex (Jungian) *see cultural complex*

Confederation of Norwegian Enterprises
  (NHO) 105
constellation of death 27
consumer, consumerism 33, 34, 36–38, 68,
  83
'contained, the' 28, 29
conversational objects 167, 168, 172
conservatism 129
Conservative party (Britain) 113, 116,
  118–119, 130
Copenhagen 52, 102
Corbyn, Jeremy 116, 119, 121
corruption (political) 21, 24, 25–26, 107,
  119
Coventry 88
Crete 127–128, 176
crime 8, 137, 158; historical 13; of the
  Holocaust 12, 90, 95; horror of 157;
  mass 151; war 11, 88, 90, 94, 95, 104, 138,
  159
Croatia 49, *87*, 176
cultural complex 165–166, 171, 172
culture 125; ancient 180; Arab 72, 75, 76,
  82; of consensus 51; dialog 49, 176, 178,
  185; elites 149; entrepreneurial 130;
  European 29, 129, 179; German 44, 45,
  85, 90, 93; Group Analytic 44; "high" 65;
  Israeli 65; Italian 48; 'memory' 10–12,
  90; Minoan 128; multi- 81; Muslim
  80; and national identity 101; Nazi 46;
  Norwegian 100, 102, 103, 104, 105,
  106; of obedience 50; patriarchal 124;
  peaceful 53; perverse 26; Polish 74, 78,
  79, 147; popular 37, 148; *post-truth* 25;
  sub- 106; Swiss 51; "welcoming" 85, 93,
  96; Western 127
Curtis, Mark 108
Czech Republic 65
Czechoslovakia 88, 91, 101

Davoine, Françoise 137, 138
death instinct 27, 28
'Deficiency Relation Disorder' 49
demi-deuil 158
democracy 10, 11, 21–22, 65, 70; anti-
  71, 126; 'European dream' of 14;
  and the European Union 51; liberal
  148; in Norway 102, 104, 105, 107;
  Parliamentary *117*, 120; secular 126
Democratic Unionist Party 116
Denmark 26, 102, 103, 114, 196
deregulation 33
Derrida, Jacques 158
'development' 8, 9, 17

development(s) 29, 178, 180; aid 101,
  106, 107; child 143; economic 21, 22,
  68; emotional 20; of the European
  Union 129, 130; of dialog culture 49;
  group process 45; human 52, 141; of
  masculinity 131; non- 24; political 53;
  in public policy 40; social 52, 83; theory
  124, 125, 128
dictatorship 9, 10, 12, 143
displacement 32, 36, 87, *88*, 88, 95, 148
dispossession 32, 33, 34; counteracting
  38–40
Divine Child archetype 131
Doré, Gustave 59
doublethink 108
Dream 155; American 9; European 9–10,
  14, 15, 17
dreamer 52, 141–144, 193, 196;
  social 186
dreams 52, 53, 95, 143, 175, 177; of children
  197; and dreamer 188, 189, 190; of the
  future 192–193; of home 192; of identity
  196–197; of illness 193; journal 137,
  141–145; of killing/being killed 192;
  and "the other" 183; recurrent 176; of
  refugees 197; of searching 196; sharing
  192; *see also* Social Dreaming Matrix
dream-telling 52, 189
'dugnad' 104
Drina river 175–176, 179, 182
Dušan (Emperor) 180

Eastern bloc 69
Eastern Orthodox Church 182
Eastern World 179
ego 94, 124, 125, 127, 128, 157; balanced
  172; collective 125, 127, 129; continental
  129; enlargement of 158; and Id 143;
  superego 25
egocentrism 14
egoist 86
Eire 116, 119; *see also* Ireland
Elias, Norbert 190
emigration 159, 181, 183
émigrés 136
Erikson, E. 143, 144, 145
Erikson Institute 135, 136
Eros archetype 131
Estonia 194, 195, 196
Ethiopia 47
ethno-nationalism 104
Ettinger, Bracha 39–40
"Eurabia" 106
Eurafrica 17

202 Index

Eurafrica: The Untold History of Integration and Colonialism (Hansen and Jonsson) 16
Europa 127–128, 131, 176, 186
Europe 186, 188; ambivalence toward 64–65; the Animus in 131; Balkanization of 176; borders of 14; Central 9, 13, 68, 149; childbirth rates in 130; Christianity of 63–64; colonial history of 17; corruption 25–26; Eastern 12, 13, 65, 68, 91, 149, 151; fascism in 10, 148; Father Complex of 128, 129; and globalization 20, 22, 28; and identity 114; immigrants from 120; and Islam 27; Israeli perceptions of 57–58, 65; Judeo-Christian 181; male/masculine aspects of 129, 130; migrants into 67; myth of 175; "Old" 179; 'others' of 16–17; post-communist 149; Puer archetype in 130; and radicalism 126; refugees in 28–30, 83, 101; repression 147; right-wing parties in 127; social dreaming matrix in 188, 191–196; terrorism 26–28; themes across 196–197; in transition 99–101; trauma in 191–194; and violence 24; war in 15, 16, 21, 47, 53, 95, 104; Western 70; *see also* Friedman, Robi; Germany; Norway; Poland
European Army 114
European Council 131
European Court of Justice 120
European defence treaty *see* NATO
European Economic Area (EEA) 103
European Economic Community (EEC) 16, 103, 112, 121
European Free Trade Association (EFTA) 104
European Parliament 115
European project 7, 9, 15, 17, 129, 148
European Union (EU) 36, 50, 67, 70, 172; and Brexit 112, 118, 120, 121, 125, 131; and egalitarianism 45; long-term project of 8–16; and memory 16–17; and Norway 103–104; refugees into 32, 114
exclusion 47–48
expulsion 15, 16, 33, 38, 47, 58, 88

Fachkräfte-Zuwanderungsgesetz 95
Faimberg, H. 157
Farage, Nigel 113, 125
FARC guerrillas 108
Far from the Madding Crowd (Hardy) 112
fascism 10, 90, 148
father 71, 76–77, 124–125, 126; assault (symbolic) on the 129, 130; Great 131; name of the 144–145; role 127
Father Complex 128

Father-world 124, 129
Fear of the Feminine, The (Neumann) 124
feminine, femininity 76, 124, 125, 126, 128
feminist: ethics 34; philosophy 39; thought 38, 40
financial bubbles 21, 23–25
financial crisis 22, 32, 36, 38
Forecki, Piotr 148
Foulkes, S. H. 165
France 8, 12, 45, 50, 53, 120; and Brexit 117; Jews in 94; 'memory law' 16; terrorism in 26, 65; and the United States 120; Vichy government 94
Free Association 165
freedom 69, 102, *117*, 144, 179; "as if" 183; as a burden 144; of choice 36, 38; of conscience 74; and equality 51; fear of losing 178; from oppression 103; price of 71; of religion 74; and stability 177; of thought 76
"Free-Floating Discussion" 165
Freud, Sigmund 39, 137, 158, 188, 190
Friedman, Robi 44–53

Gampel, Y. 156
Ganymede 131
Gaudillière, Jean-Max 137, 138
Gaza Strip 191
'generation war' 11
genocide 11, 14, 15,
German Generation, A (Kohut, T.) 135, 144
German Matrix 44
Germany 11, 34, 45, 53, 67, 95–96; anti-migration party in 36; border debate in 46; and Brexit 121; crimes of 88, 94; culture 44; East 12, 91; historic guilt of 13, 86, 87, 94; Jews in 64; and the Holocaust 87; immigration to 126; Israelis in 64–65; 'memory culture' 11, 90; mosques in 114; nationalism in 100; and Poland 70, 149, 151; post-traumatic society of 139; post-war 136; refugees in 34, 35, 91, 93; terrorism in 26; Trialog conference 163; and the United States 120; "welcoming culture of" 85; West 8, 10, 91
Gestalt 144
Ghana 91
globalization 17, 20–22, 25; anti- 114, 115; benefits of 27; bubbles of 24; idea of 26; and identity 196; and the Internet 23; mentality 28; in Norway 105; and multiculturalism 32; process of 130; progressive 82; and refugees 29
Gniewczyna 154
Good Friday Agreement 45, 119

Gould, L. 129
Great East-West Schism 182
Greece 9, 33, 36, 45
Green, A. 156
Grinberg, L. 28–29
Gross, Jan T. 149
Grossman, David 60–61
Group Analysis 49, 165
Grubrich-Simitis, Ilse 159
Guardian, The 86

Haiven, Max 36, 37
hajduks 183–184
Hansen, Peo 16
Harald (King) 100
Hardy, Thomas 112
Heller, Agnes 150
Hermaphroditus 125
Hernes, Gudmund 105
Hero archetype 131
Herzegovina 176
Hillman, James 130, 131
Hirsch, Afua 119
history 14, 15, 135, 140; of African
    Americans 94; anti-Semitic 12, 60;
    burdens of 81; colonial 16–17; 'end of'
    10; of Europe 29, 99; family 137–138,
    141; German 93, 95; of the Holocaust 11,
    136, 141, 153; of Jews 63, 64; lessons of
    9, 13–14; of mankind 76; modern 58; of
    Norway 100, 101–103, 108–109; Polish
    70; victims of 13; war 48; of World War
    II 159
Hitler, Adolph 8, 145, 178
Holocaust 11, 12; and Germany 13, 86–87, 88,
    90, 93, 95; in literature 60–63; "oblivion"
    150–151, 154; in Poland 147–156, 159;
    shadow of 58; survivors of 136, 140;
    unconscious impact of 60–63, 65
homo digitalis 30
homophobia 70
horror 88, 137, 139, 141, 179; and the
    Holocaust 61, 151, 157; memories of 89;
    of the past 8; of rape 184; shame and 142;
    of war 87
human rights 12, 13, 15, 17, 22, 28, 40, 99
Human Rights Watch 12

"I" and "non-I" 39
Icarus 131
identity 11, 26, 80, 81, 83, 144; British 119;
    collective 27; core 180; crisis 196; cultural
    82; English 116; ethnic- 100; European
    28, 29; group 165; and immigration
    197; and independence 179; individual
    27; local 126; loss of 127, 155; national

14, 82, 100, 101–102, 104, 113, 115,
    125, 148; Norwegian 102, 103; Polish
    151; Polish-Jewish 152, 154; political
    35; politics of 114, 121; Serb 181, 185;
    sovereign 122; threats to 79; traditional
    129
If This Is a Man (Levi) 150
immigrants 1, 27–29, 65, 81, *92*;
    ambivalence toward 126, 197;
    demonstrations against 148; German 94;
    illegal 115, 120; Muslim 82; in Norway
    100, 101; in Poland 153
Immigrants and Refugees (Volkan) 85
incorporation 158
Industrial Revolution 20
Institute of National Remembrance
    (Poland) 159
Institut für Demoskopie Allensbach
    (Institute for public opinion polls
    Allensbach) 96
International Dialogue Initiative 45
International Group Analytic Society
    (GASi) 44, 191
International Organisation for Migration
    (IOM) 28
Internet 22–23, 25, 28, 29, 69;
    weaponization of 116
introjection 158
invariance 21, 26, 30
Iraq 32, **73**, 108, 113; Iraqis 35, 79
Ireland 9; *see also* Northern Ireland
Iron Curtain 9, 90
ISIS 28
Islam 27, 28, **73**, 74, 76; modern 114; in
    Poland 82
Islamic terrorism 26–28, 126
Islamic world 26, 127
"Islamisation" 106
Israel 53, 60, 107, 150, 191, 192
Israeli Association for Group Psychotherapy
    44
Israeli Jews, social unconscious of 57–65
Israeli Institute of Group Analysis 44
Israelis 13, 14, 39; ambivalence toward
    Europe 64–65; and Poland 152
Italy 8, 48, 90, 126; refugees in 33, 114;
    right-wing parties in 36; terrorism in 26

James, Diane 125
Janissaries 180
Jedwabne 12, 149, 154
Jew 14, 70, 186, 189; European 15, 16;
    French 94; German 145; and the
    Holocaust 166; Lithuanian 165; and
    Nazis 46, 64–65, 138, 140; in Poland
    147–151, 153–159; and Russians 169,

170; Soviet 91; as target 120; 'Wandering' 58–60, *59*; *see also* Israeli Jews
Johnson, Boris 125
Jonsson, Stefan 16
Jung, Carl 125, 128, 131, 165–166

Kant, Immanuel 125
Kazakhstan 91
Kazimierz 155
Kfar-Saba 192, 193
Khaleelee, Olya 113
Khamenei, Ali 127
Kiel Treaty 102
Kielce 155
Kim Jong-un 127
Kimbles, Samuel L. 165–166
King, Jr., Martin Luther 198
King's Son archetype 131
Klein, Melanie 22, 23, 125, 137, 188
Kohut, Heinz 137, 138
Kohut, Thomas 135, 144–145
koinonia 178, 183, 186
Kosovo, Battle of 180
Kraków 148, 153
Krasnodar 163
Kurdistan 113
Kurds 113; Syrian 89
Kusturica 175, 176, 183

Labour Party (England) 106, 116, 118, 119, 121
LaCapra, D. 156
Lacan, Jacques 39, 139, 143
lack *see* oblivion
large group identity 165
Latvia *see* Riga
Laub, Dori 156
Lawrence, W. Gordon 129, 141, 189, 191
Leadsom, Andrea 130
Leave campaign 112, 116, 120–122, 124–125, 129; Leavers 113, 118, 120
Leder, A. 158
Lepenski Vir 179, 184
Lesbian, Gay, Bisexual, Transgender, Queer, Intersex and Asexual (LGBTQIA+) 126
Levinas, Emmanuel 39, 40
liberalism 51, 70; neo- 32–34, 37–38, 40–41, 186
libidinal 39, 130, 157
libido 158
Libya **73**, 108
Libyan Coast Guard 28
Lidice 88
Lieux de mémoire (Nora) 16

Lillehammer 105
London 115, 119, 120, 139, 196
Londonderry (Lord) 94
Long, Susan 37
loss 139
Lost in Transmission: Studies of Trauma across Generations 135
love 112, 170–172, 177, 180; affair 25; danger of 137–139
Love Is Not Praktish: The Israeli Look at Germany (Yair) 64

Macbeth (character of) 142
Macron, Emmanuel 94
Madagascar 101
'mammone' 126
'Marginalisation Disorder' 50
Markowa 154
Marshall Plan 8
Maternal Uroboros 124
matriarchate 124, 125
matrix 165, 172, 193–196; foundation 180, 183–184; German 44; individual 45; Nazi 46, 47; Soldier's 48; symbiotic 124; *see also* Social Dreaming Matrix
matrixial 39
May, Theresa 117, 119, 125, 130, 131
McHugh-Dillon, H. 35
megalomania 7, 105, 159
melancholy 157–158
members in the European Parliament (MEPs) 115
memory 83, 145, 156, 192; collective 147, 148–150, 151; common 9; cultural 166; dialogic 14; European 15, 17; European Union (EU) 16–17; Holocaust 12, 61, 147, 148–150, 151, 153, 154; national 58, 99, 103; propaganda 8; social 147; World War II 62
memory culture 8, 10–12, 13, 90
'memory law' 16
Mercury-Hermes 131
Merkel, Angela 46, 85, 126
Messiah archetype 131
metaphor 64, 158, 163; of a bird 168; for Brexit 112, 121, 127; developing 167; in a large group 169–172; of a matrix 165; Sirens as 169; of tightrope 185
metaphorization 159
migrants 15, 16, *87*, 114; assimilation of 130; attitudes towards 96; forced 32, 33, 34–36, 38, 40; policies regarding 127
Milošević, Slobodan 14
Minoan Crete 127–128, 184

Index

Minos 127, 128
'mnemocide' 11
mob 158
monstrosity 40, 94, 181
Montenegro 176
Moscow 119, 176
Mosley, Oswald 94
mother 24, 39–40, 76, 143; and child 157, 197; "dead" 156; Great 128, 131; realm of 125
Mother Russia 194
Mother-world 124, 129
mourning 23, 88, 125, 154, 156–159
Multidimensionaler Erinnerungsmonitor (MEMO) 93
Munich 85, *86*, *92*
museums 10, 102; national 14, 94
modernity 10, 12, 16, 27; post- 68, 69
More in Common 96
mosque 72, **73**, 74, **74**, 114, 192
Moyn, Samuel 12
Muslims 60, 70; Arab 76; Bosnians 14; convert 182; European 27; in Norway 106; persecution of 65; in Poland 71, 73, 74, 76, 78, 79, 80, 82, 83; Sunni 165; in Turkey 64
Muslim world 26

nameless dread 29, 186
namelessness 186
Napoleonic wars 102
Nasser, Abdul 58
National Geographic 86
National Health Service (NHS) (England) 116–117
nationalism 13, 14, 35, 74, 127, 185; ethno- 104; far-right 106, 127, 129; populist- 81, 100; ultra- 27
National Radical Camp 148
National Socialism 141
NATO 8, 114, 128
Nazi Legacy, A (Volkan) 138
Nazis 46–48, 61–65, 90, 128, 139; crimes 94, 159; era 166; neo-35, 36, 96; victims of 137
Neighbors (Gross) 149
neoliberalism *see* liberalism
Neumann, Erich 124, 125
New Public Management 33, 36
Nora, Pierre 16
Northern Ireland 45, 116, 119, 121, 122
North Korea 127
Norway 45, 99–102; and development aid 106–107; domestic terrorism in 106; and

the European Union 103–104; history of 102–103; peace negotiations by 107–108; self-image 104–105, 108–109; values 105
Norwegian Confederation of Trade Unions (LO) 105
Norwegian Refugee Council (NRC) 99
Nuremberg trials 8

Obama, Barack 126
Obcy. Inny. Taki Sam. 153
oblivion 8, 150, 153, 154
Odysseus 168
Olympic games 105
Operation 'Protective Edge' 191
Oradour 88
Origins of the Regime of Goodness, The (Witoszek)
Orpheus 168
Orwid, Maria 152
Oslo 100, 102, 105, 106
Oslo Accords 107
Other, the 4, 39–41, 87, 183, 184, 189; -Alien 80; different 48; fear of 90; and Poland 67, 68–72; protecting the 32; suffering of 86; unknown 33, 34; "unrelatable" 40
Otherness 69, 79, 81, 82, 83, 158
"Ottoman Bull" 176
Ottomans 128, 180, 181, 182

pagan 180
Pakistan 91, 100
Palestine **73**, 107; Palestinians 14, 79
Palestine Liberation Organisation (PLO) 107
paranoid-schizoid 25, 26, 125, 137, 159
Pašić (Prime Minister) 179
patriarch, patriarchal 71, 76, 77, 124, 182
patriarchate 124, 125, 126, 127, 128
patriotism 50
Permanent Structured Cooperation Pact (PESCO) 114
phantasies 25, 190
'phantastic objects' 24
pogroms 12, 57, 60, 149
Poland 10, 12, 13, 14, 35, 45, 65, 196; Arabs in 71–83, **73**; asylum seekers from 91; demographics 67; and migrants 114; mythology of 70; *see also* Holocaust; Other
Poland on the Couch project 3, 48, 49
Polish-Israeli Mental Health Association 148, 151–156
political correctness (PC) 127

206 Index

populism 135
Portugal 9, 90
postmodernity *see* modernity
post-traumatic stress disorder (PTSD) 139, 145
post-truth 25
Potsdam Conference 88
profanum 68
proletariat 20
propaganda 7, 8, 28
Prussia 44, 88
psyche 52, 124, 128, 156, 172, 178
"psychic crypt" 158
"psychic retreats" 24, 178
psychoanalysis 37, 39, 143, 165, 167; feminist 40
psychodynamics 85, 87, 112, 114
psychology 38, 44, 49, 61, 62, 80
Psychopompos archetype 131
psychosis blanche 156
Puer, the 129–131
Putin, Vladimir 9, 127, 129

Rabin, Yitzhak 107
Rees-Mogg, Jacob 119
Reflective-Citizens (RC) 175–177, 184–186
refugee crisis 14
refugees 28–30, 34–36, 40, 45, 83; ambivalence toward 197; distrust of 82; in Europe 196; in Germany 47, 85, 86, *86*, 96; identification with 87–93; in Norway 101; in Poland 148, 153; rejection of 49, 80, 81; from Syria 115
regret, politics of 14
rejection 44, 46, 47–48, 50; and acceptance 185; aggressive 79; of dispossessed 33, 34; mutual 25
Rejection Disorder 47, 49
Relation Disorders 47, 49
relationality 32, 38–40; ethics of 34
Remain campaign 112, 116, 129, 130; Remainers 113, 118, 120
reparation (psychic) 22, 23, 24, 29, 46, 137, 159
"repressed, return of the" 148
repression 11, 46, 61, 103, 124, 147
revenge 8, 12, 24, 25
Riga 14
robotisation 30
Roman Empire 128, 182
Rotterdam 88
Roudinesco, Elisabeth 158
Rumania (Romania) 88

Russia 14, 52, 60, 70, 116, 163, 195; communists 128; condemnation of 120; emboldened 119; Soviet 194; and Ukraine 163, 169, 170, 172
Russian language 142, 164

sacrum 68
Salmacis 125, 126, 127
Sand, Phillipe 141
'Sandwich Model' 51
Sataric, Jelica 185
Sassen, S. 38
Saudi Arabia 114
Savion (Tel Aviv) 151
scapegoat role 49, 51, 181, 183
Schengen zone 81, 114
Schultz, Martin 131
Scotland 114, 119, 121, 122
"Second Generation" syndrome 61
Segal, H. 21
self-destruction 181, 184
self-image 12, 15; *see also* Norway
'Selfless/Selfish Disorder' 49
Senex, the 129–130
Senfft, Alexandra 135, 137–139, 144–145
Serbia 49, 65, 175–180; Serbians 178, 180, 182
Serbian Orthodox Church 182
Serbian Patriarch 182
Serbian Reflective-Citizens 175–177
shame 48, 52, 86, 142; guilt and 95, 137, 138, 157, 177; reflexive 143
Silence Hurts: A German Family History (Senfft) 137
Singer, Thomas 165–166
Sirens (mythological) 168
Six Day War 58
Skowrowska, Joanna 191
slavery 11, 94
Slovakia 65
Smith, Adam 40
social action 37
Social Dreaming Matrix (SDM) 189, 190–198
'social dreaming' 52
'social dream-telling' 52
socialism 69, 183; national 93; *real* 69; *see also* National Socialism
social processes: unconscious 60–63
social-psychic-retreats (SPR) 175, 177–181, 183–184
Social Unconscious (SU) 57, 64, 175
Sokolovic, Makarije 182
Soldier's Matrix 48, 52; anti- 53

Son of the Great Mother archetype 131
Soviet Bloc 15
Soviet Union 8, 69, 88; former 91, 172
Spain 9, 26, 65, 90, 113, 196; Jews expelled
  from 64
Srebrenica 184
Sri Lanka 91, 107
Stalin, Joseph 14, 181, 194
Stalinism 10, 12, 14
Steiner, John 24, 28, 178
Strength, Weakness Opportunities and
  Threats (SWOT) *117*
subjectivity 37, 40–41, 143; trans- 39
Sudan **73**, 107
Sullivan, H. 157
Sumerian writing 180
Sweden 9, 26, 35, 102
Sweden Democrats 100
Syria 32, **73**, 89, 91, 113; refugees from 115
Syrians 35, 65, 79, 80
Syrian war 119

Taffer, R. 24
Talinn 14
Tel Aviv 192, 193
terror 14, 21, 24, 58, 127, 138, 141; acts of
  130; attacks 65, 95, 96, 106; environment
  of 178
terrorism 15, 29, 94, 96, 126; attacks 15;
  Islamic 26–28, 82, 126; propaganda 28;
  terrorist 191
therapist 139
therapon 139
Third Reich 136, 159, 181, 189
Third Reich of Dreams, The (Beradt) 141, 189
Tiran Straits 58
Tito, Josip Broz 178, 181, 183
Tito's Communist Youth 183
"Tito's pioneers" 183
Tongued with Fire: Groups in Experience
  (Lawrence) 191
Torok, Maria 158
totalitarianism 10, 144, 177, 178, 183
transgender 114, 126
trauma 46, 47, 53, 151, 157; 'chosen' 14,
  101; contexts 93; historical 60; of Jews
  63, 65; national 106; perpetrator
  135–145; post- 150; of rejection
  78; shared 101, 163, 166; social 58,
  61, 64, 141, 177, 179, 180; and the
  Social Dreaming Matrix 190–194;
  transgenerational 61, 136, 152, 156,
  158; transmission of 61, 135, 144, 156;
  unresolved 148; war-related 95

Treblinka 88
Trialog Conference 163–171
Trump, Donald J. 60, 119, 120, 127
'truths' 30
Tuckett, D. 24
Tugendhat, Tom 119
Turkey 15, 28, 64, 90, 91, 113
Turquet, P. M. 129
Tusk, Donald 131
Tvedt, Terje 100

Ukraine 129, 163, 170, 172, 194, 196
uncanny 28
"Underground" (film) 175, 176, 183
unemployment 25, 33, *117*
unions (workers') 20
United Kingdom (UK) 26, 36, 65, 94, 104,
  113, 120, 121; Dis- 119; economy 113;
  and the European Free Trade Association
  104; fragmentation of 122; *see also* Brexit
United Kingdom Independence Party
  (UKIP) 113, 119
United Nations Development Report 99
United Nations High Commissioner for
  Refugees (UNHCR) 28
United States of America (USA) 60, 63,
  117, 120, 128; authority of 126; financial
  crisis 22; and NATO 128; as super-state
  129
USSR 128
Utopia 12
Utøya summer camp 105–106

Vichy government 12, 99
victimhood 13–14, 181
Vienna 15, 145
Vietnam 91
Vilnius 14
Vinća 179–180, 184
violence 24, 79, 87; collective 27; excessive
  14; hatred and 120; historical 13;
  'normative' 13, 16; traumatic 11
Višegrad 175
Volatile, Uncertain, Complex, Ambiguous
  (VUCA) 117
Volkan, Vamik 14, 58, 85, 86, 138, 165
vulnerability 33, 34, 40, 41, *117*

Waldheim, Kurt 12
Wales 122
Wandering Jew *see* Jew
Warsaw 176
Washington, D.C. 107
Washington Post, The 86

208 Index

wealth and class 20
Weinberg, Haim 101
Weiwei, Ai 15
welcoming culture 85–96
welfare state 22, 32, 35, 38, 69
Western world 23, 26, 35, 69, 90, 125, 130, 179
Wilke, Gerhard 135, 136, 139, 140
Windrush generation 115, 120
Winnicott, Donald 138, 190
Witoszek, Nina 104
World War I 145, 164
World War II 7, 11, 12, 13, 21, 23; alarm sirens 169; and Britain 119; in Norway 101, 103; Polish experience of 149, 151

World Wide Web (www) 22
Wrocław 79, 148

xenophobia 27, 36, 70, 78, 100, 104

Yair, Gad 64–65
Young Man Luther (Erikson) 145
Yugoslavia (former) 14, 90, 180, 183, 196; civil wars 181; and Serbians 175–177

Zeus 127–128, 176
Zion 58
Žižek, S. 175, 183, 185
Zurich 8